SINGAPORE'S HERITAGE

through places of historical interest

DHORAISINGAM S SAMUEL *B. A. (Hons) M. A., PPA*

retired Assistant Director of Education, Singapore
past Head, Education Department,
Ministry of Defence, Singapore
former President, History Association of Singapore.

Published by Elixir Consultancy Service,
24 Cedar Avenue, Singapore 1334.

Published by
Elixir Consultancy Service
24 Cedar Avenue,
Singapore 1334.

Reprint 2006

ISBN 981-00-3185-8

Typeset and Pagemake-up by Avant Garde Typesetting & Publishing Services.
Printed by Hong Kong Offset Printing Pte Ltd

Message

"Singapore's Heritage Through Places of Historic Interest" is a welcome addition to a small collection of books written on our heritage. As Singapore undergoes rapid development, we are often engrossed in pursuits that are directly relevant to our livelihood and do not spare much thought on our past. If this trend is not corrected, more of us will grow up ignorant of our heritage.

This book uses places of interests and is written in a easily readable style. It is suitable for general reading and reference.

I congratulate Mr Dhoraisingam S Samuel for his painstaking works in the compilation of this book and hope that more individuals and organisations would emulate his good example and come forward to promote the awareness and appreciation of our heritage.

Ho Kah Leong
Senior Parliamentary Secretary
Ministry of Information & the Arts

Preface

Several books have been written by eminent persons on the history of Singapore, historic buildings and their architecture.

I have attempted to make Singaporeans proud of their heritage by introducing them to the most important places of historical interest. Through these places I sincerely hope that Singaporeans would realise how our ancestors and pioneers laid the foundations of what we proudly see today as our Republic of Singapore.

It is also my sincere desire that History teachers, their students and parents, community leaders and other Singaporeans would take time to visit these places of historical interest to derive inspiration from our past.

For example let us visit Telok Ayer Street, the centre of Chinatown in the 19th century and still a tourist attraction. The oldest Chinese (Hokkien) Temple the Thian Hock Keng, is in this street flanked by two of the oldest Mosques built by Tamil Muslims - the Nagore Dhurga and the Al-Abrar. Closeby in South Bridge Road is the earliest Hindu Temple, the Sri Mariamman Temple and just beside it is another old Mosque, the Jamae Mosque. Nearby is the Omar Mosque in Kampong Malacca. In Boat Quay were the earliest Jewish quarters and a Synagogue in a shophouse. Upper Cross Street was known in early years as the "Kampong of the Indians". Chulia Street is named after the Muslim Tamils from the Coromandel Coast, South India.

We see therefore in Chinatown since the founding of Singapore, Singaporeans of different ethnic origins embracing diverse religions have lived side by side enjoying complete racial and religious harmony.

Another example is the Jinrikisha Station erected in 1904 at the junction of Neil Road and Tanjong Pagar. The human pullers of these jinrikishas worked under extreme trying conditions, lived in cubicles, in squalor and were exposed to disease. They provided the cheapest mode of public transport. Today the Jinrikisha Station houses a seafood restaurant. Would Singaporeans who patronise this place remember those pullers who provided us the public transport?

Our ancestors came to Singapore not by invitation but on their own free will to seek a better place to toil, live and earn. They laid the foundation of our Republic and succeeding generations have built upon it to make Singapore a haven in this part of the world. Present Singaporeans should continue to make our Republic a better and more prosperous nation, above all, our motherland.

Contents

FORT CANNING

(Bukit Larangan)

History of Singapore begins here
Site of earliest fortress,
the first home of rulers,
the first signal station, religious sites, the oldest cemetery,
the first lighthouse (beacon)
first underground reservoir, the first botanical gardens,
the first Government House, underground bunkers from where
Percival decided to surrender to Japanese; military
establishment of British, Japanese, Malaysian and Singapore.
First home of Singapore Command and Staff College

The earliest settlement in this island could have been Sabara in the second century A.D. of Ptolemy's Golden Khersonese or Pu-luo-chung (island at the end of the peninsula) as referred to by Kang Tai a Chinese explorer in 231 A.D. Reference is also made by Arab sailors who mention Ma'it in the 9th century. The great explorer Marco Polo spoke of Chiamassie; perhaps it is Tamasek as Singapore was known in early times. The Javanese Nagarakretagama of 1365 seems to be first authentic documentary evidence of the settlement of Temasek.

According to the Malay Annals (Sejarah Melayu) Raja Chulan a great king of South India encamped in Temasek on his voyage to conquer China. He abandoned his enterprise and later married a princess and their son was Sang Nila Utama who became ruler of the Indianised Srivijaya Empire based in Sumatra. He took the title of Sri Tri Buana. When he landed in Temasek in 1297 he mistook an animal to be a lion and named the settlement Singapura meaning 'lion city'. He built his palace on the hill nearby (Fort Canning) and fortified it; the hill became known as Bukit Larangan (the forbidden hill) because the ruler lived there and his subjects were forbidden from ascending the hill. It was only after 1819 (the year modern Singapore was founded by Stamford Raffles) that Bukit Larangan became known as Government Hill (Raffles built his house there) and in 1859 it was renamed Fort Canning after Viscount George Canning, Governor-General of India (1857 - 1862).

Bukit Larangan was protected by a wall 16 feet broad at the base and about 9 feet high; it ended in a moat at the base of the hill which was protected on three sides - the salt marsh on the left, the sea in front and the wall on the right.

There was a monolith 10 feet high and 10 feet wide and 2.5 feet thick with writing at the mouth of the Singapore River. It was a tragedy that this ancient piece of historical evidence was blown up by the British soon after the founding of Singapore. The writing on the monolith would have thrown some light on the early history of Temasek.

Archaeological work undertaken by the National Museum and the National University of Singapore shows evidence of ruins of buildings on the summit of the hill. They can be interpreted to be the remains of a Buddhist temple or Chandi and monasteries of Buddhist priests. The excavations unearthed Malay wares, pieces of Chinese porcelain, brass coins and other artefacts.

Singapura gradually emerged as a great trading city but it became the envy of the Hindu Majapahit kingdom and empire in East Java. About 1365 the Majapahits claimed Singapura as its vassal state and demanded tribute from it. Singapura refused and the Majapahits invaded Singapura and razed it to the ground. It is recorded that some disloyal Singaporeans within the fortification secretly opened the main gates to the invaders. End of the account of this invasion says that the soil in Fort Canning is red in colour because of the blood shed by the Singaporeans on the hill during that invasion!

About 1390 Parameswara, a Palembang prince, fled from the Majapahits to Singapura where he assassinated the Siamese ruler and took control of the Settlement. Later for fear of Siamese vengeance Parameswara fled to Malaya

Underground Reservoir Fort Canning.
Top was used as a football field by British forces.

where he founded his new kingdom of Malacca about 1402.

Singapura became part of the Johore-Rhio-Lingga Empire and in the first decade of the 19th century Temenggong Abdul Rahman with a group of Malays set up a village along the Singapore River. It was with this Malay Chief that Stamford Raffles signed the Preliminary Treaty in January 1819 to establish a British settlement here.

Stamford Raffles was born in 1781 and had a poor background; he left school at an early age and joined the East India Company. He improved himself through self-study. In 1805 Raffles was appointed Assistant Secretary to the Governor in Penang which had been founded by the Company in 1786. During the Napoleonic Wars Raffles served as Lieutenant Governor of Java at Batavia from 1811 to 1816 when the Company temporarily took over the Dutch possessions in the East. These included Dutch Malacca.

After the end of the Napoleonic Wars, Raffles had to leave Batavia when the Dutch returned and he assumed his new post as Lieutenant Governor of Bencoolen in South-west Sumatra. There Raffles realised that the Dutch were re-imposing their monopolistic treaties with the local chiefs; further both Penang and Bencoolen were far away from the spice trade. Both the Straits of Malacca and the Sunda Straits, the sea routes between India and China were in the control of the Dutch. Raffles therefore felt that it was imperative that an alternative trading station should be established.

Formerly British military barracks.
Now Arts Centre, Fort Canning Park

On his own initiative he tried to set up a new base in Sumatra but his attempts were thwarted by the Dutch. The Governor-General in India was not happy with Raffles' initiatives. Finally Raffles set sail to Calcutta to convince the Governor-General that a new base should be established. In this Raffles succeeded.

The Governor-General authorised Raffles to set up the base in Acheh (north Sumatra), Rhio or Johore. Raffles could not go to Acheh for there was no approval from London; the second choice were the Carimon Islands in the Rhio Archipelago but he found them unsuitable. Raffles had then to decide on his next objective.

Raffles having worked in Penang must have known of Singapura or Temasek. He had written to his friend William Marsden in 1818, "My attention is principally turned to Johore and you must not be surprised if my next letter to you is dated from the site of the ancient city of Singapura." Major Farquhar who accompanied him was more familiar with the Rhio Archipelago and Singapura.

Further, Raffles' hydrographer, Ross also persuaded Raffles to go to Singapura.

After checking with "Orang Laut" (people of the sea) at the island now named St John's Island that the Dutch were not in Singapura, Raffles then decided to found his new settlement there. His ships anchored off the Singapore River on Thursday 28 January 1819. It is therefore clear that Raffles' first choice to establish a new British Settlement was not Singapore.

Old Gateway to the Fort

Entrance to the bunkers where Lt General Percival made the decision to surrender to the Japanese on 15 February 1942.

Building - military headquarters of Lt General Percival, Malaysian Armed Forces (1963 -65) and the first Singapore Command and Staff College.

On 30 January 1819 Raffles signed a preliminary treaty with Temenggong Abdul Rahman and a formal treaty on 6 February 1819 with both the Sultan Hussein of Johore and Temenggong Abdul Rahman, the de jure and de facto rulers of Singapore. In March 1824 the Anglo-Dutch Treaty was signed by which the Dutch withdrew all objections to the British occupation of Singapore.

In August the same year Sultan Hussein and Temenggong Abdul Rahman ceded Singapore outright to the British in return for increased pensions and cash payments.

In 1822 Raffles built his own house on the Hill and therefore it became the first Government House in Singapore. Government House was a neat bungalow 100 feet by 50 feet deep with rough plank walls, Venetian windows and an attap roof. It was later substantially reconstructed and stood on the Hill until 1859. G. D Coleman Singapore's first architect reconstructed the Government House in brick and tile after 1826. Coleman also extended the house and redesigned it in the Neo Classical style. Raffles also started the first Botanic Gardens on the North-East of the Hill and this covered the area now occupied by the Anglo-Chinese School, Coleman Street, the Armenian Church and the National Museum. Unfortunately the Botanic Gardens were abandoned in 1829 because of the lack of funds to maintain it.

The first Christian cemetery was established on the Hill which was now known as Government Hill; it ceased to be used in 1822 and the new one was consecrated in 1834.

In 1859 the military took over the Hill and lopped off 7 acres of land from the summit to build its defences which included the erection of barracks for the military which moved from Pearl's Hill. By 1861 there were extensive fortifications on the Hill including seven 68 pounders facing the sea.

The first Flagstaff was erected in 1855 and a navigation beam became the lighthouse in 1903. By 1926 the Municipality had completed a large underground reservoir which is still operational. Other buildings were erected on the Hill for the Singapore Base District Headquarters for the Malaya Command and the underground operations centre were also completed.

Between 1923 and 1927 the old fort was demolished and what remains today is only the massive gateway.

A gun was fired from Fort Canning as a salute and to warn the public of fires in the Town; it was also a time gun fired at 5.00 a.m., 12 noon and 9 p.m. This ceased in 1896.

When World War I had started Singapore Base District at Fort Canning had arranged that in case of an emergency a big gun would be fired from the Hill. It was a signal for all units of the armed forces to report to their respective headquarters at once; these included all units in the East and West coasts, those in the Clubs and homes lying within a certain distance of Fort Canning. The gun was fired when the mutiny of Indian soldiers occurred in 1915 and all units reported to their headquarters including the Straits Settlements Volunteer Force which comprised Chinese, Malays, and Eurasians. These volunteers reported to the Drill Hall at Beach Road.

During the final phase of the Battle for Singapore Lieutenant-General A.E. Percival, Commander of the British Forces, shifted his headquarters to the underground bunkers at Fort Canning. It was in the bunkers on 14 February 1942 that he met his senior commanders at 9.30 a.m. and the decision to surrender to the Japanese was reached as a counter-attack was considered impracticable. At 11.45 a.m. Percival reported the military decision to Governor Sir Shenton Thomas who was now in the Singapore Club in Fullerton Building.

On 15 February about noon the emissaries from Percival left for Ford Motor Works Bukit Timah to hand a letter to Lieutenant-General Yamashita who demanded that Percival present himself personally. In the same afternoon Percival accompanied by Brigadier Torrance (of the General Staff), Brigadier Newbigging (Chief Administrator), Major Wild (interpreter) left Fort Canning bunkers to surrender to Yamashita at the Ford Motor Works. The unconditional surrender documents were signed at 7.50 pm. and all hostilities in Singapore ceased after that.

During the Japanese occupation Fort Canning became the Defence Headquarters of the Japanese Imperial Army headed by Major-General Kawamura.

In 1945 September the British returned and soon after occupied Fort Canning.

When Singapore was part of Malaysia from 1963 to 1965 Fort Canning was taken over by the Malaysian Armed Forces; the 4th Malaysian Infantry Brigade under Brigadier Alsagoff occupied the Fort.

After separation from Malaysia the Malaysian forces withdrew to Malaysia and the Singapore Armed Forces took over Fort Canning.

The first Singapore and Command Staff College was established in 1970 in the main administrative block (after extensive renovations) once occupied by Percival and Brigadier Alsagoff. It was officially opened by the Prime Minister, Mr Lee Kuan Yew on 13 February, 1970. The author was appointed (the first Singaporean) to be a member of the Directing Staff of the College. The College later moved to Ayer Rajah and finally to its present premises in Seletar.

Today Fort Canning has been converted into a Historical Park and most of the buildings have been converted for the Arts. What still remain on the Hill are the Old Gateway, the tombstone inscriptions, the Administrative Block, the old barracks, the underground reservoir and the bunkers.

ISTANA
official residence of the President, Republic of Singapore

Source: National Archives, Singapore

ISTANA

Official Residence of the President
Republic of Singapore
(previously known as Government House
official residence of the Governor,
Straits Settlements and Colony of Singapore.
The designation of the resident
reflects the constitutional evolution of Singapore.

The Istana is the official residence of the President of the Republic of Singapore. It was previously known as Government House where the British Governor of the Straits Settlements and later the Governor of the Colony of Singapore resided. When Singapore had self government, the Head of State was known as Yang di Pertuan Negara; this title was retained when Singapore was part of the Federation of Malaysia from 1963 to 1965.

Soon after the founding of modern Singapore by Stamford Raffles in 1819 the first Government House was built on Bukit Larangan (Forbidden Hill) renamed Fort Canning in 1859 after Viscount Canning, Governor-General of India. It was a wooden house with a thatched roof and it cost the East India Company $916. The early residents of Singapore would look up the hill in the morning to see if the House was still there for it looked so light that it could be blown down by a storm! Later Coleman, Singapore's first architect extended the House and redesigned it in the Neo Classical style. The House was demolished in 1859.

In 1867 the Straits Settlements (Penang, Malacca and Singapore) were transferred from the India Office to the Colonial Office. The first Governor under the new constitution Sir Harry Ord temporarily occupied the residence called the "Pavilion" leased to the government by Dr Oxley in Grange Road. Later the Governor occupied Leonie House, also Dr Oxley's property.

Governor Ord eventually ordered that land be purchased and a proper Government House be built. Government then purchased part of the estate of Charles Robert Princep (Princep Street was named after him); the estate once extended from Stamford Road and included Mount Sophia, part of Bukit Timah and Cairnhill.

The design for the new Government House was drawn by J.F.A. McNair; he planned a well proportioned building in the shape of a cross. The architecture was Ionic/Doric with Corinthian pillars and pilasters to the towers and the roof was slated. The plaster was made with Portland cement with white sand and powdered granite. Government House was built with Indian convict labour.

The foundation stone for Government House was laid in July 1867 and the building was completed in 1869 in time to receive the Duke of Edinburgh who visited Singapore that year.

In February 1941 during the Battle for Singapore Government House came under Japanese artillery fire and bombing. Governor Sir Shenton Thomas and Lady Thomas took refuge in the Singapore Club in Fullerton Building. The Union Jack was taken down from the flag staff of Government House and hidden throughout the Japanese Occupation. In 1945 after the Japanese surrender it was rehoisted.

During the Japanese Occupation Government House was occupied by Field Marshal Count Terauchi, Commander, Japanese Southern Army and Major-General Kawamura, Commander (Syonan) Singapore Defence Forces.

Government House was reoccupied by British Governors after the war. In 1959 when Singapore attained self-government the last Governor Sir William Goode became the first Yang di-Pertuan Negara of Singapore. In the same year, Inche Yusof bin Ishak succeeded him as Head of State carrying the same title. Inche Yusof bin Ishak assumed the same title when Singapore became part of the Federation of Malaysia in 1963; when Singapore was separated from Malaysia and became an independent Republic Inche Yusof bin Ishak became its President. When he died in 1970 Dr Benjamin Sheares succeeded him. Mr C.S. V. Devan Nair became President after Dr Sheares. President Wee Kim Wee is now Head of State of the Republic.

Official functions are held in the Istana as well as in its grounds which are open to the public on certain public holidays when President Wee Kim Wee and the First Lady meet ordinary citizens of Singapore.

KERAMAT ISKANDAR SHAH

Fort Canning Park

Evidence that Fort Canning (Bukit Larangan) was not only where the palace of ancient rulers of Singapore (Temasek) was but also their tombs.

It is strongly believed that the "keramat" (the tomb of a holy person) found after the hill was cleared soon after the founding of Singapore in 1819 is that of Iskandar Shah, a king of Temasek.

According to Malay tradition the last of the five kings who ruled Singapore during its golden age in the 14th century was Iskandar Shah. Singapore was invaded and Bukit Larangan was burnt by the Hindu Majapahits from Java and all the followers of Iskandar Shah perished. The ruler managed to flee. Two years later, he founded the new kingdom of Melaka on the west coast of Malaya. Chinese sources indicate that he died about 1420.

It is believed that the first Malay king of Temasek Sri Tri Buana and his chief minister Demang Lebar Daun are buried on the Hill. It is unfortunate that their graves have not been discovered.

Raffles wrote to his friend William Marsden in 1823: "The Tombs of the Malay Kings are, however, close at hand, and I have settled that if it is my fate to die here, I shall take my place among them".

In 1819 soon after the founding of Singapore the Malays refused to ascend the Hill for fear of disturbing the dead.

By 1822 the "keramat" was venerated by Muslims, Chinese and Hindus. It is maintained by a particular Muslim family and their descendants; they have kept the incense burning at the "keramat". One familiar sight near the "keramat" is missing - the hundreds of pigeons. A notice nearby says: "No feeding of pigeons."

KERAMAT ISKANDAR SHAH (under a new roof) Fort Canning Park. Fort Canning the site of tombs of royalty.

A close-up of the Keramat Iskandar Shah (notice the incense burner)

THE FIRST BOTANIC AND EXPERIMENTAL GARDEN

In Fort Canning Singapore started by its founder Stamford Raffles on Bukit Larangan / Government Hill now Fort Canning in 1822.

It may be a surprise to most Singaporeans that the first Botanic Garden was started by Stamford Raffles in 1822 on Bukit Larangan, later known as Government Hill (Fort Canning).

Raffles instructed Farquhar, the Resident, that a Botanic and Experimental Garden be set up on Government Hill; an area of 48 acres was allotted for this purpose.

The Botanic and Experimental Garden was started on the north and north-east slopes of Fort Canning and included the present site of the National Museum, the National Library, the Armenian Church and the Anglo-Chinese School, Coleman Street.

In August 1819 after Raffles had returned to Bencoolen he sent to Farquhar 125 nutmeg plants, 1,000 nutmeg seeds and 450 clover plants and seeds to be planted in the allotted area.

The man Raffles appointed to supervise the Botanic and Experimental Garden was Dr Nathaniel Wallich, a Dane, born in Copenhagen.

Dr Wallich had served as a surgeon in Calcutta and had also been Superintendent of the Botanic Garden there. In Singapore Dr Wallich became a prominent resident. He served on the Land Allotment Committee in 1822. Mount Wallich (named after Dr Wallich) next to the present Ministry of National Development Building was cut down to provide the soil to reclaim what is today Raffles Place (Commercial Square), Cecil Street, Robinson Road and Shenton Way.

Raffles took a personal interest in the Botanic and Experimental Garden and on his visits to Singapore he looked after it from Government House on Government Hill.

The Botanic and Experimental Garden, was a failure. It was abandoned after 30 June 1829. The main reason given was that it was not economical. It cost the settlement $60 per month (a large sum of money in early Singapore) to upkeep it.

For almost 30 years there was no Botanic Garden in Singapore until the present one was begun in 1859 in Napier Road. Eighty acres were set aside for the Garden which was officially opened to the public in 1874 by the

Governor Lieutenant General Sir Andrew Clarke who presented two horned rhinoceroses. The Garden also flourished as a zoo for 20 years when it was abandoned in 1905.

It was here that H.N. Ridley, the Director, planted the first rubber seeds that led to the foundation of the rubber industry of Malaya.

Botanic Gardens
Napier Road

THE OLDEST CHRISTIAN CEMETERY IN SINGAPORE

Fort Canning

A reminder to Singaporeans that we enjoy a very high degree of health and medical care; in early Singapore many died of malaria and cholera epidemic. The tombstones remind us of those who died at an early age because of these epidemics.
The tombstone of George Dromgold Coleman, (is still here) first government architect - left his mark on Singapore's architecture.

The earliest Christian cemetery was close to the flag-staff on top of Government Hill (Fort Canning). This cemetery ceased to be used by the end of 1822; all traces of this burial ground have also disappeared except the inscriptions on tombstones now embedded in the wall surrounding it.

The new cemetery was consecrated by Bishop Daniel Wilson, the Bishop of Calcutta on 4 October 1834 and was ready for use in 1835. This cemetery was a burial ground for members of the Anglican Church and other Protestants. In 1835 the Roman Catholics were allocated the southern half of the cemetery and the line demarcating Protestant and Roman Catholic graves was a brick wall with two arches constructed in 1846. However, this demarcation was not strictly adhered to until 1845. Two mortuary chapels stood on either side of the entrance to the cemetery.

The north gate to the cemetery was designed by Captain Charles Edward Faber, the Superintending Engineer of the Straits Settlements.

The earliest grave marked by the tombstones now embedded in the wall surrounding the old cemetery is that of John C. Collingwood of the ship "Susan"; the tombstone was erected in 1821.

Prominent persons who were buried in the cemetery included George Dromgold Coleman, the first Government Architect, Superintendent of Public Works and Executive Officer of the Convicts and Surveyor. Coleman was also a building contractor and he surveyed the islets for the new Keppel Harbour. Coleman was an Irishman. He was engaged by Sir Stamford Raffles to build Raffles' House (the first Government House) in Fort Canning in 1823. The house was built with timber and later it was reconstructed in brick and tile in neoclassical style. The old Government House looked so fragile that the early residents of Singapore always looked up in the morning to see if it was still there or blown off by the wind!

Coleman built other buildings in Singapore; these included the Old Court House (now Parliament House), the first St Andrew's Church (between 1835

Oldest Cemetery at Fort Canning Park

Tombstone of G. D. Coleman, Singapore's first architect, Fort Canning Park

and 1837), the Armenian Church (1834) and the original Raffles Institution. Coleman also built his own house at No. 3 Coleman Street which was demolished in December 1965 and is the site now occupied by the Peninsula Hotel. His house was earlier converted to a hotel (London Hotel).

Coleman left Singapore on 25 July 1841 after having served Singapore for 15 years. He returned to Singapore in 1843. On 27 March 1844 Coleman died at the age of 48 after a short illness and was buried in Government Hill. A conspicuous monument was raised at his tomb and it still stands as a tribute to the architect to whom the pioneers of Singapore owe so much. The inscription on the tombstone commissioned by his widow reads as follows:

> *For many years the*
> *Superintendent of Public Works*
> *In this Settlement*
> *The important duties of which Department*
> *He was acknowledged to have discharged with zeal*
> *and ability*
> *While the many public improvements*
> *Which he originated and carried out into effect*
> *Will long attest the value of his services.*

Coleman's widow eventually married William Napier, the first law agent in Singapore.

Others buried in the old cemetery were members of the civil service, and early pioneers including Chinese Christians.

The gravestones and memorials were imported from Calcutta, India. Tombs were mostly constructed of brickwork and plaster and many inscriptions cut in granite. A Chief Justice of Singapore, a Russian Consul, the Post Master General and few others were buried in the cemetery. These tombstones now stand close to the road at Canning Rise.

By 1863 the entire cemetery was taken up and the tombstones were falling to pieces. In 1865 the bodies were exhumed and reburied in Bukit Timah Road near Newton Circus a site agreed to by the Municipal Commission. The memorials and tablets are embedded in the north and south walls surrounding the old cemetery in Fort Canning.

The cemetery at Newton Circus was later converted into a public park. The bodies were once again exhumed and reburied in the Christian Cemetery in Chua Chu Kang.

Today the old cemetery is part of the Fort Canning History Park. Young Singaporeans reading the obituaries inscribed in the wall will realise that many people died young in early Singapore because of disease. How fortunate we are today living in a clean Singapore with excellent medical services!

THE MOSQUE AND ROYAL MAUSOLEUM OF TEMENGGONG ABDUL RAHMAN WHO SIGNED THE PRELIMINARY TREATY WITH STAMFORD RAFFLES TO ESTABLISH A BRITISH SETTLEMENT IN SINGAPORE 1819

Telok Blangah

The Mosque (previously the reception hall) of the Temenggong Abdul Rahman whose tomb is in the Royal Mausoleum where a Rajah of Pahang, Rhio, and Lingga Empire is also burried.

Sir Stamford Raffles returned to Singapore three years after the founding of the Settlement. He was displeased with the progress it had made under Major Farquhar, the Resident of Singapore. This was in 1822. Raffles therefore appointed a committee to reorganise the Town and to decide where the different races ought to settle.

On 14 March 1823 Raffles arranged for the Temenggong Abdul Rahman who signed the preliminary Treaty with Raffles in 1819 to establish the Settlement and his followers to vacate the village (kampong) at the mouth of the Singapore River and resettle in a new village (Kampong Bahru) in Telok Blangah. This was Singapore's first urban renewal project.

The Temenggong's new area stretched from Tanjong Pagar to Telok Blangah and covered approximately 200 acres of land. He built his house here and on his new land he grew spices, fruit and gutta percha. He became prosperous.

The Temenggong's Istana (Palace) was demolished. Later the Batu Shoe Factory occupied the site. The factory no longer exists but has been replaced by other modern buildings. The present Mosque which belongs to the Government of Johore (Masjid Kerjaan Johor) was previously a reception hall of the Temenggong's residence.

Next to the Mosque on a hillock is the Royal Mausoleum; it includes the royal tomb of the Rajah of old Pahang, Johore, Rhio and Lingga Empire. Temenggong Abdul Rahman who died in 1825 is also buried there and the various tombstones in the Mausoleum are indicated in a legend placed against a wall.

In front and behind the Mausoleum among numerous other graves is the

State of Johore Mosque.
Once the reception hall of Temenggong Abdul Rahman
Telok Blangah

Royal Mausoleum, Telok Blangah
Temenggong Abdul Rahman who signed Preliminary Treaty with Stamford Raffles 1819 buried here.

Other tombstones in the Mausoleum

special bathing area (now covered with dense trees) of Temenggong Abdul Rahman. There was a running stream which flowed from Telok Blangah Hill (Mount Faber) to the bathing enclosure.

Singaporeans who pass Telok Blangah Road just before they reach the World Trade Centre will easily recognise the two buildings between Kampong Bahru Road and Temenggong Road. In the Mausoleum is the Tomb of Temenggong Abdul Rahman who made it possible in 1819 for Raffles to establish a British Settlement in Singapore.

SULTAN'S GATE - THE ISTANA (SULTAN'S PALACE)

Sultan Hussein signed the Treaty
with Raffles and ceded Singapore
as a British Settlement in perpetuity
Descendants of the Sultan still live here

On 6 February 1819 Raffles acknowledged Hussein as "His Highness the Sultan Hussein Mahomed Shah, Sultan of Johore" and signed a treaty with him. Another Treaty was concluded in June 1819 defining the boundaries of the new Settlement. A final Treaty of Friendship and Alliance between the East India Company, Sultan Hussein and the Temenggong was negotiated in 1824 by John Crawford, the British Resident. In August 1824 in exchange for cash payments and annual pensions Sultan Hussein and Temenggong Abdul Rahman ceded to the East India Company the perpetual title to Singapore and all islands within 10 miles of its shores.

In 1822 Stamford Raffles drew a master plan for Singapore and he assigned specific areas for different races to live in.

Kampong Glam was allocated to the Malays, Bugis and Arabs. The village derives its name from the glam trees found in abundance there. Temenggong Abdul Rahman was resettled in Telok Blangah.

Sultan's Gate was the seat of Malay royalty in Singapore. Raffles reserved Kampong Glam for Sultan Hussein Shah and his descendants.

Sultan Hussein built a palace for himself soon after the founding of Singapore. He brought his whole family and hundreds of followers from Rhio. His son Sultan Ali built Sultan's Gate between 1840 and 1843. Sultan Hussein died in 1835 and was buried in Melaka.

It is lamentable that John Crawfurd, the Resident, tried to oust the Sultan and the Temenggong from Singapore and made their lives miserable. In September 1824 Crawfurd freed 27 female slaves who had escaped from the Sultan's palace. The following month Crawfurd drove a road to Kampong Bugis through the Sultan's compound smashing down his wall! He, however, failed to dislodge the chiefs and their continual residence in Singapore. This rash act brought considerable embarrassment to the British Government.

The style of Sultan's Gate reflects G.D. Coleman's work but there is no evidence that it was Coleman who built it.

Sultan's Gate is painted in strong yellow, the colour of Kings the world over.

The descendants of Sultan Hussein receive about $70,000 annually from

SULTAN'S GATE - The ISTANA (Sultan's Palace), Kampong Glam
Built in 1840 by Sultan Ali, son of Sultan Hussein who signed the treaty with Stamford Raffles and transferred sovereignty of Singapore to the British.

the Singapore Government. Finance Minister Dr Goh Keng Swee said in Parliament on 18 December 1967, that this was an "obligation which we have inherited from the distant past..." The Istana occupied some 66 acres of land which was given by the British government for the use of the heirs of the Sultan. In 1897 the Court of Singapore ruled that the land belonged to the Colony of Singapore and not to the Sultan's descendants but they were allowed to use it. In 1967 there were 23 beneficiaries.

SULTAN'S MOSQUE

North Bridge Road

One of the oldest Mosques in Kampong Glam - the area allocated by Stamford Raffles for Sultan Hussein Shah of Singapore - became a Malay and Arab Settlement.

The first Sultan's Mosque was built about 1824 when North Bridge Road ended at the junction of Arab Street. To erect the present Mosque, North Bridge Road was extended and Jalan Sultan was diverted to provide the space needed for the Mosque.

Sultan Hussein Shah, who signed the Treaty handing Singapore over to the East India Company, was given a sum of $3,000 by the Company to build the Mosque. Financial help also came from local Muslims.

The management of the Mosque was in the hands of the Muslim community. A member of the Sultan's family was responsible for its general administration.

In 1879, fifty-five years later, a special committee was set up to manage the Mosque. Sultan Alauddin Alam Shah nominated the five members of its administrative committee. This system of management continued up to April 1914 when the Colonial government established a Board of twelve Trustees for the Mosque.

In the early twentieth century decision was taken by the Trustees and leading Muslim residents of Singapore to erect a new Mosque because the old one needed substantial repairs. The estimated cost for the new Mosque was $200,000 and a campaign was launched to raise the funds.

The construction of the present Mosque was begun in 1925 and was completed by the end of 1928. A British architect designed the new Mosque in arabesque style with domes, minarets and balustrades. A special feature of the Mosque is the springing of domes from bases formed of many glass bottles.

While the construction of the new Mosque was in progress a part of the old one was used for regular prayers.

The latest renovations of the new Mosque were carried out and completed in September 1968.

The Sultan's Mosque stands in the midst of Kampong Glam the area allotted by Stamford Raffles for Sultan Hussein Shah whilst Temenggong Abdul Rahman was relocated with his followers to Telok Blangah - the first urban renewal project in Singapore. Close to the Sultan's Mosque is the Sultan's Palace - known as Sultan's Gate. The successors of the Sultan still receive an annual pension from the Singapore Parliament. In the precincts of the Mosque is the graveyard of the grandson of Sultan Hussein, Sultan Ali.

Sultan's Mosque, North Bridge Road
First Sultan's Mosque was built in 1824; the present one in 1928. Located in Kampong Glam - area allocated for the Sultan by Sir Stamford Raffles.

THIAN HOCK KENG TEMPLE

158 Telok Ayer Street

Gazetted as a national monument on 6 July 1973

The point for disembarkation of early Chinese immigrants and oldest Chinese Temple in Singapore. The main deity Ma Cho Po protected the immigrants during their long voyage across the South China Sea to the new settlement of Singapore.

Chinese Temples in the early 19th century served as cultural community and education centres; God and deities protected their lives; the Temples helped the pioneers to maintain their cultural heritage, their values and identity.

The Thian Hock Keng Temple had its beginnings as a joss house on Telok Ayer Street when the early Chinese immigrants especially from the southern provinces of Kwangtung, Kwangsi, Foochow, Amoy and Canton came in their crowded junks soon after Sir Stamford Raffles founded the settlement of Singapore. Large scale immigration began in 1830s.

The immigrants .came from South China for political and economic reasons. The Chinese Emperor tended to concentrate on the welfare of his subjects in the north and north-west of China where his traditional enemies were. Shi Huang-ti built the Great Wall in 226 B.C. against the Tartars. The first capital of China was Nanking and later Peking - both in the north. Chinese officials from the capital travelled south to raise taxes and South Chinese resented this. They gradually developed an anti-government attitude. This led them to form secret societies to protect themselves from oppressive officials. There were also economic problems. A large number of South Chinese decided to leave China to seek their fortunes in Singapore.

The junks (generally described as "hell ships") from South China were overcrowded with immigrants who disembarked at Telok Ayer Basin.

Telok Ayer until the 1880s was on the water front. It was in 1887 that the Telok Ayer Basin was filled with earth from Mount Wallich; Cecil Street and Robinson Road to Shenton Way were swamps.

It was on the shore that the immigrants built their joss house for Ma Cho Po (Mother of the Heavenly Sages) some time between 1821 and 1822 to thank the Goddess for having brought them safely across the South China Sea.

The joss house was rebuilt as Thian Hock Keng Temple between 1839 and 1842 with funds collected from wealthy men like Tan Tock Seng, a Hokkien merchant. A large sum was also received from owners of Chinese junks from China, Siam and Java. All the building materials, the pine wood, the granite

Thian Hock Keng Temple, Telok Ayer Street
Oldest Chinese Temple and point of disembarkation of early Chinese immigrants

The main altar

pillars, the carvings and the craftsmen were all brought from China. The statue of Ma Cho Po arrived in Singapore in April 1840 and there were large scale celebrations in Telok Ayer Street.

The Temple is square. It has a central hall leading to a large courtyard and another courtyard with an altar of Kuan Yin. This Temple like all Chinese Temples has symbols and designs intended to promote the health and happiness of the worshippers.

The decorations remain almost intact today. They are richly ornamental and reflect traditional Chinese temple architecture in China.

The Temple was completed at a cost of Spanish $30,000. In the courtyard is the Bodhisattva, Kuan Yin, two pagodas each with an octagonal base. Strong beams support the curving, wide eaved roof. The type of structures dates back to the Han Dynasty or even earlier. The hexagonal and two octagonal pagodas, two in this Temple, were popular especially during the Sung Dynasty.

Inside the Temple is also a special plaque presented to the abbot in 1907 by the Qing Emperor.

At the entrance to the Temple is a very low granite wall or barrier over which the devotees have to cross to enter the Temple; this is a reminder to Singaporeans and visitors that this was built to prevent the sea water entering the Temple during high tide. Today the sea is far away from Telok Ayer Street.

Telok Ayer Street was the centre of Chinatown in the early years and South Chinese met in the Temple even to settle disputes among the devotees and hold meetings of the Hokkien community.

The biggest event of this Temple in the past and at present is the celebration of Ma Cho Po who has blessed countless number of Chinese with luck and protection to become the most worshipped deity in the world today.

According to the legend Ma Cho Po was a young girl who performed supernatural feats: healing the sick, walking on the water and foretelling the future. She is the sixth daughter of a Jujian sailor who lived during the Sung Dynasty (960-1279). The original name of Ma Cho Po was Lin Muonjiang and she undertook many miraculous rescues at sea. For her divine intervention the Empress gave her the title Tian Hou (Queen of Heaven) and Tian Fei (Lady in Waiting to Heaven). Ma Cho Po is a sea Goddess worshipped by millions of Chinese all over the world; the Chinese pray to her for safe journey before embarking on a voyage.

Ma Cho Po was a symbol of peace to the early Chinese immigrants who toiled to bring prosperity to their descendants in Nanyang. The older generation called her Tian Hou (Tien Fu Gong) or fondly as Ma Cho Po in Hokkien. The Thian Hock Keng Temple was exclusively devoted to Ma Cho Po for a few decades in the early years.

Masjid Omar Kampong Melaka off Havelock Road

On either side of the Thian Hock Keng Temple are the old Mosques built by Tamil Muslims, the Nagore Dhurga Shrine and the Al Abrar. Behind these in South Bridge Road is the oldest Hindu Temple, the Sri Mariamman Temple. Next to this Hindu Temple is the Jamae Mosque. Just further down is the Omar Mosque and Kampong Malacca in Havelock Road

In Boat Quay were the Jewish quarters and the Synagogue in a shop house. At the end of Telok Ayer Street is the Telok Ayer Chinese Methodist Church.

Chinatown has indeed been a fine example of racial and religious harmony in Singapore since the founding of Singapore in 1819.

NAGORE DURGHA SHRINE

(originally known as Shahul Hamid Durgha)
Telok Ayer Street

Old Tamil Mosque built by early Tamil immigrants in Chinatown; a cultural centre, a meeting place and house of worship by pioneers. Built next to the Thian Hock Keng Temple - a unique feature even in early Singapore - religious and racial harmony.

This was gazetted as a national monument on 29 November 1974.

The Nagore Durgha Mosque was built between 1828 and 1830. It is therefore one of the earliest houses of worship in Singapore. This Mosque is also known as Masjid Moulana Mohammad Ally and is in memory of the holy man Shahul Hamid of Nagore, South India.

Land was granted to one Kaderpillai in 1827 and provision was made that no building of wood and attap should be erected. By the Court Order of 15 June 1893 a board of new trustees was appointed; they were M. Mohamed, V. Hameed, S. Saiboo Ghany, K. Mohamed Ismail and T. Chinna Tamby.

The Mosque has flutal Corinthian pillars, fan lights over windows, a pierced Islamic balustrade and two stepped minarets.

The Mosque must have been not only a house of worship but also a meeting place of early Tamil Muslims and a cultural centre as well. A unique feature of even early Singapore was its religious and racial harmony for this Mosque is located next to the oldest Hokkien Temple, the Thian Hock Keng Temple; both are located in Telok Ayer Street, the centre of Chinatown.

Nagore Durgha Shrine, Telok Ayer Street
One of the oldest Tamil Muslim Mosques next to Thian Hock Keng Temple.

MASJID AL ABRAR

Telok Ayer Street

Old Mosque built by early Tamil Muslims in Singapore
Symbol of early immigration of Tamils to Singapore

It was gazetted as a national monument on 29 November 1974.

The original Masjid Al Abrar was a thatched hut put up after 1827. It was not until 1850-55 that the brick building was erected. The land lease is for 999 years held originally by Hadjee Puckery Mohamed Khatib bin Shaik Mydin a Trustee for the Muslim community.

Al-Abrar is also known as Koochoo Pally (A small Mosque). The Mosque is surrounded by a brick wall with two plain minarets and a dome.

By order of Court on 21/11/1910 trustees were appointed to look after this Mosque. The trustees were K. Mohamed Eusofe, E Thamby Ravooter, S. Kanisah Maricayer, V. M. Kader Bux and J. Sultan Abdul Kader.

Masjid Al Abrar Telok Ayer Street
Another old Tamil Mosque

SRI MARIAMMAN TEMPLE

oldest Hindu Temple in
Singapore built by Naraina Pillay.

Naraina Pillay
first Indian and Tamil pioneer
of Singapore; accompanied Stamford
Raffles in 1819; the first brick maker
and building contractor of Singapore;
the earliest Indian community leader
of Singapore.

Sri Mariamman (Rain maker) Mother Goddess,
protective deity; the Temple centre of early
South Indians to sustain their identity, culture and heritage.

Gazetted as a national monument on 6 July 1973

Naraina Pillay was a government clerk in Penang and would have come to the attention of Stamford Raffles who was in 1805 the assistant secretary to the Governor of Penang which was founded by the East India Company in 1786. Raffles must have found Naraina Pillay a dependable, honest and versatile person that he selected him to accompany him during his second visit to Singapore in May 1819.

Soon after his arrival in Singapore, Naraina Pillay established himself in Singapore. He became a business man with all the qualities of a leader and pioneer; he had his fingers in so many pies. He set up the first kiln in Singapore to bake bricks and also became the first building contractor in the Settlement. Jane Beamish and Jane Ferguson in their book "A History of Singapore Architecture" write: "Pillay started the first Singapore brick company, an operation that was to make him not only rich but a fundamental contributor to the history of Singapore's early architecture".

Naraina Pillay opened a shop to sell cotton piece goods which were in great demand in Singapore. A tragedy hit Naraina Pillay when fire burnt his shop and he went bankrupt in 1822. Raffles helped Naraina Pillay to restore his fortunes. This is clear evidence of Raffles' concern for the Tamil pioneer who became once again a wealthy merchant. He had a shop in Commercial Square (Raffles Place).

Later, he asked a few carpenters, brick-layers and cloth merchants from Penang to come to Singapore to join him; one such merchant was Viahpoory.

In early 1823 Naraina Pillay obtained the present site to build the Sri Mariamman Temple in South Bridge Road.

Sri Mariamman Temple - oldest Hindu Temple in Singapore founded by Naraina Pillay, first Tamil pioneer who accompanied Raffles to Singapore in 1819. First brick maker and building contractor of Singapore.

Sri Mariamman Temple, South Bridge Road

The first site offered by the government for the Temple was in Telok Ayer Street but there was no fresh water close to the site. The Resident, Major William Farquhar then offered an alternative site near the Bras Basah stream (the present Stamford Canal). The exact location is not known. The Town Planning Committee eventually advised Naraina Pillay to build the Temple on the present site at South Bridge Road.

Hindu civilisation dates from very ancient time and Hinduism in its quintessence is a belief in the universality of ONE GOD, Brahman the infinite. The essence of the Hindu religion is the oneness of life in all its manifestations. God is one and is seen in three of his major aspects: Brahma, the creator, Vishnu, the preserver (who remedies evil to preserve the good), and Shiva, the destroyer and procreator; these three are represented by three deities.

Sri Mariamman the Mother Goddess nourishes and protects all beings. Sri Mariamman is associated with rain; she gives life, nurtures and sustains it. She is the source of all energy without which nothing moves in this world; she has various forms which describe her attributes in eloquent appearances. The Mother Goddess is also called Devi, the divine, the celestial and the first to be worshipped; she is the gentle and loving Nirmala, the pure, peerless or incomparable. She also carries the name of Kalyani and Sumangali or Shankari, one who confers happiness and prosperity. As Rajeswari she is the ruler of the Universe and as Kali, the deity that destroys evil.

The deity Mariamman can be traced as far back as 4,000 years ago to the Indus Valley civilisation of Mohenjo-daro and Harappa in North West India and it is believed to be a Dravidian civilisation.

The worship of the female aspects of Shiva is a major feature of the Navaratri Festival.

The fire-walking ceremony also held in this Temple has direct bearing on the "Mahabharata", the great war which embroiled the whole of ancient India, but the conflict centres on the rivalry of two closely related Aryan clans, the Kauravas and the Pandava brothers, fighting for the possession of the Doab, the territory between the Ganges and the Jumna. Duryodhara (the eldest of the Kauravas) artfully provoked Yudhisthra (the eldest of the Pandavas) to play dice and by trickery caused him to lose his kingdom, his brothers, his own person and his wife, Thirobathi.

The ceremony is held here because the idol of Thirobathi is installed in it and she is considered as an "avatar" (a re-incarnation) of the universal Mother.

The boat caulking Indian community who lived in Jalan Sultan and had migrated from Poigaiyur, Nagapatanam, installed their village deity Thirobathi Amman in the Temple and managed the fire-walking ceremony until 1975.

The fire-walking ceremony is a purification one; it is a ceremony where a devotee submits himself to walk over fire as a fulfilment of a vow or as an act of repentance of his sins or as a form of penance.

Several rituals are conducted in the Temple before the actual fire-walking.

The fire pit is about 3 metres long and is filled with firewood and ignited; when the flames die down they leave behind a pit of smouldering embers.

The Temple's head priest carrying a "karakam" (water vessel containing various items in it) on his head leads the devotees across the fiery pit. When they have crossed the pit they step on to a pool of milk.

The fire-walking demands from the devotee deep devotion, abstinence of worldly pleasures and fasting. No harm comes to the devotee who has devoutly and with piety prepared himself for the ceremony. Women devotees are not allowed to walk across the fiery pit but walk around it.

NANYANG CHO CLANMEN'S ASSOCIATION SINGAPORE

103 Onan Road

First member of the Cho clan was Cho Ah Chee
the ship's carpenter of "S.S. Indiana"
in which Raffles travelled to
Singapore in 1819

No. 1 Lavender Street was the attap house of Cho Ah Chee the carpenter of the ship "S.S. Indiana" in which Sir Stamford Raffles travelled to Singapore in 1819.

It is believed that Raffles gave the house to Cho Ah Chee in recognition of his services at the time of the founding. The house has been demolished and a small public park has taken its place.

Cho Ah Chee established the Ning Yeung Wei Kuan in South Bridge Road in 1822 probably the first Overseas Chinese Association. He built an assembly hall and a temple for men who migrated to Singapore from the Toi San District of Canton. Cho Ah Chee died in 1830 and was originally buried in Ann Siang Hill. Later his body was exhumed and reburied in the Peck San Teng Cemetery in Thomson Road.

Cho Ah Chee was the first member of the Cho Clan Association. Its headquarters are at 103 Onan Road.

Cho Clan Association Joo Chiat
Cho was Raffles' carpenter on ship "S.S. Indiana"

Cho's residence in Lavender Street was in this location.

Jamae Masjid, South Bridge Road, another old Tamil Mosque

JAMAE MASJID (MOSQUE)

218 South Bridge Road

Tamil Muslims' Mosque - one of the oldest Mosques in Singapore Tamil Muslim pioneers of Singapore - merchants, traders, businessmen and shopkeepers - contributed to Singapore's economic prosperity from early Singapore.

Some of the earliest pioneers and immigrants to come to Singapore soon after its foundation were the Chulia Muslims (Tamil Muslims from Coromandel Coast, India). A number of them settled in Chulia Street (named after them); earlier the street was called Kling Street.

Because of the large number of Tamil Muslims in Chinatown three of the oldest Mosques are located in this area: the Jamae Masjid, the Nagore Durgha and the Masjid Al Abrar.

The Jamae Masjid was built as early as 1826 under the leadership of Ansar Sahib. The building in its present brick form was completed between 1830-1835 and the land on which it stands is on a 999 year lease dated 24 November 1881 made between the Governor of the Straits Settlements and five Trustees of the Indian Muslims Management Committee.

The Mosque has two stepped minarets and intricate decorations. It has a large prayer hall and a very spacious courtyard. Next to the Mosque is the oldest Hindu Temple in Singapore - the Sri Mariamman Temple.

TELOK AYER CHINESE METHODIST CHURCH

Telok Ayer Street

Gazetted as a national monument on 23 March 1989
Another example of the "March of Methodism" in Singapore.

Benjamin F. West a medical doctor had his clinic in rented premises in Japan Street renamed Boon Tat Street; there he not only had his medical practice but he also practised as a Christian missionary; he had converted some of his patients to Christianity. It was in 1889 that he was appointed to head the Chinese Christian work and later in 1897 the Reverend Ling Ching Mi of the Foochow Conference was sent to take charge of the Chinese missionary work in Singapore. In 1901 Reverend W.G. Shellabear arrived with two Chinese pastors, one Hokkien speaking and the other Foochow to head the missionary work among the Chinese.

In 1913 the congregation moved from the rented shophouse to worship in the Fairfield Methodist Girls' School in Neil Road. As the number of worshippers increased it was felt that a distinct Church should be built for the Telok Ayer congregation. A piece of land was purchased and the present Church was built on it. The corner stone was laid on 9 January 1924 and the French firm of Bross and Mogin were the architects.

Architecturally the building represents the eclectic style, the "Singapore eclectic", a combination of Eastern and Western influences. This particular style was fashionable during the period between 1918 and 1930 when many houses were built with this type of architecture. Such houses are located in various parts of Singapore including Katong, Jalan Besar and Emerald Hill.

The Church has a colonnade ground floor with the exterior of the Roman Doric and Tuscan order; it has a flat roof with a Chinese pavilion on it; the windows are quasi Venetian and Chinese.

In the early 20th century members of the Church provided welfare service to those in the neighbourhood; this included writing letters in Chinese (for the illiterate) to their relatives in China.

During World War II the Church was used as a refugee camp for about 300 persons and the descendants of some of these are members of the Church today. To protect the refugees a special front wall was built to the Church building; it remains today to remind the congregation of the Japanese Occupation.

Telok Ayer Chinese Methodist Church
Telok Ayer Street

Telok Ayer Chinese Methodist Church celebrated its centenary on 23 March 1989.

The Church represents another lap in the "March of Methodism" in Singapore when congregations speaking Chinese dialects, English, Malay and Tamil appeared in different parts of Singapore.

CHINATOWN

Early settlement of Chinese immigrants - locality assigned by Stamford Raffles in 1822; living and working under extreme conditions they contributed to the development of Singapore.
Chinatown in Singapoe is unique in the world.

In November 1822 Stamford Raffles wrote to the Town Committee in Singapore about his plans for the layout of the Town and the setting of the various major ethnic groups in the island. These major ethnic areas were for the poor but the rich could settle anywhere they chose to.

"The Chinese," Raffles wrote, "will form by far the largest portion of the community" and he assigned the south-west of the Singapore River to them. They should also be settled according to the provinces they came from in China and be under the immediate control of their respective chiefs for the maintenance of law and order.

Raffles also suggested that the streets in Chinatown should run as far as practicable at right angles and the artisans - blacksmiths, carpenters and others should be concentrated in certain areas. For the sake of uniformity Raffles specified that the shophouses and houses should be built in brick and tiled and each house should have a verandah or covered passage five feet wide to provide an open space where the dwellers in the crowded houses could have fresh air and also where food hawkers could operate. The houses and shophouses were built in neat rows and in the centre was an air-well open to the sky. This served for the collection and storage of water, for ventilation and light.

Chinatown became a crowded place particularly after the 1830s when the large scale emigration from South China took place. The occupants of these shop-houses or terraced houses lived in cubicles - sordid, dark, grimy and self-contained living areas. The corridors that divided the cubicles were narrow. The entire belongings of the dwellers were in the corner of the cubicle - the storage boxes and a board which doubled up at night as a bed.

Until 1935 the night soil (collected in buckets) was carried through the front door. Later back lanes were created and the buckets were removed from there. How fortunate Singaporeans are today living in Housing and Development Board flats with modern sanitation, water supply and electricity!

Despite the hard living conditions, the Chinese to sustain their cultural heritage, their traditions and identity, built several Chinese Temples in the area, had their own singing halls and "wayang" (opera) theatres.

Old buildings, Chinatown

Renovated building Chinatown

Unfortunately there were also government licensed opium dens (opium was one of the main sources of revenue), illegal gambling houses and brothels. There were also rickishaw depots and most of the coffee shops were patronised by the rickishaw pullers.

Secret Societies originated in South China operated in Chinatown and it was a major problem in early Singapore.

Sago Street was named by the Cantonese, "Street of the Dead" where the funeral clothes, paper models of cars and houses were sold. There was Sago Lane where the death houses were ; "these are where the sick go ostensibly for treatment but where chances of recovery are almost nil". Inmates of these death houses simply wasted away slowly and then after death were moved to the funeral parlours. Many died of epidemics like cholera and malaria.

In Chinatown lived the Sam Sui women who were extremely industrious workers who carried earth which was a back-breaking occupation.

These women came from three districts of Kwantung: Sam Sui, Shun Tak and Tong Koon. The Sam Sui women were found predominantly in Upper Chin Chew Street, Upper Nanking Street and Eu Tong Sen Street. Upper Chin Chew Street was nicknamed "Black Cloth" street because of the colour of the clothes of these women. The Sam Sui women wore scarlet head-dress, loose black "samfoos" (jacket and trousers) and lived in cubicles. These Cantonese women rarely married and led a life of frugality but they were colourful and conservative; they kept largely to themselves. They were generally kind and had a sense of humour; they ate plain food - rice and vegetables - but sent regular remittances to their families in China.

It was estimated that by 1941 there were several thousands of these Sam Sui women working and contributing to the economic growth of Singapore.

Most of those who lived in Chinatown worked in the tongkangs, twakows and lighters and ferried goods from sea going vessels to the several warehouses along the Singapore River; many worked in the early years in the spice plantations and later in the Singapore Harbour and the Dockyard.

Other races also dwelt in Chinatown. There were a large number of Indians; proof of this is the number of old Tamil Mosques and the oldest Hindu Temple in Chinatown. Upper Cross Street was also known as "Kampong of the Indians" where a number of Indian spice traders and boatman lived. Indonesians lived in "pondoks" (lodging houses); one such example is the one still at 32 Club Street off Upper Cross Street. Near Havelock Road is Kampong Malacca and one of the oldest Mosques. Near North Canal was the early quarters of the Jews as well as their oldest Synagogue.

During the Battle for Singapore Chinatown was bombed daily by the Japanese. The heart of Chinatown was roughly an area of 30 acres with almost 20,000 crammed into it. There were no air raid shelters in Chinatown because the British authorities had bungled their air-raid policy. Many had to cower in their crowded homes or lie panic stricken in filthy monsoon ditches. The Japanese bombers made indiscriminate raids on Chinatown and the casualties mounted day by day.

The Civil Defence unit comprised mainly Chinese who were brave and worked around the clock, clearing roads, and debris; rescue workers had to extricate the victims in bombed buildings and death lorries had to be manned to collect the unclaimed bodies for mass burials in deep pits. To show respect to the different races the bodies were grouped according to the races and kept apart in the pits.

Many in Chinatown and whose homes were bombed and had become homeless sought refuge in the several Chinese Temples and in the Telok Ayer Chinese Methodist Church.

Despite urban renewal projects several parts of Chinatown are still intact and Singaporeans should visit these areas (some renovated) to realise how our ancestors had lived and toiled to make Singapore what it is today.

'Pondok' (Indonesian lodging house) in Club Street, Chinatown

MINISTRY OF LABOUR BUILDING

Havelock Road

The building housed the Chinese Protectorate which supervised and protected Chinese immigrants. It formed a link between the Chinese masses and the Colonial government.

Large scale Chinese migration to Singapore from South China occurred during the 1830s. The early British officials were unable to control and protect the migrants. In 1867 the control of the Straits Settlements was transferred from the India Office to the Colonial Office and a Straits Settlements Legislative Council was established to pass laws for the Straits Settlements. Though various laws were passed, their implementation was not effective largely because there were no colonial officials who could speak the different Chinese dialects.

William Pickering was a Chinese Interpreter in Singapore in 1872. He spoke several Chinese dialects. He was appointed as the first Chinese Protector in 1877 and he established the Chinese Protectorate. The early Chinese immigrants called Pickering, "Mr Pinkiling".

The Chinese Protectorate was first set up in a shop-house in North Canal Road. It moved to Havelock Road in 1886 to larger premises. These were demolished in 1930 and the present building was erected.

Ministry of Labour Building, Havelock Road previously the Chinese Protectorate.

The officials of the Chinese Protectorate had very responsible duties; they had to deal with in-coming immigrants, check abuse in the coolie traffic, licence the vessels and go on board in-coming Chinese junks and ships. They had also to register societies, prevent forced prostitution and protect Chinese women and girls. In the 1870s, 80% of the women were sold to the brothels. The population of Chinese in 1884 was 60,000 Chinese men and 6,600 women. Chinese immigration by 1873 was 103,000 when there was great demand in the tin mines in the Malay States for Chinese labour.

Responsibilities of the Chinese Protectorate increased when its officials had to keep surveillance over Chinese political parties like the Communist Party of Malaya and the Kuomintang branches.

The Chinese Protectorate no longer served its purpose after World War II. Its various functions were taken over by the Immigration, Labour, Social Welfare and Education Departments. In 1955 the Labour Front Government established the Ministry of Labour and Social Welfare. In 1959 the People's Action Party Government formed the Ministry of Labour and Law.

Today when Singaporeans pass by the massive building of the Ministry of Labour in Havelock Road they are reminded of the difficult tasks undertaken by the Chinese Protectorate. William Pickering is remembered in two streets: Pickering Street and Upper Pickering Street.

Another view of the MInistry of Labour Building

YUE HAI QING MIAO

Phillip Street

One of the earliest Chinese Temples in Singapore; built for worship of the spirits who protected the traders who travelled between Singapore and China; a meeting place for the Teochew Clan.

Yue Hai Qing Miao means the "Temple of the Calm Sea built by the Guanzhou people". Phillip Street was then close to the sea. This is one of the oldest Taoist Temples in Singapore and it began as a small shrine like the Temple in Telok Ayer Street as early as 1826. The present Temple was built in the 1850s; it was both a Temple and Teochew Clan Association.

This Temple had close ties with China since its inception. The imperial signboard in the Temple premises proves this; Emperor Guang Xu of the Qing dynasty presented this to the Abbot of the Temple.

Statues of the Heavenly Father (Yuan Tian Shang Di) and the Queen of Heaven (Tian Hou) sit in the right and left wing altars of the Temple.

Yue Hai Qing Miao is a twin temple, built in the traditional classical design. It stands in the midst of the high rise buildings and is close to Raffles Place. Today, it is not easy to locate it but once it occupied a prominent position beside the sea. Traders returning from China disembarked from their junks and went into this Temple to offer their prayers and gratitude for their safe arrival - such was the faith of our ancestors.

Yue Hai Qing Miao
One of the oldest Chinese Temples - a place of worship and meeting place for the Teochew clan.

THE MAGHAIM ABOTH AND THE CHASED EL SYNAGOGUES

Jews - among early pioneers and businessmen

Oldest Synagogue in Boat Quay; old Jewish quarters in Chinatown

The first Jews in Singapore can be traced to 1830 when traders of the Jewish faith came to the settlement of Singapore. By 1833 there were 22 Jews: 18 males and 4 females; in 1846 there were 6 Jewish merchant houses in Singapore. By 1858 there were 20 Jewish families in Singapore.

The earliest Synagogue was in Synagogue Street behind the old Central Police Station and for 30 years it served the Jewish community in Singapore. Later it was sold to be used as a shophouse. This building was demolished after the Japanese Occupation. The first Jewish quarters were in Boat Quay, off South Canal Road, behind the Hill Street Building which today houses the Oral History Department, the Archives, the Film Censor's Office and the Public Trustee's Office. Later, the Jews moved to North Bridge Road, Sophia Road, Wilkie Road, Dhoby Ghaut, Waterloo Street, Prinsep Street and Selegie Road.

In 1873 the Jewish community bought a piece of land from government in Church Street now known as Waterloo Street and the present Synagogue known as the Maghaim Aboth (Shield of our Fathers) was built there; the consecration was on 4 April 1878. In 1924 extensions were made to the Synagogue.

Famous Jews include Manasseh Meyer who in 1870 established the firm of Joshua Brothers. Nissim Adis owned the land now occupied by the Supreme Court and he built the Grand Hotel del'Europe. By 1900 the old Jewish Cemetery in Orchard Road next to one of the oldest Hindu Temples, the Sivan Temple, was closed and a new burial ground was opened in December 1900 in Moulmein Road.

By 1910 about 500 Jews had settled in Singapore and because of dissension in the order of service and specific rituals a new Synagogue was completed in 1905. It was a private Synagogue built by the Mannasehs in Oxley Rise and they named it Chased El Synagogue. Manasseh Meyer had a special chair in an alcove near the Abel and around this his family was seated during the prayers. Manasseh Meyer's, residence, the Belle Vue was close to the Synagogue.

Maghaim Aboth - Synagogue Waterloo Street Jews - pioneers and businessmen.

Chased El Synagogue
private Synagogue of Sir Manasseh Meyer, Oxley Rise

Manasseh Meyer donated $150,000 towards the Raffles College Fund and the Manasseh Meyer Block was named after him. It remains untouched in the Bukit Timah Campus - now the Institute of Education. In 1941 the Jewish population in Singapore had risen to 844.

During the Japanese Occupation the Jews were interned in various stages, in 1942, 1943 and 1945. They were interned at Sime Road Camp and Changi Gaol.

There were several eminent Jews in Singapore. Today the most well-known is David Marshall, the first elected Chief Minister of Singapore and presently Singapore's Ambassador to France. Others include J. Grimberg, Harry Elias both eminent lawyers.

BELLE VUE HOUSE

Oxley Rise

Once residence of Manasseh Meyer the well-known Singapore Jew, pioneer and philanthropist.

Belle Vue House was erected by Singapore's first architect Coleman in 1842 for Dr Oxley, the well-known government surgeon in the 1830s. Dr Oxley also owned the nutmeg plantation on the hill which was named after him.

In 1857 Dr Oxley left Singapore. The house was eventually bought over by Sir Manasseh Meyer, the eminent Jew who added a second wing to the residence which was within walking distance to his private synagogue, the Chased El Synagogue built in 1905. The Manasseh Meyer family still occupy Belle Vue House, Oxley Rise.

Before Manasseh Meyer purchased the House it was acquired and converted into a boarding house for the Anglo-Chinese School at Coleman Street. The Board of Trustees of the Boarding School included prominent Chinese businessmen Tan Jiak Kim, Tan Hap Seng and Tan Boo Liat.

Belle Vue House

KAMPONG BUGIS

Kallang

Early settlement of the Bugis from Macassar, Celebes.

The home of the Bugis is Macassar, Celebes, They played an important part in the political development of the Malay Peninsula in the 18th century. They were great warriors and this enabled them to extend their political influence to Kedah and Perak and established a Bugis Sultanate in Selangor.

Soon after the founding of Singapore Bugis traders came to the settlement. By 1820 the "Pallari", the distinct Bugis vessels, were a familiar sight in the Kallang River. About 500 Bugis with their chief Arong Bilawa in 1822 fled from Macassar to Singapore to settle down here. Raffles in his master plan for the settlement allotted to the Bugis the land between Kampong Glam and Rochore River. In the late 19th century Kampong Bugis developed along the north side of the Rochore River.

During the Japanese Occupation a number of Bugis were resettled in Pontian, Johore and others moved out to Beach Road and Arab Street.

Today the Bugis have been assimilated into the Malay community and live in the Housing and Development Board flats.

Kampong Bugis, original home of the Bugis - near the Kallang Gas Works

BAWAEANESE PONDOK
(lodging house)

64 Club Street
ChinatownA social institution to assist early Indonesian Immigrants to Singapore

The Pondok Peranakan Gelam Club at 64 Club Street in Chinatown was founded in 1932 by early settlers from Pulau Bawean.

There were pondoks in Blair Road, Everton Road, Spottiswoode Park, Duxton Hill, Serangoon Road and Jalan Besar; some of them are still there. The Baweanese who established these pondoks came from an island north of Java and south of Kalimantan Indonesia.

They set up the pondok for the new migrants from their district or village. The migrants took on various jobs as gardeners, horse-carriage drivers and syces with the assistance of those who had already settled in Singapore.

The pondok was a social institution that helped the Baweanese to cope with life in a foreign land. It was based on the principle of mutual help and on strict sanctions to uphold the honour of the institution.

Pondoks were shophouses. Married couples used the bedrooms upstairs while singles and children slept downstairs on wooden platforms. Every couple had its own stove and when a misunderstanding arose the head of the pondok (pak lurah) would settle it. Meals were generally prepared by their kinsmen and the partakers paid for them. Rentals were paid to the head or his assistant. Even government fines imposed on individuals were met by the pondok. Punishment was meted out to members who threatened other families; the pondok members would decide the punishment even expelling the member.

By 1860 there were about 3000 Javanese and Baweanese in Singapore.

Very few pondoks are left in Singapore as most of the occupants have moved into Housing and Development Board flats.

The early Baweanese lived in harmony with Chinese and Indians in early Singapore.

A Pondok

Inside a pondok in Dalhousie Lane
Note the long wooden platform where bachelors slept

JINRIKISHA STATION

NEIL ROAD
TANJONG PAGAR

Jinrikishas were the cheapest means of public transport until the end of World War II; this building remembers the men who toiled to provide this service.

The Jinrikisha Station in Neil Road was constructed in 1903 to ease the heavy load of the Station in Middle Road. It stands on a triangular plot at the junction of Neil Road and Tanjong Pagar Road and has a curved corner at the junction of these two roads. An extra storey was added to the roof, a lantern-shaped structure.

Today the Jinrikisha Station building is a seafood restaurant.

The Middle Road Station (Office of the Registrar of Vehicles) until recently served as the Work Permit Office of the Ministry of Labour.

The jinrikisha was invented in Japan in 1869. It meant "man-powered carriage"; in the Jinrikisha Ordinance it means "a wheeled vehicle for the conveyance of passengers drawn by one or more men." The jinrikisha was introduced to Singapore in 1880 from Shanghai. It became the main mode of transport in Singapore and the cheapest. In Malay the jinrikisha was called "kreta Hong Kong".

The jinrikisha provided additional employment for a section of the Chinese immigrants in the Colony. The owners of the jinrikisha came from South China primarily from Foochow and Canton. There were about 1000 owners in the 19th century and each had 1 to 20 jinrikishas which had to be registered and licenced. These owners hired them out to pullers on two shifts: 6 am to 2p.m. and 3 p.m. to midnight; sometimes the shift ran from 5 p.m. to 3 a.m. the following morning.

The jinrikisha took the largest proportion of the traffic in the Colony; it was also the cheapest and the most convenient for commuters. The distance the jinrikisha carried its passengers extended from several hundred yards to about two miles. By the early 20th century the jinrikisha became the pride of the road and it was patronised by shoppers, hawkers, colonial officials tourists and even prostitutes. The jinrikisha and their pullers became part of the scene near hotels, markets and in business districts; they could be seen plying in South Bridge Road, New Bridge Road, Collyer Quay, Raffles Place and Tank Road. The pullers particularly competed for the right to operate the lucrative Raffles Hotel pitch. In 1923 about 400 of the pullers fought for this right. The Duxton area in Tanjong Pagar used to be the battleground where pullers from different clans fought one another often to protect their monopoly of the jinrikisha trade.

The jinrikisha pullers were hard-working and suffered to earn a meagre livelihood. They were exploited by their prosperous owners who collected a very high percentage of their earnings. The owners made a fortune; the cost

Jinrikisha Station, Neil Road
Jinrikishas pulled by men who led hard lives and lived under trying conditions provided the cheapest means of public transport. Today this building houses a restaurant.

of a jinrikisha was $25 and its licence $12 per annum. The fare generally was 3 cents for half a mile or 20 cents for one hour; between 1904 and 1916 the rate was 50 to 60 cents per day for a first-class jinrikisha (a puller and a runner behind it for the safety of the passenger) and 15 to 32 cents for a second class one. The Europeans were selective; they looked for pullers who were strong, experienced and had muscular legs!

The pullers lived in lodging houses in different parts of the town; these were known as jinrikisha depots. They had inadequate ventilation, they were foul and thick with filth; they were breeding grounds for cholera. These depots had one or more large rooms; the average had two to three rooms and the largest six to nine rooms in the building. The pullers slept on wooden beds in tiers, on canvas or straw cots in the centre of the room and on the floor in the passageway.

In the early 20th century one of the major occupational groups residing in Tanjong Pagar were the jinrikisha pullers and one of the depots was located at 135 Tanjong Pagar Road.

As the jinriksha was a means of transport on public roads the Singapore Municipality established a Jinrikisha Department in 1888 to register the vehicle. The necessary Ordinance was passed for its periodic inspection; it also provided for fines and even seizure of the vehicle in certain circumstances.

The pullers were bachelors in their early twenties. They were young men in search of a livelihood and experience. They generally returned to China with their hard-earned savings every 6 to 10 years. Though life was tough the pullers kept up their morale with a quasi-kinship that bound them to each other. Some of them married young women between the ages of 16 to 20; most did not marry because they did not see a future in Singapore and therefore did not raise a family here.

The jinrikisha traffic increased as the years went by and the population of Singapore grew. The following figures give an indication of the growth of the jinrikisha traffic:

Year	No. of jinrikishas
1883	2,000
1893	13,041
1902	22,629
1911	26,072
1924	28,800

The Jinrikisha Department coped with the ever increasing number of pullers by renting houses in Beach Road, South Bridge Road and Fort Canning for the inspection and registration of jinrikishas. It became necessary to build a new headquarters. A multi-storey department was built in 1899 at a cost of $34,000 at the junction of Middle Road and Prinsep Street. The quadrangle was used for inspecting vehicles and the ground floor for impounding them. The building had quarters for officers and the Registrar's Court.

The implementation of the Ordinance was not an easy task; there were grievances by both the owners and their pullers and these led to four major jinrikisha strikes in 1903, 1919, 1920 and 1938.

When Singaporeans pass by the stations in Middle Road and Neil Road they should remember the hard-working, thrifty and suffering jinrikisha pullers who provided early Singapore with the cheapest means of public transport. These pullers were an intrinsic part of the early social history of Singapore. Today the jinrikisha has been replaced by the trishaw. Some trishaw riders still wear blue shorts and shirts of the type worn by pre-war jinrikisha pullers. The trishaw riders today are generally seen near markets and at Waterloo Street. They carry numerous tourists for a tour of Chinatown and "Little India" in Serangoon Road.

When Singaporeans dine in the air-conditioned seafood restaurant at the former Jinrikisha Station in Neil Road let us not forget the early immigrants, the pullers, who toiled day and night under harsh conditions to provide Singapore with the cheapest means of public transport now replaced by the Mass Rapid Transport System.

RAFFLES PLACE (COMMERCIAL SQUARE)

Earliest commercial centre - offices of Agency Houses and Departmental Stores

Soon after the founding of Singapore in 1819 traders from South-east Asia, the Middle East, Europe, China and India began to arrive. Agency Houses were established. Stamford Raffles and the first Resident Major Farquhar found it necessary to establish a Commercial Centre. Major Farquhar suggested that Rochore would be a suitable site for the Centre but Raffles suggested the swampy area next to the Singapore River. Raffles also said that the other side of the town would be deserted and no settlement would be formed for a 100 years. It was necessary therefore to reclaim this area by filling it with earth excavated from Mount Wallich. This was the first reclamation project in Singapore. With the labour of 300 "coolies" comprising Chinese, Malays and Indians the hill was completely cut down, drains, hollows and streams were filled up. Work was completed after 3 or 4 months.

On the reclaimed land Commercial Square (now Raffles Place) emerged; the Square was 200 yards by 50 yards with a garden in the centre. Agency Houses then set up their offices in Commercial Square; the offices were on the ground floor while the top floor was used as living quarters. Raffles allowed businessmen irrespective of race to establish their offices there. One of the earliest to have his business premises there was Nairaina Pillay who accompanied Raffles on his second visit to Singapore. Nairaina Pillay set his textile business there.

Four banks were established in Commercial Square; they were the Oriental Bank of London, the Chartered Mercantile Bank of India and China, the Chartered Bank of India, Australia and China and the Asiatic Banking Corporation.

In January 1832 a public house and hotel was started at the northern end of the Square; it included a Billiards Room and a Refreshment Hall, the first of its kind in Singapore created by the owner John Francis. The Street was named Tavern Street and renamed Bonham Street now between the Bank of China and Malayan Banking Berhad.

A proposal to put up a portrait of Raffles in the Square was not carried out.

Several fire wells were made in the Square. They were covered by square plate flap doors and lay level with the ground. The Square was laid out with paths and ornamental trees.

Dr Jose D'Almeida, the surgeon, had his dispensary and his business firm of Jose D'Almeida and Sons in Commercial Square. Dr Almeida, a pioneer, died in Singapore and was buried in the old cemetery in Fort Canning. The streets around the Commercial Square were De Souza Street, Market Street and Chulia Street (known earlier as Kling Street).

Hong Kong and Shanghai Bank, the Straits Trading Company, Whiteaway and Laidlaw Departmental Stores, Robinson's and later Asian stores like Gian Singh's and Naina Mohamed appeared in Commercial Square which was renamed Raffles Place in 1858. In 1864 the auctioneer John Gimmill erected the first public drinking fountain which is now in the grounds of the National Museum.

When Japanese planes dropped bombs on 8 December 1941 Raffles Place was one of the targets. Robinson's was hit but it continued its business until British Surrender. In 1942 when refugees from Penang and Kuala Lumpur poured into Singapore, many of them needed clothes but had no money.

Singapore's Commercial Square (Raffles Square/Raffles Place) site chosen by Sir Stamford Raffles

Raffles Place
Mass Rapid Transport (MRT) Station - once where horse-carts, gharries and rickishaws provided public transport.

Robinson's sold these refugees clothes on credit. After the Japanese Surrender these grateful clients settled their debts. Robinson's was established in 1858. Tragedy fell on Robinson's on 22 November 1972 when fire completed gutted it. It now functions in Centre Point in Orchard Road.

Commercial Square was also the most lucrative stand for the jinrikishas.

Some of the old firms and banks are still located in Raffles Place. Skyscrapers have appeared in and around the Raffles Place. A Mass Rapid Transport Station is located at Raffles Place. The entrances to it are designed in neo-classical style very similar to that of the entrances to the old cemetery in Fort Canning.

Raffles Place even in the early years used to be deserted after 5 pm but before that there was a never ending stream of traffic - carriages, gharries largely driven by Malays and Indians, rickishaws and foot passengers.

GEMMILL FOUNTAIN

(originally installed in Raffles Place now in
the grounds of the National Museum)

First public drinking fountain
"for the use of all nations"

The auctioneer John Gemmill donated the public drinking fountain which originally stood in Raffles Place in 1864 but is now relocated in the grounds of the National Museum.

The inscription in the fountain reads:

For the use of all nations
at
SINGAPORE
This drinking fountain
of pure water is the gift of
JOHN GEMMILL
formerly of this island
and now of London
1864

The fountain still works. Water spurts from the mouth of the lion when a button is pressed.

Gemmill Lane off Club Road in Chinatown was named after John Gemmill.

Gemmill Fountain

INDIAN OLD/CONVICT SETTLEMENT

GAOL GATES
(now demolished)
Between Bras Basah Road and Stamford Road

Indian convicts provided labour for early buildings and road projects in Singapore; they cleared jungles and filled swamps and helped to build among others the St Andrew's Cathedral, the Istana, government offices, early defence works and Horsburgh Lighthouse.

British Bencoolen (founded in 1685) in South West Sumatra was a British penal settlement. Indian convicts were transported there for various petty crimes.

The Anglo-Dutch Treaty 1824 created two spheres of influence in the East Indies - British and Dutch. British Bencoolen was exchanged for Dutch Malacca so that Penang, Malacca and Singapore came under British influence in the Malay Peninsula.

When Bencoolen was vacated, the British transferred the Indian convicts to Singapore in 1826. The convicts first occupied the Temenggong's Village (vacated by the Temenggong who moved out to Telok Blangah) near the Singapore River. Later they moved to permanent buildings erected for them between Bras Basah Road and Stamford Road.

At one time there were about 2,000 convicts. They were deployed as labourers for the Public Works Department and were generally well-behaved and hard-working; they were supervised by their own fellow convicts. They contributed much towards the early development of the Settlement: they built some of the most beautiful buildings existing today - the Istana and St Andrew's Cathedral; they built our early roads and filled up swamps to create Commercial Square (Raffles Place), Thomson Road and Bukit Timah. They were stone cutters for the Horsburgh Lighthouse and labourers for construction of early Singapore defence works.

The name "Klings" was given to Indians. One theory is that the chains of the Indian convicts clanged and the word "Kling" was derived from the sound. Actually the word "Kling" referred to Kalinga a place in India. The word "Kling" was used more than 300 years before the founding of Singapore. The Tamils were referred to as Klings in Portuguese Malacca (1511-1641) and Kampong Kling was already a distinct settlement in Portuguese Malacca and Dutch Malacca (1641-1824).

Site of old Indian Convict Settlement - Bras Basah Road

The Indian Mutiny of 1857 spread baseless fear in Singapore. In 1867 when the Straits Settlements were transferred from the control of the India Office to that of the Colonial Office the convicts were transferred to the Andaman and Nicobar Islands in the Indian Ocean.

Indian convict labour contributed much to the very early development of Singapore.

PEARL'S HILL

New Bridge Road

Chinese had spice plantations on Pearl's Hill before the arrival of Stamford Raffles in 1819

Pearl's Hill was named after Lieutenant James Pearl Royal Navy owner and commander of the ship "Indiana" which brought Stamford Raffles to Singapore in 1819. Lt Pearl purchased the Hill in May 1822 from the East India Company. Later he sold it to the government after his retirement for 10,000 rupees.

On Pearl's Hill the Chinese had their spice plantations before the arrival of Stamford Raffles in 1819. The first Paupers' Hospital and Seamen's Hospital were also located there. The Paupers' Hospital later moved to Balestier Plain as Tan Tock Seng Hospital before the Hospital was finally moved to its present site in Moulmein Road.

Pearl's Hill became the Police Headquarters and later the Ministry of Interior and Defence after Singapore became a Republic in 1965. Subsequently the Ministry was separated into two Ministries - the Ministry of Home Affairs and the Ministry of Defence. The latter moved to Minden Road.

Pearl's Hill, Old site of Paupers' and Seamen's Hospitals. Chinese pioneers had spice plantations here before Raffles came to Singapore.

Tablet at the entrance of Tan Tock Seng Hospital.

TAN TOCK SENG HOSPITAL

Moulmein Road

Hospital built by pioneer Tan Tock Seng at his own expense "for the diseased of all Countries".

On Pearl's Hill was the first Chinese hospital or Poor House built from profits made in Government Pork Farms. For the diseased and the poor an attap building was erected but because of the poor facilities the Chinese avoided using it.

In 1844 a Chinese merchant Cham Chan Seng bequeathed $2000 and another merchant $5000, to the hospital.

On 3 February 1844 a public meeting under the chairmanship of Tan Tock Seng affirmed that the Chinese community was most anxious to build a hospital. The foundation stone of the new Paupers' Hospital at Pearl's Hill was laid. A tablet (dated 1854) in front of the main entrance to the present new wards in Moulmein Road reads as follows:

THIS HOSPITAL
for the Diseased of all countries,
was built A.D. 1844
at the cost of
Seven Thousand Dollars
wholly defrayed by
TAN TOCK SENG.
The wings were added,
and large improvements effected,
at a cost of
Three Thousand Dollars,
wholly defrayed by
TAN KIM CHING,
son of the founder.
This Tablet is erected by the
COMMITTEE OF MANAGEMENT
1854.

At the same time the foundation stone of the European Seamen's Hospital was laid.

Tan Tock Seng Hospital was managed by a committee; the meals for the patients were paid for by contributions from the public while the government provided the medicines and medical services. When facilities in the Hospital were found inadequate, additions were made to the buildings; the costs were met by Tan Kim Ching, the eldest son of Tan Tock Seng. By 1854 the additions were completed. An inscription engraved in stone at the hospital gate acknowledged the donation of $7000 by Tan Kim Ching.

Old Tan Tock Seng Hospital wards now part of The Kwong Wai Shiu Hospital, Serangoon Road

New wards of Tan Tock Seng Hospital, Moulmein Road.

During the Indian Mutiny in 1857 both Tan Tock Seng Hospital and the European Seamen's Hospital were converted into military establishments. Tan Tock Seng Hospital was set in swampy ground on Balestier Plain, Serangoon Road in 1860. Government erected three blocks of buildings for the Hospital and by 1884 Tan Tock Seng Hospital had become a well managed Hospital in Singapore. In 1867 a female ward was added at the expense of Lee Seo Neo, the widow of Tan Tock Seng. (The Kwong Wai Shiu Hospital occupied the site and three wards of Tan Tock Seng Hospital are still used by the Kwong Wai Shiu Hospital).

Tan Tock Seng Hospital was generously supported by the Chinese. The rich Arab merchant Syed Ali bin Mohamed Aljunied donated the rental of $1200 per annum of five acres of land in Victoria Street, Queen Street and Arab Street to the Hospital to meet expenses of the Hospital. The Hospital was overcrowded, had no proper drainage and food supply was limited. The average deaths were two per day. Mr Dunman the Chief of Police even sent cart loads of slaughtered fighting cocks on his raids during cock- fights. In 1909 the present buildings at Moulmein Road were erected at a cost of nearly half a million dollars. Government met the cost of the land and buildings. Loke Yew donated $50,000 and Wee Boon Teck $4,000. The Governor Sir John Anderson decided the new Hospital should carry the name of the founder Tan Tock Seng. A separate ward for the blind was built and named after its donor Ong Kim Wee who gave $12,000 for that purpose.

Tan Tock Seng was born in 1798 in Malacca and later migrated to Singapore. He began as a vegetable, fruit and fowlseller and later opened a shop and went into business with Whitehead and Company. Governor Butterworth made Tan Tock Seng a Justice of the Peace; he was the first Asian to be given this honour. He was a philanthropist who contributed to numerous charities. He died in 1850 at the age of 52 years leaving behind his widow, three sons and three daughters.

Tan Tock Seng Hospital is an apt memorial to this great philanthropist and pioneer who was deeply concerned over the sick in early Singapore.

OLD THONG CHAI MEDICAL INSTITUTION

No 50 Eu Tong Sen Street

The oldest charitable Medical Institution in Singapore catering to all ethnic groups and a core social organisation within the Chinese community in early Singapore.

It was gazetted as a national monument on 6 July 1973 by the Preservation of National Monuments Board which owns this building.

"Thong Chai" means "Benefit to All". Thong Chai Medical Association has been appropriately named because it manifests the spirit of mutual assistance among the early Chinese settlers. It is the oldest charitable institution in Singapore. It was endowed in 1867 by the philanthropist Gan Eng Seng (the founder of Gan Eng Seng School) and other prominent leaders including Khoo Cheng Tiong and Choo Yoke Lam. The Institution was managed by a Committee comprising leaders of various clans.

The two-storey building built in the South China palace design with three halls, two courtyards and ornamental gables was completed in 1892.

Thong Chai provided free medical services to the poor of all races, a unique feature of early Singapore. Patients received their medicine free of charge at designated dispensaries. In 1911 during an outbreak of malaria Thong Chai became a centre for the distribution of free quinine.

The Institution also served a social purpose within the Chinese community. Public meetings were held there and it was regarded as the headquarters for the Chinese guilds.

The Chinese Chamber of Commerce at its inception functioned in a room in Thong Chai until the Chamber moved into Wee Ah Hood's residence in Hill Street. The new Singapore Chinese Chamber of Commerce and Industry Building now stands at 47 Hill Street.

Thong Chai is the only monument owned by the Preservation of Monuments Board. It was restored at a cost of $440,000 and is rented out to an Arts and Crafts dealer.

Old Thong Chai Medical Institution, Eu Tong Sen Street. Oldest charitable medical institution catering to all ethnic groups and a core social organisation within the Chinese community in early Singapore

PO CHEK KIONG

TAN SI CHONG SU
15 Magazine Road

Early Assembly Hall and Temple of the TAN clan in Singapore. Clan Associations still play a significant role in Singapore.

It was gazetted as a national monument on 29 November 1974.

In 1876 through the efforts of Tan Kim Ching (eldest son of Tan Tock Seng) and Tan Beng Swee, the institution known as Po Chek Kiong was built in Magazine Road near Kampong Malacca (opposite the Ministry of Labour building) and on the bank of the Singapore River - one of the busiest commercial areas of early Singapore.

Po Chek Kiong served as the assembly Hall and Temple of the Tan clan. One part of the building is still used as a repository of ancestral tablets. Another section was once used as a Chinese School. There is a large reception room.

Po Chek Kiong, Tan Si Chong Su
oldest Tan Clan Association Temple, Magazine Road

All the wooden carvings and granite dragon pillars were imported from China and the architecture classical Southern Chinese. Singapore's Chinese Temples were largely designed in this tradition.

In the Temple are relics donated to the Temple and these include a bell and a drum; in an annex is a unique miniature marble pagoda - another special feature of this Temple. The Boddhisatva, Kuan Yin, is also installed in this Temple.

Tan Kim Tian and Tan Hong Keat were the first President and the Vice President respectively of this ancient institution which still stands today.

Tan Siew Sin, a member of the Tan Clan, and Federal Minister of Finance when Singapore was part of Malaysia, unveiled a plaque to commemorate the renovation of the Temple in 1964.

Exquisite Marble Pagoda

THE ARMENIAN CHURCH OF ST GREGORY

HILL STREET

THE OLDEST CHURCH IN SINGAPORE
Built by Armenian pioneers of Singapore
Agnes Joaquim (an Armenian)
grew the Vanda Miss Joaquim orchid - the
national flower of Singapore.
The Church was gazetted as a
national monument on 6 July 1973.

Three Armenian trading firms established themselves in 1821 soon after the founding of Singapore in 1819 by Stamford Raffles. Aristarchus Sarkies and Arratoon Sarkies of Malacca came to Singapore in August 1828 and established the firm of Sarkies and Moses. Three Armenian brothers set up Raffles Hotel in 1886. They were Arshak Sarkies, Aviet Sarkies and Tigran Sarkies. They also built the Adelphi Hotel.

The small Armenian community conducted Church services in rented premises. In 1827 it began to raise funds to build their own Church. For this purpose it was granted a piece of land by the Singapore government at Hill Street where the Church still stands. This site was part of the Botanical Garden at the foot of Government Hill (Fort Canning) facing Hill Street. Earlier the Armenian community was unsuccessful in securing a site facing the esplanade.

In 1834 the elders of this community commissioned George Dromgold Coleman, Singapore's first architect, to design and build the Armenian Church. Construction started in 1835 and the building was completed in January 1836; the contractor was a Malabari (an Indian). The consecration of the Church was conducted in the Armenian language on 26 March 1836 by the priest Rev Eleazar Ingergolie.

The Church was dedicated to St Gregory the Illuminator, the first monk of the Armenian Church. It is believed that the design of the Church was based on the Mother Church at Echmiadzin in North Armenia.

The total cost of the building in 1835 was 5058.30 Spanish dollars. About a quarter of this was subscribed by Armenians in Calcutta, Java and Europe and other communities in Singapore. Twelve Armenian families in Singapore gave the rest.

Originally there was a conical dome and a bell tower with a ball and cross; these were replaced in 1853 by a beautiful spire by the architect Maddock.

Internally the Church is circular and superimposed on a square plan with projecting porticos in a cruciform pattern. Externally the most outstanding features are beautifully proportioned Roman Doric columns and pilasters.

The Armenian Church of St Gregory oldest Church in Singapore

The Memorial Garden in Armenian Church grounds

The Armenian Church is an architectural treasure, one of Coleman's finest buildings in Singapore.

In 1909 electric lights and fans were installed in the Church, the first in Singapore to enjoy electricity.

The Memorial Garden in the grounds of the Armenian Church is of special historical interest. The Armenian pioneers were buried in the old cemetery in Government Hill and after 1865 in the Bukit Timah cemetery. All the tombstones that could be recovered from the Bukit Timah cemetery were assembled in 1988 to form the Memorial Garden.

The tombstone of Agnes (Ashen) Joaquim is in the Memorial Garden. She grew the orchid, Vanda Miss Joaquim which is now the national flower of the Republic of Singapore.

Just behind the Church is the parsonage, rebuilt in 1905 as a memorial by Nanajan Sarkies to her husband John Shanazar Sarkies, the distinguished scholar and merchant who died in 1904. Today the parsonage is used as a Counselling Centre by the Church of England.

The Armenian community never exceeded 100 members. There is an Armenian priest who conducts regular services with other Christians at the Church.

The Church of St Gregory is a credit to the Armenian pioneers whose religious zeal inspired them to build the oldest Church in Singapore. Several members of this community were pioneers who had contributed to the economic prosperity of particularly early Singapore.

GIOK HONG TIEN TEMPLE

Havelock Road

Faith in God and deep-rooted culture sustained the early immigrants to the Settlement of Singapore

Giok Hong Tien Temple in Havelock Road was built on "a peaceful and wholesome street with the hill at the back and the Singapore River in front - a fortunate geomantic position." A plaque at the Temple is dated 1887. It is therefore one of the oldest Chinese Temples in Singapore. The Temple is syncretic. There are Taoist and Buddhist deities and a statue of Confucius. The Temple is dedicated to the Jade Emperor, the Supreme Deity of Taoism. There are altars for the Goddess of Yin and the God of Yang, the Registrar of Births.

Cheang Hong Lim, the prominent merchant after whom Hong Lim Green was named built the Temple.

Giok Hong Tien Temple, Havelock Road, one of the oldest Chinese Temples

The architecture is classical Chinese; there are wild dancing dragons on the roof statues of the Sun, Rain, Wind and Thunder Gods. They ward off danger and evil. There are also beautiful flying fish dragons which are symbols for success and achievement. The interior displays exquisite wood and granite carvings.

This Temple played an important spiritual role in early Singapore and continues to do so at present.

TELOK AYER MARKET

("Low Pa Sat")
Raffles Quay

First market built by the Municipal Commission;
Telok Ayer the landing point of Chinese emigrants from junks in early Singapore and the centre of Chinatown.
This market was gazetted as a national monument on 6 July 1973

In 1822 Stamford Raffles instructed that a market be built on a site selected by Colonel Farquhar, the Resident of Singapore. By 1825 the first wet market, an octagonal structure in Victorian style was constructed. It cost the Settlement a sum of $4,316. It was designed by George Drumgold Coleman, Singapore's first architect. By the year 1841 the market was found inadequate for the growing population in Chinatown and a decision to demolish it was then taken.

Telok Ayer Market ("Low Pa Sat"), Raffles Quay
Present market built in 1894 - first to be built by the Municipal Commission.

Plans for a new market were prepared by James MacRitchie, the Municipal engineer; he proposed a similar octagonal structure to occupy an area of 5500 square metres. A Glasgow company submitted a tender for a cast iron building for £13,200.

Three thousand cast iron parts were shifted out to Singapore from Glasgow and assembled at the present site at Robinson Road on land reclaimed in 1880. Work on the foundation was carried out between 1891 and 1893. Telok Ayer Market was completed in 1894; it was a distinctive octagonal structure with 8 entrances and surmounted by fan shaped patterns. A fountain was also erected in the centre of the market and it stood there from 1895 to 1901 when it was removed to Orchard Road Market in 1902. The author is unable to trace the eventual fate of that fountain.

Opposite Telok Ayer Market stood Telok Ayer Police Station designed by Sir Henry McCallum. The building was demolished in 1957 and the first multi-storey car park was built on the site.

In 1986 Telok Ayer Market which had operated as a food centre was dismantled and the 3000 cast iron pieces were tagged and logged into a computer for restoration; by 1989 the restoration was completed at a cost $6.8 million.

The Singapore Tourist Promotion Board called for tenders for the use of Telok Ayer Market and Scotts Holdings won a 30 year lease for a $8.3 million project which would transform the Market into a festival market place with retail stalls, food courts, restaurants and entertainment.

Telok Ayer Market would now serve Singaporeans especially those in Chinatown in its new role and should regain its past glory.

MAJESTIC THEATRE

New Bridge Road

Tien Yien Moh Toi Theatre
for Cantonese Operas built in 1927 by Eu Tong Sen
converted into a Cinema

The Majestic Theatre in New Bridge Road was built by the rich philanthropist Eu Tong Sen in 1927 as the Tien Yien Moh Toi Theatre for Cantonese operas. Later it was converted into a cinema for Chinese films and renamed as Queen's Theatre; the name was changed again as Majestic Theatre. The Southern Hotel adjacent to Majestic Theatre was also built in 1927. Both are still landmarks in Chinatown.

Majestic Theatre (previously Cantonese operas were staged here)

SOUTHERN HOTEL

The tallest building in Chinatown in the early years; the first hotel to have lift service in Singapore.

Southern Hotel in the heart of Chinatown was built in 1927 and was the first hotel to be installed with a lift. In the early twentieth century Southern Hotel was the tallest building in Chinatown.

The ground floor before the outbreak of the Pacific War was occupied by offices while the hotel rooms were on the top floors. On the fourth floor was a popular Chinese restaurant and a tea house was located on the roof terrace (which still remains today). Occasional operas were staged there as an added attraction of the Hotel.

The Hotel is a land mark in Chinatown. It is a dignified old world charm with special metal railings and grills. It stands amidst tall Housing and Development Board flats. The Chinatown Point Shopping complex almost faces the hotel across the street.

Southern Hotel, once the tallest building in Chinatown and first hotel to have lift service.

ELGIN BRIDGE

Elgin Bridge built because of increased business in the South of the Singapore River and construction of North and South Bridge Roads.

The first bridge across the Singapore River was a wooden one; it was called Presentment Bridge. The Presentment Bridge was augmented by a ferry service to facilitate more persons crossing the River because of the narrowness of the bridge.

By the 1840s the Presentment Bridge divided the road that was constructed into North Bridge Road and South Bridge Road.

By the turn of the century more business was carried on in the South of the Bridge and the Chinese called South Bridge Road Tuo Po (big town in Fujian) and North Bridge Road Sio Po (small town).

The Bridge underwent reconstruction three times and the present Bridge, Elgin Bridge, was named after a former Viceroy of India. It was built in 1925.

Elgin Bridge

CAVENAGH BRIDGE

Singapore River

Cavenagh Bridge is named after the last Governor of the Straits Settlements - Colonel Orfeur Cavenagh (1859-67). He was succeeded by Colonel Sir Harry St George Ord (1867-73), the first Governor of the Straits Settlements when Penang, Malacca and Singapore became a Crown Colony. Singaporeans could express their views in the Straits Settlements Legislative Council which was established in 1867 under the new constitution.

The Bridge was manufactured in Scotland in 1868 by P.W. MacLellan, Engineers, Glasgow. The Bridge was assembled by Indian convicts, the last major project undertaken by them. Built in 1869, it saved residents the trouble of crossing the Singapore River by ferry to Empress Place. It cost 1/4 cent each trip.

The use of the Bridge was prohibited to any vehicle of which the laden weight exceeded 3 cwt. and to all cattle and horses.

Old Postcard photo of Cavenagh Bridge

Cavenagh Bridge built in 1869

The Old Police notice on the Cavenagh Bridge still stands today.

COLEMAN BRIDGE

Bridge built to link
North and South of the
Town; named after G.D.Coleman,
Singapore's first architect.

G.D. Coleman was Singapore's first architect and superintendent of Public Works. He built several of the Republic's historic buildings.

The present bridge across the Singapore River is the replica of the Iron Bridge built in 1886 to meet increased traffic between North and South of the Town. Eight of the iron lamp posts of the old bridge were preserved and re-erected at the new Coleman Bridge. The present bridge is the fourth one to be erected at the same location and built by the Public Works Department in May 1990.

Coleman Bridge

ANDERSON BRIDGE

This bridge is named after Sir John Anderson, Governor of the Straits Settlements. It was built in 1909 jointly by the government of the Straits Settlements and the Municipal Commissioners of the Town of Singapore. The President of the Municipal Commissioners was E. C. Broadrick, and the Municipal Engineer was R. Peirce. The bridge was built by A. Butments - The Westminster Construction Co Ltd and the contractors who did the superstructure was Howarth Erskine Ltd. The plaque on the bridge is of stone specially brought out from Egypt.

Anderson Bridge

THE ALKAFF MANSION

Telok Blangah Green

Symbol of affluence of Arabs - pioneers, businessmen, property owners, traders and patrons of education and charities who have contributed from the earliest times towards the prosperity of Singapore.

The Alkaff Mansion is located at Telok Blangah Green encompassing an area of 780 square metres and overlooking a beautiful park of 19 hectares with the sea down below. Thus the Mansion commands a panoramic view.

The Mansion was owned by the Alkaff family whose ancestors arrived in Singapore from Indonesia in 1852; the first to come was Shaik bin Abdul Rahman. The Alkaffs were great traders who had a lucrative business between India and Indonesia in spices, coffee and sugar. Later the Alkaffs were also involved in property business.

The Alkaff Mansion was built by Syed Abdul Rahman Alkaff who came to Singapore from Yemen. Located on Bukit Jagoh (the old name for Telok Blangah Green), the Alkaff Mansion was built primarily as a retreat for the Alkaff family and also to entertain their numerous clients and guests of different races. Sometimes the hill was referred to as Mount Washington by the American guests who were entertained there by the Alkaffs. Not only a variety of food was served to their guests but entertainment with floor shows and music was provided in the terraces of the Mansion.

It is not clear why the Alkaff Mansion was abandoned after World War II and the Mansion went into a state of disrepair. In 1986 the Singapore Tourist Promotion Board became interested in the Mansion and awarded the restoration of this unique Mansion to Hotel Properties Limited to restore the past glory of the Mansion into a restaurant and yet retaining the old world charm of the Alkaffs.

The Alkaffs had other holidays bungalows in Pasir Panjang and Pender Road but they lived in a large mansion where the Methodist Publishing House (MPH) stands today before they moved into their new home in Lloyd Road.

Syed Abdul Rahman Alkaff also owned the Hotel de L'Europe, a famous hotel for Europeans and distinguished visitors to Singapore; he also ran the "Europe Garage" - cars and carriages were hired out to the public and thus he could be called the pioneer in car rentals in Singapore. It is believed the Alkaffs sold the Hotel because they were against the sale of liquor on the premises.

Alkaff Mansion, Telok Blangah Green (previously known as Mt. Washington)

Burial ground for the Aljunieds - Jalan Kubor

The old Moorish style Arcade Building in Raffles Place was also built by him in 1888; the offices and shops were located on the first storey while the ground floor was reserved for their horse carriages which were also used as public transport. The Arcade Building was sold and the new building - the Alkaff Building - is now in Market Street.

Syed Shaik Alkaff developed, what is now Sennett Estate off MacPherson Road, the Alkaff Lake Gardens which was a typical Japanese tea gardens with an excellent restaurant, tea kiosks and an artificial lake reminiscent of old Japan. There was also boating in the lake. The Alkaffs bred and trained their horses in the neighbourhood and also had both a bicycle and motor cycle racing track.

In 1949 the Alkaffs sold the land with the gardens to the Sennett Realty Company for $2 million. The earth removed from the hillock which represented Mount Fuji was used to fill the beautiful lake to become the playing field of Willow Avenue Secondary School.

In Sennett Estate today we have the Alkaff Mosque and Alkaff Avenue. What is presently Potong Pasir was owned by the Alkaffs who leased the land to Indians who reared cattle in the area.

Alkaff Mosque Sennett Estate

Before the invasion of Malaya by the Japanese, the British Army requisitioned the land in the Alkaff Gardens to build a camp for the Indian troops.

Immediately after the British Surrender in February 1942 many Indian prisoners of war were accommodated in the camp behind barbed wires for a period before they were transferred to the main camp in Port Dickson on the west coast of Malaya.

The other wealthy and prominent Arab families were the Alsagoffs and the Aljunieds.

Syed Abdul Rahman Alsagoff came to Singapore with his son Ahmad and established his firm Alsagoff and Company in 1848. His son Ahmad married Raja Siti, the daughter of Hadja Fatimah, of Bugis royalty and who built the historical Hadja Fatimah Mosque in Beach Road. The Alsagoffs also started the Arabic School in Jalan Sultan in 1912.

A large section of Geylang Serai formed part of the "Perseverance Estate" which belonged to the Alsagoff family. The Alsagoffs had also served as Municipal Commissioners from 1872 to 1898 and from 1928 to 1933.

Syed Omar Alsagoff owned a large estate where he lived in a palatial bungalow and entertained Europeans lavishly at Bukit Tunggal near Chancery Lane. He served dinners on gold plated plates, forks and knives. There was also a lake there which was one of the attractions of old Singapore and canoes

Alkaff Gardens
(now Willow Avenue Secondary School Field)

could be seen afloat in it. After his death his sons developed Bukit Tunggal Estate in the 1920s. The Alsagoffs had property in Paya Lebar and elsewhere.

The tomb (the Keramat) of the holy man Habib Nor bin Mohamed Al-Habshi was built by Syed Mohamed bin Ahmad Alsagoff about 1890 and is still maintained by the Alsagoff family.

Syed Omar bin Ali Aljunied who was an Arab pioneer was one of the most respected local merchants with extensive business; he had amassed a large fortune and his nephew Syed Mahomed bin Haroon Aljunied had a large mansion in High Street.

Syed Omar owned a large burial ground at Jalan Kubor off Victoria Street and also built a Mosque in Bencoolen Street; his son built the Omar Mosque at Kampong Malacca, near Havelock Road. Syed Allie bin Mohamed Aljunied donated the rental of some of his property towards the funds of Tan Tock Seng Hospital. The Aljunieds also dug wells behind Fort Canning, Selegie Road and elsewhere; these were large wells with granite sides and supplied water to the early residents of Singapore.

Syed Alwi Road off Serangoon Road is named after Syed Allie and Aljunied and Upper Aljunied Roads are named after this wealthy Arab family.

The Alkaff Mansion and Arab institutions in Singapore are permanent reminders to Singaporeans of the affluence, the business acumen and contribution of the early Arab families towards the development and prosperity of Singapore. Their descendants are continuing their contribution to our Republic.

PARSI ROAD

Parsis were early pioneers of Singapore who were philanthropists and contributed to the economic prosperity of Singapore.

In early Singapore several Parsis migrated here in 1829 and became merchants of some standing. Cursetjee was a well-known Parsi and a partner and founder of the store of John Little in Raffles Place. Mount Wallich was known earlier as Cursetjee's Hill. John Palmer (Palmer Road named after him) was originally a Calcutta merchant (Mount Palmer later became fort Palmer) went bankrupt in 1827 and sold part of the Hill to a Parsi who turned it into a Parsi burial ground.

In June 1864, the Parsi firm of Byramjee Hormusjee Cama and Company started a school for the teaching of English in Tanjong Pagar. The school functioned for several years at the personal expense of Cama as a free school for Chinese children and others. End of the first month there were 103 pupils mostly Chinese. It closed after his death.

Parsi Road

Mistri, a Parsi, started the Phoenix Aerated Waters Factory; there was another, the Framroz Aerated Waters Factory. It was Navroji Rustomji Mistri who generously donated the Children's Ward in the Singapore General Hospital and the plaque was laid in the ward by his brother H.R. Mistri.

The Parsis are followers of one of the World's oldest religions - Zoroastrianism. Today they number about 100 many of whom are notable personalities in the business and industrial communities. They are represented in our Inter-Religious Organisation of Singapore.

READ BRIDGE

Singapore River

An old map in 1881 shows Merchant Bridge later replaced by Read Bridge to give greater height over the Singapore River to allow "tongkangs" (boats) to pass beneath it during high tide. W.H.M. Read Singapore's pioneer and businessman laid the first cylinder in 1887 at the bridge which was officially opened by the Governor on 18 April 1889.

Read Bridge

CLARKE QUAY

River Valley Road

Former Centre for entrepot trade and hub of Singapore's commerce

Until the 1970s the Singapore River hummed with activities. Many bumboats carried various cargoes from the ships on the outer roads to the warehouses on its banks. The River ends at Clarke Quay which is just behind the hotel (New Otani Hotel).

Clarke Quay was named after Sir Andrew Clarke, the Governor of the Straits Settlements who was responsible for the signing of the famous Pangkor Treaty in 1874 by which the British intervened in the Malay States, first with Perak and later with the rest of the Malay States. By this Treaty British indirect rule over the Malay States was established.

The bridge that links the banks is Read Bridge (originally Merchant Bridge) named after the well-known businessman W.H.M. Read. It was

Singapore River, Warehouses on either bank; owned by individuals and Agency Houses.

officially declared open by the Governor in April 1889. A lane is named after the wealthy Chinese pioneer and timber merchant Tan Tye; there is also Cannery Lane where pineapple canneries were located.

On one side of Clarke Quay is one of the earliest Agency houses, the Paterson Simons which built their godowns here in 1893. On the other side is the godown of the Towkay Tan Yoke Nee who built the classical Chinese house in Clemenceau Avenue, for many years the headquarters of the Salvation Army.

Along the Singapore River next to the River View Hotel is the "Warehouse" (a godown converted to a disco) - an ingenious idea. The author discovered that on 21 February 1852 the prominent Chinese businessman Tan Kim Seng had set a precedent; he held a ball on the first floor of his warehouse in Battery Road. There was a great deal of mirth when two queques were interlocked during a Waltz.

Clarke Quay is to be restored to its past glory. Those who walk there to enjoy the restaurants and other attractions will bring life to sleepy Clarke Quay.

Clarke Quay is a reminder of the boatmen who toiled day and night to make Singapore the centre of entrepot trade in South-east Asia and also of the enterprising merchants who made this possible.

Clarke Quay, River Valley Road
Centre for entrepot trade; godowns and warehouses of Singapore's pioneer merchants and Agency Houses.

CLIFFORD PIER

Built by Woh Hup
Expertise developed by early Singaporeans

Clifford Pier is named after Sir Hugh Clifford, Governor of the Straits Settlements (1927-29). It was officially opened by Governor Sir Cecil Clementi (1930-34) on 3 June 1933.

Previously the Pier was known as Johnston's Pier. This was dismantled in July 1933. Johnston Pier was erected in 1854 and named after one of the first businessmen and a founder of the Chamber of Commerce, Alexander Laurie Johnston, a friend of Stamford Raffles.

Clifford Pier was built by the Singapore contractors Woh Hup. Steel piles were hammered into the seabed to create the foundation of the Pier by the local company which had then acquired the expertise to complete the task. The Pier has a unique architecture and today it is still a busy one.

Clifford Pier (previously Johnston's Pier)
Built in 1933 by Singapore Contractors Woh Hup.

old photo

ST ANDREW'S CATHEDRAL

Coleman Street

The oldest Anglican house of worship.
During Colonial era the Governor and other British officials attended regular worship services here
Gazetted as a national monument on 6 July 1973

As early as 1823 Stamford Raffles, selected a site for an Anglican Church; this site adjoined the Plain (Padang).

The jungle and an area occupied by European residents and sepoys had to be cleared for the construction of St Andrew's Church.

The foundation stone was laid on 9 November 1835. When the Church was under construction there were rumours that men were going round beheading people as thirty human heads had to be sacrificed to appease the spirits! The government offered a reward of $500 for information on these rumour-mongers.

G.D. Coleman was the architect who built the Church which was similar to St George's Church in Penang and St George's Cathedral in Madras. The Church of St Andrew was completed in 1834. It opened for services on 1 October 1834 and it was consecrated on 6 October 1834 by the Bishop of Calcutta. A spire was added by J.T. Thomson in 1842 because the Church looked like a Town Hall, College or Assembly Room. Before the erection of this Church the Anglican congregation worshipped in an overcrowded Chapel at the junction of Bras Basah Road and North Bridge Road.

The Church of St Andrew was used until 1852 and after that it was considered unsafe for the congregation because it was in a dangerous state of disrepair. Further, it was also struck twice by lightning.

The architect of St Andrew's Cathedral was Colonel Ronald MacPherson of the Madras Army. A memorial cross to MacPherson still stands in the Cathedral grounds. The construction was in the hands of Captain McNair of the Royal Artillery who used Indian convicts for labour.

The architecture is early English Gothic. One of the interesting features of the Cathedral is the coating of the interior walls and pillars with a composition made from shell lime. This lime had been mixed with the whites of eggs and coarse sugar or jaggery and the paste was mixed with water in which husks of coconuts had been soaked into it. The walls and pillars after a period of drying were rubbed with rock crystals or rounded stones until they took on a beautiful polish. They were dusted with fine soapstone powder leaving a remarkably smooth and glossy surface. The walls and pillars were so hard that it was almost impossible to drive a nail into them.

On 4 March 1856 Bishop Daniel Wilson laid the foundation stone and consecrated it in January 1862. The Cathedral was opened for services on 1 October 1861. In 1856 the St Andrew's Mission launched the "first evangelistic outreach of the Anglican Church in Singapore and produced new congregations using Hokkien, Tamil and Malay in their worship." In 1909 C.J. Ferguson-Davis became the first Bishop of Singapore.

The Central Light or window in the Cathedral was dedicated in 1861 to the memory of Sir Stamford Raffles, the founder of modern Singapore.

A tablet in the Cathedral reads:

> *To the memory of Sir Stamford Raffles, Kt. the illustrious Founder of the Settlement of Singapore. This window is dedicated by the citizens A.D. 1861.*

The window over the West Door commemorates Colonel MacPherson. In the North Aisle there is the memorial to those members of the congregation who died in the 1915 mutiny that broke out at Alexandra Barracks. Other tablets commemorate those who died during the Second World War. A bell

St Andrew's Cathedral
British Colonial officials worshipped here

presented to the Cathedral by Maria Revere, wife of Joseph Balestier, the first American Consul, and four Standards from Second World War formerly in the North Aisle are now in the National Museum.

In 1942 during the Japanese invasion of Singapore the Cathedral's nave was converted into a casualty station to care for the wounded and when all hospitals were overcrowded with the casualties by the constant bombing and artillery fire by the Japanese invaders. The Nave's floor was blood-stained and in the yard were bombed out military vehicles.

The Cathedral was open for worship during the Japanese invasion. General Percival attended a communion service on 15 February 1942 before he surrendered to the Japanese on that day.

Bishop Wilson and other European clergy worked in the Cathedral during the first year of the Japanese Occupation. However, in March 1943 Bishop Wilson was arrested and made a prisoner-of-war. Daily prayers were conducted for internees in Changi Gaol by Canon Jack Bennett and others responsible to Bishop Wilson who gave devoted service to all races in captivity.

Bishop Wilson was one of the 57 internees who were interrogated in the "Double Tenth Incident" at Changi. The Japanese had suspected that a spy ring was operating in Changi Gaol and had assisted a daring British raid at the Singapore Harbour on Japanese vessels which were sunk.

Normal worship services were resumed after the Japanese Surrender in 1945.

"... St Andrew's Cathedral will continue to be as it has been throughout its history, a centre of Christian outreach and witness to the whole of Singapore" (Frank Lomax - Vicar).

Memorial with a Maltese Cross in St Andrew's Cathedral grounds for Colonel Ronald MacPherson, designer and builder of the Cathedral.

Parliament House
Built as the residence of John Argyle Maxwell but became Singapore's first Court House. Oldest government building in Singapore.

PARLIAMENT HOUSE

Symbol of Parliamentary Democracy and Rule of Law in the Republic.
Oldest government building in Singapore.

Parliament House (after extensive renovations) was originally built as the residence of John Argyle Maxwell a Java merchant and was bought over by the Government to establish the Court House.

Maxwell had served in the Home Guards and later came to Singapore from Java to become one of the three magistrates in the Settlement of Singapore. He commissioned G.D. Coleman to design a two- storey house in 1826 which was completed in June 1827.

Maxwell was granted a lease of 999 years but he never occupied the house; he rented it out to the government at 500 rupees per month.

The Courts were held in the part of the building close to High Street and in the Central Room while the side rooms became the office of the Resident Councillor. The ground floor was used by the Land Office.

A central tower which still stands was perhaps used as a lookout tower for ships in the outer roads. An announcement was presumably made from there and the early residents lined the Singapore River to receive the new visitors and also details of their cargo in the vessels.

An addition of a single storeyed building was made in 1839 and this became the new Court House which opened in October 1839.

Later in September 1841 Thomas Church, the Resident Councillor purchased the buildings on behalf of the Government.

In 1854 the building was found unsuitable as a Court largely because of the noise from the adjacent Stephen Hallpike's shipbuilding yard.

Extensions to the Court House were made in 1875, 1901 and 1909. Alterations were also made to the architecture of the buildings. The buildings were transformed from the Palladian style to Victorian architecture.

The buildings served as the Supreme Court until 1939 when the new Supreme Court on the site of the former Hotel de L'Europe was completed.

The Old Court House became semi-derelict and after World War II it became the first office of the Public Relation Officer, Colony of Singapore.

In 1954 alterations and renovations were made to convert the building into the Assembly House (the legislature) which was officially opened by the Governor Sir John Nicoll on 7 July 1954. Today it is Singapore's Parliament House - the symbol of parliamentary democracy, the Rule of Law of the Republic of Singapore.

Parliament House is the oldest government building in Singapore.

Parliament House designed by G. D. Goleman and built in 1827.

SUPREME COURT BUILDING

St Andrew's Road

Symbol of Justice

The Old Court the present Parliament building, was the house of John Argyle Maxwell. It was bought by the government and court proceedings were held on the first floor. In 1839 an annexe was built and the Court moved there. Because of the noise from Hallipike's Boatyard the Court moved to Central Building at Empress Place. In 1875 the Court returned to the old Maxwell House and occupied the new wing.

Central Building became the venue for the Straits Settlements Legislative Council established in 1867 when the Straits Settlements were transferred from the India Office to the Colonial Office.

In 1939 the Court moved to the present Supreme Court Building which was the site of a house built by Coleman in 1823. This house was converted into the London Hotel in 1845 which later became Hotel de L'Esperance and then Hotel de L'Europe. A syndicate bought this hotel and rebuilt it into the Grand de L'Europe. This was demolished and the Supreme Court constructed between 1937 and 1939. The architect was F. Dorrington Ward.

On 3 August 1939 Sir Shenton Thomas, Governor of the Straits Settlements, officially declared the Supreme Court Building open.

The Corinthian and Ionic columns and the sculpture are the work of the Italian Cavaliere Rudolfo Nolli. The architecture of the Supreme Court Building was intended to harmonise with that of City Hall next door.

It was the last example of British Imperial architecture in Singapore. It has been commented that the building and the dome are too high for the width of the building. City Hall and the Supreme Court are the most imposing buildings facing the sea.

Supreme Court Building, St Andrew's Road
Symbol of Justice officially opened on 3 August 1939 by Governor, Sir Shenton Thomas

THE BRONZE ELEPHANT STATUE

PARLIAMENT HOUSE

Singapore-Thai close relations go far back into history

King Chulalongkorn of Siam was 16 years old when his father King Mongkut (Rama IV) died in 1868. Siam was therefore under a Regent before Chulalongkorn was crowned King Rama V. King Mongkut, more than anyone else preserved the independence of Siam at a time when other states in South-east Asia had come under European domination. King Mongkut also opened Siam to European influence and began its modernisation.

Chulalongkorn continued the modernisation process; he centralised the government and made reforms in local administration. He travelled to Java and India to study methods of administration. He abolished the practice of prostration in the royal presence and also slavery in 1874. The King had his education under European teachers and he sent his subjects to study in British Universities.

The first Siamese King ever to leave his kingdom and travel overseas was King Chulalongkorn and he chose to visit Singapore in 1871. He and his Queen landed in Singapore on 15 March 1871; they were accompanied by two brothers of the King, two Ministers and retinue of sixty-six. They were received by the Officer Administering the Government, Colonel A.E.H. Anson. A military band and troops paraded along Battery Road in the King's honour and a gun salute was given from the warships in the roads.

The royal couple stayed in Government House (Istana). Prominent Chinese residents including Tan Kim Seng, the Thai Consul, presented an address at Town Hall and the King responded appropriately in English. The royal couple visited Tan Tock Seng Hospital and made a donation of $1,000 to the Hospital. They attended a flower Show at the Botanical Gardens. The King was present at the Speech and Prize Giving Day at Raffles Institution. Seventeen Siamese boys were students there. The royal couple left Singapore on 23 March 1871.

Soon after his return to Siam, King Chulalangkorn presented the Elephant Statue to the Singapore Government; it was originally placed in front of the Victoria Memorial hall where the Raffles Statue now stands. In 1919 when Singapore celebrated the centenary of it founding, the Raffles Statue which was at the Padang close to St Andrew's Cathedral was bought to its present site.

The Bronze Elephant Statue was moved to stand opposite the Old Court House (Parliament House).

The Bronze Elephant Statue is a reminder to Singaporeans of the close relationship Thailand has with Singapore.

Bronze Elephant Statue, Parliament House.
Gift of King Chulalongkorn of Thailand, 1871

RAFFLES STATUE

Opposite Victoria Memorial
Concert Hall

To commemorate the founder of modern Singapore;
The inscription on the statue was written
by Lim Koon Tye, an old Rafflesian.

The inscription on the statue of Raffles reads as follows:

This tablet to the memory of
Sir Stamford Raffles to whose
foresight and genius Singapore
owes its existence and prosperity
unveiled on February 6th 1919
the 100th anniversary of the
foundation of the Settlement.

The bronze statue of Sir Stamford Raffles was cast by T. Woolner at a cost of $20,446.10; it is 8 feet high mounted on a granite base and was originally erected in the Esplanade at its far end (close to the Singapore Recreation Club and opposite today's Satay Club). At the feet of the statue lies an object which looks like a map or scroll dropped by Raffles.

The statue was officially unveiled by the Governor of the Straits Settlements, Sir Frederick Weld, on 27 June 1887, Jubilee Day, to celebrate the 50th anniversary of Queen Victoria's reign. Present at the ceremony were Tengku Ali of Singapore and Temenggong Abu Bakar of Johore.

In 1919 when Singapore celebrated the centenary of its foundation the statue was removed from the Esplanade and installed where it stands now and occupied the site where the Bronze Elephant Statue donated by King Chulalongkorn in 1871 stood. The Elephant Statue was taken away and placed opposite the Old Court House, the present Parliament House.

The memorial tablet at the base of the statue was unveiled by the Governor of the Straits Settlements, Sir Arthur H.Young in the early morning of 6 February 1919. There was a large assembly comprising residents of Singapore and representatives from Penang, Malacca, the Federated Malay States and the Unfederated Malay States.

The President of the Municipal Commissioners, Mr W.Peel, on behalf of his Committee, presented the Governor with a small medal struck in commemoration of the historic occasion. The ceremony ended with laying of wreaths by representatives from several public institutions and organisations; these included representatives from Raffles Institution, Raffles Girls' School, the Straits Chinese British Association, the Chinese Chamber of Commerce, the Chinese Advisory Board and the Po Leung Kuk Committee.

Statue of Sir Stamford Raffles in front of Victoria Memorial Hall

To get the best inscription for the statue a competition was held and the best entry came from Lim Koon Tye, an old Rafflesian who was awarded the sum of $25.

Sir Stamford Raffles died on 4 July 1826 at Highwood House, Hendon, England from an epileptic stroke.

The best eulogy on Raffles comes from Munshi Abdullah who wrote:

> *There are many great men besides him,*
> *clever and handsome, but in good*
> *disposition, amiability and gracefulness,*
> *Mr Raffles had not his equal, and were I*
> *to die and live again such a man I could never*
> *meet again, my love of him is so great.*

During the Japanese Occupation the statue was removed and kept in the Museum. After the return of the British, the statue was re-installed at the same site in 1946 by Governor Sir Franklin Gimson.

Note Raffles Statue near the St Andrew's Cathedral in 1887; it was removed in 1919 to its present site opposite Victoria Memorial Hall.

Empress Place Building
previously included the Chambers of the StraitsSettlements Legislative Council, the Secretariat and other government departments. Presently venue for historical and cultural exhibitions.

EMPRESS PLACE BUILDING

The old seat of Government and Government Offices

Empress Place
Old Court of Justice
Legislative Council Chambers
Colonial Secretariat

Today the building in Empress Place close to the Singapore River and Cavanagh Bridge is known as Empress Place Building officially opened by the Second Deputy Prime Minister Mr Ong Teng Cheong on 7 April 1989. The Building is now the venue for historical and cultural exhibitions. One section of the Building is occupied by a Chinese Restaurant.

The central part is the oldest of the Empress Place Building erected between 1864 and 1865. It became the new Court House when the Court moved out of John Argyle Maxwell's house, the present Parliament House because of the noise created by Hallpikc's Boat Yard nearby. In 1875 the Court moved back to an annexe of Maxwell House and the central part of Empress Place Building became the Chamber for sittings of the Straits Settlements Legislative Council established in 1867 when the Straits Settlements became a Crown Colony. New wings were added to the Empress Place Building in 1903, 1911 and 1920.

The rest of the Empress Place Building was occupied by various government departments which included the Secretariat, Treasury, Education Department, the Medical Services Department and the chambers of the Attorney-General.

Just before the British surrender to the Japanese, Treasury officials burnt stacks of bank notes for fear of them falling into Japanese hands.

Before the complete restoration of the Empress Place Building the Immigration Department, The Registry of Citizenship and Majlis Ugama Islam Singapura occupied various parts of the Building.

VICTORIA THEATRE AND MEMORIAL HALL

Empress Place

Singapore's cultural centres from early Singapore

In the early years soon after the founding of Singapore the British held their dramas and operas in the old Assembly Rooms at the foot of Fort Canning where Hill Street Police Station stands. When the old Assembly Rooms went into disrepair the trustees decided in 1854 to build a new one for the growing town of Singapore.

The foundation stone for the new Town Hall was laid by the Governor, Colonel W.J. Butterworth on 17 March 1855 and the building was completed in 1862 by John Bennett, the Municipal Engineer. To meet the cost of the building the government of India gave a grant of $3,000.

Temporarily the Municipal Commissioners occupied some rooms for their offices in the Victoria Theatre.

In 1902 decision was taken by the government to build on to the Town Hall a Memorial Hall to Queen Victoria. The foundation stone for the Victorial Memorial Hall was laid by Governor Sir Frank Swettenham on 9 August 1902 and the building was completed in 1905. The older part became the Victoria Theatre. The Straits Trading Company donated a clock and chimes in 1906; the clock chimed every hour but was silenced from 9 pm and 7 am. because of complaints by the patrons of the Grand Hotel de L'Europe nearby. Renovations were carried out in 1915 when a crown was placed on Victoria Memorial Hall.

In February 1942 during the Battle for Singapore Victoria Memorial Hall became an improvised hospital when all hospitals were overcrowded with the wounded and the sick.

After the Japanese surrender in 1945 the Victoria Memorial Hall was used in March 1947 as the venue for trying the Japanese war criminals associated with the massacre of the Chinese; it was known as the Sook Ching Trial. Those tried included Major General Saburo Kawamura, Commander of the Syonan (Singapore) Garrison, and Colonel Masyuki Oishi, Head, Syonan Kempeitai (Military Police). They were found guilty and sentenced to death; five other Japanese received life sentence. The other venue where other Japanese war criminals were tried was the Goodwood Park Hotel.

General Elections were held in Singapore since 1948 and the Victoria Memorial Hall was used for the briefing of Election officials and for the counting of the ballot papers. The Victoria Memorial Hall was also the venue of several public meetings and the People's Action Party held its inaugural meeting there on 21 November 1954. In the 1970s the Victorial Memorial Hall was renovated to serve as a concert hall.

Victoria Theatre and Memorial Hall

At the Victoria Theatre today concerts and cultural shows are held by the various ethnic groups. Many of these shows are sponsored by the Ministry of Information and the Arts. At Victoria Memorial Hall (now the Victoria Memorial Concert Hall) the Singapore Symphony Orchestra performs regularly to packed audiences. Cultural shows are also held at the Singapore Conference Hall, the Kallang Theatre, the Sub-Station and elsewhere.

The Arts Festival cultural programmes and the numerous plays and concerts are held in both the Victoria Theatre and the Victoria Memorial Concert Hall. These symbolise the maturing of the arts of both the East and the West in the Republic of Singapore.

STEPHEN HALLPIKE'S BOAT YARD AND BLACK SMITH SHOP

Hallpike Street

South-east Asia's boat yard that first built the gun boats with a 3 pounder gun.

Stephen Hallpike owned the boatyard from 1836 until his death in 1844 at the age of 61.

Boat making and repairs were carried out in the north bank of the Singapore River. The lane leading from High Street to the Singapore River was known as Hallpike Street. This is the lane that today leads to the Food Centre near the Attorney-General's Chambers. In fact the street plate was on a wall of the Chambers building. It is now missing.

Singapore River was for a long time an important centre for boat making. It was Singapore which first built the gun boat in South-eat Asia.

Mrs Hallpike ran a boarding house in High Street in the 1830s. The noise produced from the boat yard was one of the reasons why the Old Court House (Parliament House) was vacated and a new Supreme Court built in 1939.

Hallpike's Street, Singapore's first Boat Yard and Black Smith Shop located in bank of Singapore River

HIGH STREET

The first to be built in Singapore in 1819

High Street was the first street to be constructed in Singapore by the first town planner Lieutenant Henry Ralfe, Gunnery Officer, Bengal Artillery, East India Company. Ralfe and his soldiers had to clear some part of the jungle near the shore to create a meeting place for the signing of the preliminary treaty with Temenggong Abdul Rahman in 1819.

In the same year Hill Street and North Bridge Road were laid out. The streets were simply named: Hill Street was at the foot of Government Hill, North Bridge Road because it was north of the Singapore River and later South Bridge Road because it was south of the River. When a new bridge was built the road was named New Bridge Road.

High Street used to be the most import street in the city and was the main shopping centre before Orchard Road overtook it.

High Street
First Street built in Singapore in 1819.

ATTORNEY-GENERAL'S OFFICE

High Street

The Attorney-General's Office Building was the first Government Printing Office.

The Attorney-General's building was built in 1910 in High Street as the Government Printing Office. It moved to its present premises in Upper Serangoon Road in 1976.

Later the building was occupied by the Public Works Department before it was renovated to become the Attorney-General's Chambers.

Attorney General's Office, High Street
previously the Government Printing Office; built in 1910.

THE DALHOUSIE (GOVERNOR-GENERAL IN INDIA) OBELISK

EMPRESS PLACE

A permanent reminder to Singaporeans of the days when Singapore was administered by the East India Company through the Governor-General in India.
Marquis Dalhousie was Governor-General of India from 1848 to 1856 and Governor of the Straits Settlements (Singapore was part of it) was directly answerable to him.

In India, Dalhousie was recognised as an active modernist but incurred the displeasure of the Indians with his infamous "doctrine of lapse" by which he annexed Indian princely States where the rulers had no direct heirs to succeed them.

Marquis Dalhousie was the second Governor-General of India to visit Singapore; the first was Lord William Bentick in March 1829.

Marquis Dalhousie and Marchioness Dalhousie arrived in the settlement of Singapore on 17 February 1850 in the man of war "Feroze" which was anchored in the roads. He was received by the Governor, the Temenggong, European residents and the heads of various Chinese clans.

During their three-day stay, the Governor-General and his wife visited the oldest Chinese temple the Thian Hock Keng in Telok Ayer Street. At the farewell ceremony the Chinese community organised a procession of Chinese children up Government Hill (now Fort Canning) as a display of their loyalty to the British. Before his departure Marquis Dalhousie donated a sum of 1,000 rupees to the Tan Tock Seng Hospital.

As a permanent memorial to that visit the residents of Singapore decided to erect an obelisk by means of a $5 subscription fund. The following persons in May 1850 served on the Committee of the Dalhousie Testimonial:

G.G. Nicol
M.F. Davidson
J. Guthrie
Tan Kim Seng
Joaquim D'Almedia
H.C. Caldwell
Ang Choon Seng
and Seah Eu Chin

Dalhousie Obelisk, Empress Place
Symbol of British Colonialism

The Dalhousie Obelisk was completed by the end of 1850 and the plaque on the Obelisk used to read as follows:

> *the mercantile and other non official members*
> *of our community, Europeans and Asiatics deeply*
> *impressed with a sense of the great benefits*
> *the Settlement cannot fail to derive from the*
> *visit of the Most Noble the Marquis of Dalhousie,*
> *Governor-General of India*

The Dalhousie Obelisk was designed by John Turnbull Thomson who planned the spire for St Andrew's Church, and built the Horsburgh Light House on Pedra Branca; he also surveyed Keppel Harbour.

The Obelisk was removed from its original position to its present site a little further from the mouth of the Singapore River to make way for the construction of Connaught Drive and Anderson Bridge.

After his return to India Marquis Dalhousie brought the Straits Settlements under the direct control of the Governor-General; previously the Bengal Presidency was responsible for the Straits Settlements.

CITY HALL

National symbol and where important national ceremonies are held. Singapore's first Prime Minister declared self-government here in 1959 and independence through Malaysia in 1963. Mr Lee Kuan Yew and Mr Goh Chok Tong were sworn in here as Prime Ministers.

City Hall was previously known as the Municipality. It occupied the site of a private house of two pioneers: Dr William Montgomerie of the East India Company and Thomas Church, the Resident Councillor. The house was built by Singapore's first architect, G.D. Coleman.

Soon after the founding of Singapore, municipal matters were under the jurisdiction of the magistrates and later a Municipal Committee was established in 1851. The Municipal Committee comprised Thomas Church, as Chairman and members which included the Superintendent of the Convicts, a Representative from the Court and two other Europeans.

It was only in 1856 that a proper Municipal Council was set up. It looked after street lighting, water supply, maintenance of roads, in 1864 gas supply and 1906 electricity. The Municipal Health Department was opened in 1887 and the Municipality also controlled public transport provided by the jinrikishaws.

From 1856 to 1897 the Municipality functioned from a room in Town Hall and later the offices were moved to Finlayson Green in 1893.

The present building was completed in 1929 in Grecian architecture with dignified columns by F.D. Meadows, the Municipal architect.

In 1856 meetings of the Municipal Commissioners were open to the public.

In May 1858 the first Town Engineer and one person who was both the Surveyor and Architect were appointed by the Municipal Commissioners.

The Singapore Gas Company, a London Company carried on business in Singapore for 38 years sold its business to the Municipality in 1901.

During the Japanese Occupation the Municipality carried on the normal duties.

One of the major ceremonies held during the Japanese Occupation was the appearance of Subhas Chandra Bose the Indian leader who addressed a mammoth rally of Indians on 24 October 1942 standing at the Municipality steps to get their support for the Indian National Army.

Admiral Lord Louis Mountbatten, Supreme Commander, South-East Asia Command, accepted the surrender of the Japanese who were represented by Lieutenant General Seishiro Itakagi. It was also on the City Hall steps that a ceremony was held to remember the Singapore patriot and martyr Lim Bo Seng.

The City Hall
(previously the Municipality Building erected in 1929)
A national symbol - national ceremonies are held here.

On 22 September 1951 Singapore was proclaimed a City by Royal Charter granted by King George VI and Sir Franklin Gimson the Governor presented the Charter to the Municipal chairman.

The first mayor of Singapore was sworn in at City Hall on 24 December 1957. In 1959 Mr Lee Kuan Yew proclaimed self-government on the steps of City Hall. Again here he made the declaration of independence for Singapore in 1963. Mr Lee Kuan Yew was sworn in as Prime Minister in City Hall and so is his successor, Mr Goh Chok Tong.

After the first fully elected City Council in 1957 multi-lingualism was introduced at City Council meetings.

When the first President of the Republic Inche Yusof bin Ishak died on 23 November 1970 his body lay in state at the City Hall for the people to pay their last respects to him.

For Singaporeans City Hall will also be the proud symbol of our constitutional development and it is from City Hall that President, Prime Minister and Cabinet, Members of Parliament and Singaporeans witness the National Day rally which reflects our achievements in all spheres of life.

TAN KIM SENG FOUNTAIN

ESPLANADE

A commemoration to a Singaporean who was responsible for the supply of fresh water to the Town of Singapore and erection of the Singapore Water Works.

Tan Kim Seng came from Malacca to Singapore in 1840. He had a humble beginning but through perseverance rose to be a very wealthy man. He founded Kim Seng and Company, a trading house on Boat Quay. Tan Kim Seng was a leader among the Chinese; he was often asked to settle disputes among them.

On 18 November 1857 Tan Kim Seng offered a sum of $13,000 for a supply of water to the Town from Bukit Timah. This water was to be carried through pipes on the main roads in Singapore. The Secretary of State for India praised the public spiritedness of Tan Kim Seng.

Plans were made and various schemes had been suggested but nothing was actually done with regard to the water supply. There were meetings of the Municipal Council and much correspondence with the government on the subject about the unnecessary delay in implementation. Several places were proposed for reservoirs which included the New Harbour, Bukit Timah and Thomson Road.

During this period especially in 1862 Singapore had experienced severe droughts and no plans had yet been implemented for water supply into the Town. Money was, however, spent on a lot of earthenware drain pipes which were of no use for the project. A number of these pipes was laid at Kandang Kerbau. There was even an advertisement in the local paper stating that unless a large quantity of water pipes on board a vessel in the harbour had been taken delivery, the captain of the ship would get rid of them in the manner he desired. Money was also wasted by the Government Engineer who hoped that water would run uphill through pipes.

In recognition of Tan Kim Seng's farsightedness and generosity the Municipal Council erected in 1882 a large fountain in Fullerton Square in front of the Exchange Building (Fullerton Building) to commemorate him. On 19 May 1882 an opening ceremony was performed by the President of the Municipal Commission, Mr Thomas Scott, in the presence of the Chief Justice Sir Thomas Sidgreaves, the Colonial Secretary Sir Cecil Clementi Smith and Tan Kim Seng's son, Tan Beng Swee. Scott paid tribute to Tan: "Without Tan Kim Seng's generous gift, probably our water supply would have been a thing of the future instead of an accomplished fact."

Tan Kim Seng Fountain

The fountain was built by Andrew Handyside and Co Ltd, Derby and London. Around the fountain is inscribed the following: "This fountain is erected by the Municipal Commissioners in commemoration of Mr Tan Kim Seng's donation towards the cost of the Singapore Water Works."

In 1925 the fountain was moved to the Esplanade (Queen Elizabeth Walk) next to the "Satay Club" when Fullerton Building was being constructed.

Singaporeans are deeply indebted to Tan Kim Seng.

SINGAPORE CRICKET CLUB

The Padang

A symbol of British and European exclusiveness in the Colonial era; an exclusive Club for the "Tuan Besars" (big bosses) of the Colony.

Before the present Clubhouse was built the first one was a humble square hut where the cricketers kept their gear. At one time before 1852 the cricket bats, pads and other equipment were stored in the Masonic Hall nearby at Coleman Street.

A meeting was called in October 1852 to establish the Singapore Cricket Club but the modest Clubhouse served its members from 1859 to 1870. The second, a single storey Clubhouse, was completed in 1877; in 1884 the third Clubhouse was erected on a cast iron frame with verandahs all round. It was built in two levels; the upper level was ladies' viewing gallery.

In 1906 extensions were made to its square central core; a three dimensional appearance was given to the Clubhouse by the addition of the jail roof above the main one. Two wings were added in 1922.

The membership of the Club was kept exclusively to British and European residents of Singapore and it therefore became a symbol of British colonialism.

Cricket was the most popular sport in 1902 and 1903 and the Governor of the Straits Settlements, Sir Frank Swettenham, was both the President of the Club as well as its cricket captain. Cricket was not played on Sundays for a long time because of the services at the St Andrew's Cathedral nearby.

The membership of the Club in 1940 was 1093, the highest number before the outbreak of the Pacific War.

Even when the Japanese were advancing through Central Malaya the Singapore Cricket Club functioned normally with the members having their favorite whiskey and soda. The British believed that Singapore was invincible, the Japanese myopic and their aircraft were made of rice paper. It was a reflection of the British superiority complex. When the Battle for Singapore had begun the members were crestfallen.

During the Battle for Singapore the Club was converted into a temporary hospital to meet the mounting casualties. In February 1942 a bomb was dropped by a Japanese aircraft in Empress Place close to the Club's car park.

When the Japanese occupied Singapore they converted the Club into a luxurious restaurant and bar for Japanese military officers and Japanese girls served as waitresses. The restaurant was named Yamato Butai. Field Marshal Count Terauchi, the Commander of the Southern Army, hearing this ordered it be closed. In July 1942 it became a Japanese military officers' exclusive club where meals were served even during lunchtime.

Singapore Cricket Club - Club exclusively for "Tuan Besars" (big bosses) - Europeans until 1959.

The first President of the Club was L.T.R. Glass and full membership only was opened to Asians after the end of World War II. The first Asian President of the Club was Justice Mr. T.S. Sinnathuray.

Mr Lee Kuan Yew, the Prime Minister, accepted the Club's invitation to become The Visitor on 12 December 1970 and in his address to the Club said, "There is an indefinable quality about this club which no other club can match - it bridges the transformation from what was to what is, and represents our capacity to meet what will be."

SINGAPORE RECREATION CLUB

The Padang

Symbol that the Eurasians have been part of our Singapore community from early times.
Eurasians in the Singapore Volunteer Corps fought courageously against the Japanese invaders; a Director, General Staff, Singapore Armed Forces in its formative phase, was a Eurasian; the first non-European Commissioner of Police was also a Eurasian.

Other than Singapore Eurasians quite a number of Eurasians of Portuguese and Dutch origins migrated from Malacca to Singapore in the early years.

To provide sporting facilities for the Eurasian community the first Singapore Recreation Club was in a building in Waterloo Street. The new Clubhouse at one end of the Padang opened on 23 June 1833. The pavilion was raised in November 1885.

The monthly subscription for the Club membership then was $1 per mensem and $2 as entrance fee. The first president of the Club was J. R. McFarlane.

When the Singapore Volunteer Company was formed in 1881 it comprised mainly of Europeans and Eurasians and a separate Eurasian Volunteer headquarters and Club opened in Beach Road in February 1927 because of the excellent work of the Eurasian Company. Even when the Volunteer Cadet Corps were formed in Raffles Institution, St Joseph's Institution and Anglo-Chinese School in 1906 most of the cadets were Chinese and Eurasians.

During the Malayan campaign and the Battle for Singapore the Eurasians fought valiantly alongside the British forces against the invading Japanese troops. There is a tablet inside the Club to commemorate all the Eurasians who died during World War II (1939-1945). At the Kranji Memorial names of Eurasian volunteers who died in the war are also inscribed there.

Under the Japanese Occupation the Eurasians were also persecuted for having been pro-British. The Japanese decided to settle a large number of Eurasians in the proposed Fuji Village in Bahau, Negri Sembilan; the project was a failure.

The Singapore Recreation Club was converted into an outpatient clinic during the days of the Japanese Occupation.

After Singapore was separated from Malaysia in 1965 the Singapore Armed Forces (SAF) were established and Mr Campbell who served as a prisoner of war along with the British forces helped to organise the SAF and was given the rank of a Brigadier and became Director, General Staff.

The Eurasians are a part of the Singapore community and the Singapore Recreation Club is a reminder of their eminent position in the pre-war period. There are today about 10,000 Eurasians in Singapore serving in the various professions in government service including the SAF and the Singapore Police force as well as the private sector.

The Eurasian Association of Singapore has planned a Eurasian Heritage Day in 1991 which besides including a programme of dance, music and food will also hold an exhibition in the National Museum to depict their history through photographs and artefacts.

After the Clubhouse was renovated the Prime Minister, Mr Lee Kuan Yew officially declared open the building. Today the membership to the Club is open to all ethnic groups in Singapore. The present president is Mr E. C. Tessensohn. Honorary members of the Club include Mr Lee Kuan Yew, Mr E.W. Barker and Mr David Marshall. Dr E.W. Sheares and Professor E.S. Monteiro were also Honorary Members of the Club.

Singapore Recreation Club, The Padang
(once exclusively for Eurasians) now open to all ethnic groups.

DHOBY GHAUT

Bras Basah Road

Site where early Indian dhobies washed their laundry

Indian dhobies (laundrymen) in early Singapore washed their laundry in the stream which used to be known as Sungei Bras Basah - a rivulet - that flowed from Orchard Road to the sea. Today it is the Stamford Canal. The Chinese called the road beside it "Lau Chooi Koei" (Flowing Water Road).

The dhobies dried their laundry in the open space between Bras Basah Road and Stamford Road. Bras Basah Road (west rice road) was once called Church Street and College Street because of the several Churches and Schools in that locality.

Dhoby Ghaut opposite Cathay Theatre

Old Flag Staff Mount Faber

MOUNT FABER

Formerly Telok Blangah Hill
Old Signal Station,
Observatory and half
completed fortress

Telok Blangah Hill is close to the old village of Temenggong Abdul Rahman who was resettled there by Stamford Raffles and became known as Kampong Bahru (new village) as it replaced the old kampong along the Singapore River. This first resettlement could be called the first urban renewal project in Singapore.

The Hill maintained the old name of Telok Blangah Hill until July 1845 when it was renamed Mount Faber after Captain Faber of the Madras Engineers.

Captain Faber built the narrow winding road to the summit for the new Signal Station (the old one was in Blakang Mati, now Sentosa). Adverse criticism was made about the narrow road which still leads to the summit of the Hill. The *Free Press*, a local newspaper commented "... stupidly narrow road to the top....two persons meeting can barely pass each other. ... so much of renown is bestowed up him." It also asked who changed the pretty and appropriate Malay name of the hill. The new Signal Station on Mount Faber was known in Malay as Bukit Bandara (Flag Hill).

In May 1851 a new Flagstaff was erected on the hill. A month later it was struck by lightning and destroyed. An Observatory was built on the Hill in 1905.

In 1857 Indian soldiers (sepoys) mutinied against their British Officers in India. The Settlement government feared that the local Indian sepoys might also revolt. It therefore decided to convert Mount Faber into a fort. Defence work was carried out and granite emplacements for guns were completed half-way up the Hill. Mount Faber never became a Fort.

Today Mount Faber is a popular tourist attraction and the Signal Station is still there; it is here that one boards a cable car to Sentosa.

Hong Lim Green (Park);
in the middle stood the Singapore Chinese Recreation Club House. Club founded in 1885.

HONG LIM GREEN

(HONG LIM PARK)
New Bridge Road

Hong Lim Green was Singapore's first private public garden created and maintained by Cheang Hong Lim - business man and philanthropist.

Hong Lim Green today is known as Hong Lim Park and maintained by the government.

Cheang Hong Lim was a wealthy businessman. He ran opium and spirit farms which at that time were very lucrative enterprises. His partners were also well-known and prosperous businessmen - Tan Seng Poh and Tan Yeok Nee.

Cheang owned a private fire-brigade which was manned by 37 firemen; his fire-brigade fought fires in the Town. Cheang was a property owner and sat on the Po Leong Kok Committee. In 1875 he contributed liberally to build a free school for boys of all ages and creeds to study at the Telok Ayer Grammar School at Cheang Wan Seng Place. He was the largest subscriber to provide Maxim guns for the Singapore Volunteer Artillery Unit.

In August 1875 he petitioned successfully to the government to cease further burials in Peak Island (now Pulau Kusu). There were two shrines (Toa-pek-kong Kusu and Data Kramat) on the island.

Cheang Hong Lim's most interesting contribution to Singapore was his donation of $3,000 to convert the space in front of the old Central Police Station into a public garden. This was the first private public garden in Singapore and he employed two gardeners to maintain it.

Hong Lim Green (Park) was a popular venue for election rallies. Today it is a popular park and has a stage where public concerts are performed.

The Singapore Chinese Recreation Club (founded in 1885) House was erected at Cheang Hong Lim's expense. It stood in the centre of Hong Lim Green for many years. The Club had some outstanding national players in cricket and hockey. The Club House and field have now disappeared.

Cheang Hong Lim died on 11 February 1893.

Peranakan Houses, Petain Road

Close up of a Peranakan House

PERANAKAN PLACE

Orchard Road

The Peranakan Chinese (The Babas and Nonyas) are an indigenous community evolved over the centuries in Melaka, Penang and Singapore. They were an affluent community and contributed substantially to the social and economic development of Singapore.

The Peranakan Chinese (the Babas and Nonyas) are an indigenous people of Singapore. Their ancestors evolved in Melaka, Penang and Singapore. In the Indian language "peranakan" means "speakers of a foreign tongue". In the Melaka Sultanate (1402-1511) Malay was the lingua franca and people who spoke foreign languages were known as Peranakans; so we have Peranakan Chinese, Peranakan India, Peranakan Arab, Peranakan Java, Peranakan Yahudi.

The Peranakan Chinese are also known as Babas and Nonyas. Their Chinese ancestors married or made union with local women; speak little or no Chinese. They speak Baba Malay. They are "Chinese in spirit and traditions but Malay in form" (Felix Chia in "The Babas" published by Times Books International, Singapore 1984). The Singapore Babas are an offshoot of the Melaka Babas who speak a Malay patois with Chinese words and phrases of the Hokkien dialect. The spelling and pronunciation of Malay words are different from those of Malay words.

The Nonya lady wears a dress which is of Malay origin; it is a "sarong" - a long tunic stretching down to the ankles. The tunic is won with a set of 3 "kerosangs" or brooches. She carries on the head the "sanggol sipot", a snail-shaped hairdo with 3 large pins in the shape of snails ("sipot"). They wear beaded slippers called "kasot manek manek".

The religion of the Peranakan Chinese is a mixture of Taoism, Buddhism and Confucianism and they celebrate and observe the major Chinese festivals which include Chinese New Year's Day, Cheng Beng and All Souls' Day. They also have their own traditions, ceremonies and customs for weddings, birthdays and other auspicious occasions.

A unique feature of the Peranakan Chinese is that after a wedding they usually sing the "Dondang Sayang", composing and reciting "pantun" (4 line verses) to express their emotions.

The Babas and Nonyas eat with their fingers like the Malays and Indians. Nonya food is very spicy including the "sambal blachan" (Chilli and shrimp paste). Their variety of cakes is very tasty. They chew betel leaf ("seray" in Malay) which they keep in a small metal box called "tumpat seray".

They have their own distinct porcelain, Nonya ware, which include tea pots, cups and bowls and their own distinctive Baba furniture. Nonya jewellery is also unique; all these reflect the affluence of the Peranakan Chinese community.

Peranakan Chinese architecture is distinct; it is Chinese Baroque or Neo-Classical European design that originated in Melaka. Their houses are located generally in Cairnhill, Joo Chiat, Petain Road, Tanjong Pagar, Serangoon, Geylang, Katong, Tanglin and Blair Road.

In the early years the Peranakan Chinese also had their special games; these included the "cherki" card game played with a pack of 60; there was also the "chongkak" game played with a wooden board and 98 cowrie shells.

Today the Peranakan Chinese are marrying among the mainstream Chinese and the community is getting smaller; many of them are Christians.

The Babas were very pro British. They sent their children to English Schools and they served in the Straits Settlements Volunteer Corps. Many of the Babas were also eminent persons who contributed immensely to the social, educational and economic growth of Singapore from the very early times. Well-known among the Peranakan Chinese before the outbreak of the Pacific War were Sir Ong Song Siang, the author of "One Hundred Years of the Chinese in Singapore" first published in 1902 and is still an invaluable source book and Dr Lim Boon Keng, a leader of the Chinese community, a member of the Straits Settlements Legislative Council and Chairman, Chinese Overseas Association during the Japanese Occupation.

Peranakan Place, Orchard Road

THE CENTRAL SIKH GURDWARA (TEMPLE)

Towner Road

The Sikhs have been a small but vibrant component of our Singapore community from very early Singapore. Their Temple is their community centre to sustain their culture, values, faith and identity.

The Gurdwara (Sikh Temple) is the most important institution of the Sikhs. Both men and women have rights and equal say in religious matters.

The Scriptures of the Sikhs are contained in a 1430 page book called the Sri Guru Granth Sahib which is found in all the Gurdwaras. It forms the basis of Sikh meditation, their understanding of God and their world outlook.

The first Sikhs numbering 165 from Punjab, India, came to Singapore to be employed as policemen in the Straits Settlements Police Force in 1881.

Central Sikh Temple, Towner Road

Eventually they became members of the 500 strong Sikh Contingent of the Straits Settlements Police Force. These policemen worshipped in the Police Barracks on Pearl's Hill.

After World War II in 1945 the Sikh contingent was disbanded and the equipment of their Gurdwara was transferred to the Central Sikh Temple in Queen Street; the books were handed to the Sikh Missionary Society of Malaya.

The original Central Sikh Temple, a bungalow erected in 1912 stood at 715 Queen Street. It was reconstructed in 1921. In 1940 an Ordinance was passed to administer the Sikh Temple and it was known as "The Queen Street Gurdwara Ordinance".

As a result of urban re-development the site was acquired by the government and the Temple was vacated. The government provided a new site for the Central Sikh Gurdwara at Towner Road. The new and large Temple built by donations from the Sikh community was officially opened by President Wee Kim Wee on 16 November 1986 on the occasion of the 518th birthday of Sri Guru Nanak Dev Ji, the founder of the Sikh Faith.

Silat Road Sikh Temple

SILAT ROAD SIKH GURDWARA

The first Sikh Temple to be constructed in the visible shape of a Temple with a dome and arches was completed in 1924 in Silat Road.

In the 1930s the Temple was neglected because of dissension in its congregation. During the Japanese Occupation (1942-45) widows and orphans were accommodated in and around the Temple premises. The Baba Karam Singh Samadh in the Singapore General Hospital grounds, Outram Road, was transferred to the Silat Road Gurdwara in 1968.

There are Sikh Temples at Niven Road, Sophia Road and Wilkinson Road. These Temples are not only places of worship but also venues for Sikh community to meet.

The Sikhs who migrated to Singapore are today a small but vibrant community whose religious activities and welfare are in the hands of Sikh organisations like the Sikh Advisory Board and the Khalsa Association which has its own premises and which conducts various activities including Punjabi classes. Members of the Sikh community continue to serve in the Civil Service, the Singapore Armed Forces, the Singapore Police Force, and in various professions and businesses. There is today a Sikh member of Parliament.

Because of their strong religious faith the Sikh community was able to introduce Sikh Studies in the Singapore school curriculum and teach the subject in the schools. The community celebrates events like the birthday of Guru Nanak and Guru Gobind Singh. The Sikh Bangra dance is a vibrant attraction during Singapore National Day rallies and a popular item in cultural concerts in the Republic.

The Sikh population has grown throughout the years; in 1921 it was 2,000 and in 1931, 3,500; in 1957 it was 7,000; today it is about 12,000.

SALVATION ARMY HEADQUARTERS BUILDING

No. 207 Clemenceau Avenue

former house of Towkay Tan Yeok Nee; Only remaining house in Singapore built in the traditionalChinese architecture;Tan Yeok Nee - a merchant pioneer of Singapore
It was gazetted as a national monument on 29 November 1974.

The house of Tan Yeok Nee ("Towkay" in Chinese means "boss" and generally referred to a wealthy person) was built in 1885. It is the best example of Southern Chinese architecture that remains in Singapore. A small number of "towkays" (wealthy businessmen) built large houses in the Chinese tradition in the early years in Singapore. Tan Yeok Nee's house (Salvation Army Headquarters) is the only building now that reflects that tradition. The earliest in that tradition was the residence of Tan Seng Poh built in 1869 and later used as the Chinese Consulate.

The house of Tan Yeok Nee has a distinctive Chinese roof, curved eaves, spectacularly carved mythical beasts on the roof, stone carvings and massive granite piers; all imported from China.

Tan Yeok Nee was born in 1827 in the village of Sa-Ling in China; he died there on 21st May 1902 at the age of 75. He came to Singapore at an early age and began life as a cloth pedlar. The Temenggong's family in Telok Blangah became his customers. He became friendly with Temenggong Abu Bakar of Johore who made him a Captain China of Johore and gave him the Kanchu papers. By 1866 he had become a prosperous gambier and pepper trader in Boat Quay. With Cheang Hong Lim and Tan Seng Poh, he ran the Singapore and Johore Opium and Spirit Farms.

The laying of a railway affected the house of Tan Yeok Nee. The line ran from Keppel Harbour in Tanjong Pagar through New Bridge Road near the Singapore General Hospital to Tank Road which was the southern terminus and main railway station.

Because of the noise, dust and dirt that affected the Tan family the house was vacated and acquired by the government to be used by the Railway Station Master of the Tank Road Station as his residence.

Later the house was given as a trust to Bishop Ferguson of the Anglican Church. It became the St Mary's Home and School for Eurasian girls for about 20 years. In the 1930s the house was purchased by the Anglican Church from the government. In 1940 the Salvation Army bought it from the Church of England for $50,000 and made it their headquarters.

In 1942 the Japanese Imperial Army occupied the premises. When the

House of Tan Yoke Nee, Clemenceau Avenue
Headquarters of the Salvation Army

British returned to Singapore after the Japanese surrender in 1945 the Salvation Army had to carry out extensive repairs to the building before they could occupy it. Sir Franklin Gimson, the first Governor of the Colony of Singapore, officially opened the Salvation Army Headquarters on 6th July 1951.

Before Tan Yeok Nee built this beautiful house he made Hotel de la Paix in Coleman Street his residence. The house of Tan Yeok Nee reflects the affluence of the "towkays" of early Singapore and their natural attachment to traditional Chinese architecture. Today the house still stands as a fine example of that tradition.

GOODWOOD PARK HOTEL

SCOTTS ROAD

Club of early German community in Singapore and War Crimes Court; Tower Block gazetted as a national monument on 23 March 1989

The Teutonia or the German club was built in 1900 for German residents of Singapore. The architect of the new building was R.A.J. Bidwell of Swan and MacLaren Co Ltd.

The Club was officially opened by the acting Governor of the Straits Settlements, Sir Frank Swettenham on 21 September 1900. The Club held various classical musical concerts and the funds raised through them benefited several local charities and the Tan Tock Seng Hospital.

The outbreak of Workd War I in 1914 brought an end to the Teutonia Club when it was acquired by the British custodian of enemy property. The building served as an electric power-station for the next eight years. In 1929, the Manessah family, purchased the building at an auction and turned it into the Goodwood Park Hotel.

During the Japanese Occupation (1942-45) the Goodwood Park Hotel was used by the Japanese as their military headquarters and as a residence for senior military officers.

In 1945 the British Military Administration used the building as a War Crimes Court during the trials of Japanese war criminals; the world was shocked to hear of terrible atrocities committed by the Japanese in Singapore. The trials were witnessed by relatives of the victims from the United Kingdom, Australia and elsewhere including Signapore. About 135 Japanese were tried, convicted and executed at Changi Gaol. One of them, a former commander of the prisoner-of-war camp, was sentenced to be shot at Changi beach - the same place where two Australian and two British soldiers were shot by his orders.

In 1947 the Hotel was restored; the facade at the entrance built in 1900 was retained but the distinctive tower of the Hotel removed in 1950 and later restored in 1959 was not in the original shape but it blends with the rest of the building.

The Hotel was built in the South German style with ornamental work, with large semi-circular gable end flanking the entrance. The whole of the beautiful arrangement is topped by an octagonal tower and pointed tiled roof. The rustication on the windows is a special feature of the architect, Bidwell.

Goodwood Park Hotel

Cathedral of The Good Shepherd, Queen Street

CATHEDRAL OF THE GOOD SHEPHERD

Queen Street

Expansion of the Roman Catholic Church - the French Mission Singapore.It was gazetted as a national monument on 6 July 1973

Stamford Raffles gave a Malacca priest land on a 999 year lease to build a Catholic Church in 1822. Rev Mgr Courvezy got the site from Bonham, the Resident Councillor. The present St Joseph's Institution stands on that site. The first Roman Catholic Chapel was a modest building which cost $700, met from public subscription; it had no tower or spire.

By the end of the 1830s Bishop Hilary Courvezy, Vicar Apostolic of Malaya, thought of extending the small chapel but Father Beurel persuaded him to keep the site for a school and select a different one for the Church.

The corner stone was laid by John Connolly on 18th June 1843; a tablet in the Cathedral confirms this. The corner stone was blessed by Bishop Courvezy. A building appeal fund was launched in 1840.

The Cathedral was built to a design by Denis Leslie McSwiney. It was opened and blessed by Father J.N. Beurel, the parish priest on 6th June 1846. The building is in the form of a crucifix in Renaissance style - a steeple at one end and Greek pillars supporting the roof. The building cost $20,000. The steeple was added in 1847 by C.A. Dyce, Sheriff for the Settlements of Singapore, Malacca and Penang. The marble paving from Antwerp was installed in 1860; the nave was extended in 1888 and consecrated on 14th February 1897 by Bishop Rene Fee.

The relics of Saint Laurent Imbert, the first priest to visit the few Catholics in Singapore in December 1821, are preserved in the Cathedral.

During the Battle for Singapore the Cathedral was converted into an emergency hospital.

CHURCH OF ST JOSEPH

225-A Queen Street

Expansion of Portuguese Roman Catholic Mission in Singapore.

The first Church of St Joseph was erected on a site chosen as early as 1822. Rev Father Vincentre de Santo Catharina used the funds left for constructing the Church by Rev Francisco de Silva Pinto i Maria, head of the Portuguese Mission. The foundation stone was laid on 14 December 1851 and the building was completed in 1853 but in 1906 the Church was pulled down and the present building replaced it in 1912.

The present Church of St Joseph cost $15,000 to build it and gifts were also sent from the King of Portugal. There is a tablet in the Church dated 1 January 1919; it was placed by the congregation which recognised the "generous aid towards completion of the Church" by Father Castro, Bishop of Macao. The Church was designed in the Gothic style by the architect firm of Swan and MacLaren; the central tower is octagonal in design with a dome and flanked by two small towers.

Next to the Church is the Priests' House of St Joseph's Portuguese Mission built in 1912.

St Anthony's School was opened in 1889 by Father Jose Pedro Sta Anna da Cunha in a small shop house in Middle Road. Later the school moved to a compound house in Victoria Street near the Church in 1886. In 1893 the girls were separated from the boys who occupied the ground floor of the Parochial House. In 1894 the Society of the Canosianas Sisters in Italy took charge of the Girls' School.

It is interesting to note that the French and Portuguese Missions contended for the honour of evangelising and pastoring in Singapore and this led to papal intervention in 1886. The Pope decided the respective spheres of influence by the two Missions.

The building of the Church of St Joseph and other Churches opened by the Portuguese Mission is an example of the early expansion of the Roman Catholic Church in Singapore.

Roman Catholic Church of St Joseph (Portuguese Mission)

Priests' House of St Joseph's Portuguese Mission built in 1912

CHURCH OF ST PETER AND PAUL

Queen Street

Extension of the work of the Portuguese Mission in Singapore

Father Paris built the Roman Catholic Church of St Peter and Paul between 1869 and 1870 and also donated three beautiful bells to the Church. Pedro Tan No Keah influenced the men among the Chinese Roman Catholics to subscribe liberally towards the fund for erecting the Church of St Peter and Paul.

Most of the Chinese and Indian Roman Catholics moved from the Cathedral of the Good Shepherd to worship in the new Church soon after its completion. When the Chinese Roman Catholic community in the Town had increased the Cantonese congregation since 1910 worshipped in the Roman Catholic Church of the Sacred Heart in Tank Road.

Church of St Peter and Paul, Queen Street
Portuguese Roman Catholic Church

WESLEY CHURCH AND ANGLO-CHINESE SCHOOL

Canning Rise and Coleman Street

"The March of Methodism" - its Church and school in Singapore; Methodist Contribution to Singapore

William Fitzjones Oldham (1854-1937) arrived in Singapore in 1885 to establish the first Methodist Episcopal Church in Malaya and Singapore. On 1st March 1886 the first school was started with 13 pupils at 70 Amoy Street in a shophouse when Oldham had raised $6,300 from his Chinese friends and $6,000 from the Colonial Secretary McCabe. English was taught in the morning and Chinese in the afternoon in this school, "the Chinese merchants undertaking to pay all current expenses, the missionary not charging for his time and labour".

The enrolment gradually increased and when it reached 104 it was necessary to look for larger premises. The school was resited at Coleman Street on a land granted by the Municipality; a boarding school and a residence for missionaries were also erected there.

To increase the enrolment, the principal of the school had to visit homes to invite pupils to join the school. Pupils travelled to school on foot, by bicycle, rickshaw or horse-carriage.

The Methodist Episcopal Church in Coleman Street was born on Sunday 22nd February 1885 when Oldham was appointed the pastor on a salary of $70 per mensem. Later he was also appointed as the chaplain to the British troops. This Church stood on the site of the present Anglo-Chinese School, Coleman Street. The architecture of the Church was in harmony with that of the Armenian Church and the Cathedral of the Good Shepherd nearby; it had a broad triangular top borne by noble pillars. It is "toned down, Gothic Revival" with red bricks, Gothic tracery, mullion details in white stone or stucco with impressive wooden cross beams.

The new Gothic Church at Canning Rise was completed in 1909. D. McLeod Craik, Swan and MacLaren were the architects. Renovations and additions were made to the building. On 7th January 1910 the name "Wesley Church" replaced the "Methodist Episcopal Church".

The Methodist Church began to expand and soon Churches were established where services were held in Chinese, Malay (for the Straits Chinese) and Tamil. A number of girls' schools was also set up. A Tamil Boys' School was established opposite the present "Tekka" market in Serangoon Road.

Wesley Church, Canning Rise, Built 1909

Old building of Anglo-Chinese School in Cairnhill occupied in 1928.
In 1950 it became the premises of the first Teachers' Training College.

A Continuation School was also added to the School at Coleman Street and was named Oldham Methodist School. In 1923 it was decided to build a new school at Cairnhill and in 1928 the building opened as a secondary school.

During the Japanese invasion of Malaya and Singapore the building at Cairnhill was damaged; there were foxholes and trenches and a tunnel ran round the entire building. With the Japanese Surrender the school reopened on 1 October 1945 after repairs were carried out with the help of Japanese prisoners of war.

Just before the fall of Singapore, Bishop Edwin F Lee and 22 American missionaries left Singapore on the advice of the American Consul but several remained in Singapore. Rev H.B. Amstutz (later Bishop) was a prisoner of war. He returned after captivity to re-establish the Church and Schools in Malaya and Singapore.

In 1950 the building was taken over by the government and it became the first Teachers' Training College for Singapore. The school occupied the new premises at Barker Road.

The old Anglo-Chinese School Building at Cairnhill is now an Arts Centre. Its unique architecture is retained.

The first premises of Anglo-Chinese School at 70 Amoy Street. School founded on 1 March 1886 (Photo taken in June, 1991)

PRESBYTERIAN CHURCH

Stamford Road

Expansion of the Protestant Missions

In 1856 Rev McKenzie Fraser was the first minister to the Presbyterian congregation in Singapore and the mission to the Chinese was undertaken by Tan See Boo, a catechist and convert from Amoy and who later set up the Chinese Presbyterian Church in 1867.

Rev Fraser began his Church ministry in Singapore by conducting his services in the Missionary Chapel. In 1872 the Missionary Chapel became an affiliate of the Presbyterian Church of England.

The Presbyterian congregation secured a parcel of land in the town in 1875 to build a Church; this is the site occupied by the present Presbyterian Church of Singapore in Stamford Road. The foundation stone of the Church was laid on 1 August 1877 by the Officer Administering the Government of the Straits Settlements - Colonel Anson.

The Church was erected at a cost of $20,000 and the congregation then comprised 42 members and by 1910 the number had reached 340; at that time about one quarter of the members came from Malaya.

During the Japanese Occupation (1942-45) the Church was used by the Japanese as a supply base for Japanese civilians and the building suffered much damage. Most of the Church records were also lost during those dreadful years.

After the Japanese surrender in August 1945, Rev Greer who had been interned in Changi Gaol during the occupation, re-opened the Church for regular services in 1947.

Presbyterian Church, Stamford Road

CONVENT OF THE HOLY INFANT JESUS AND ITS CHAPEL

Victoria Street

Catholic education for girls in English and Chinese medium of instruction; orphanage for girls and home for abandoned babies in early Singapore

The Convent of the Holy Infant Jesus (CHIJ) was founded in Victoria Street by Rev Mother St Mathilde with three Sisters, Sr Gaetau, Sr Appolinaire and Sr Gregoire. Soon after their arrival in Singapore in the ship "Hoogly" in 1854 they started the Convent with 14 fee-paying pupils, nine boarders and 16 orphans.

In 1856 the Convent was extended when Rev Father Beurel acquired Caldwell's House for $4000. By 1894 the enrolment was 167 and in 1904, 300 and the School presented its candidates for the Junior Cambridge Examination.

The first commercial classes were started in 1926. Boys were also admitted in the early years and one of its pupils is Mr David Marshall, the first elected Chief Minister of Singapore and at present Singapore's Ambassador to France.

A new wing was added in 1909 for which the government gave a grant of $20,000; this wing included the hall and new classrooms. In the same year the beautiful Chapel was completed. The special feature of the Chapel are the stained glass panes, the work of Flemish artists and donors were from several countries including France, Ireland, England and the Philippines.

The stained glass panes have been described as "a consummate piece of workmanship a divinely mosaic - the flawless transparency of which will be struck through with rays of God's transcendent beauty." Stained glass panes include the apsidal series encircling the high altar. The aisle windows depict the twelve apostles bearing their distinctive symbols.

Further extensions were made to CHIJ when in 1931 it acquired the Van Dyke Hotel adjoining its grounds. Two years later St Nicholas Girls' School opened in Victoria Street to educate girls in Chinese.

Prior to the outbreak of World War II, CHIJ educated girls in both Chinese and English and the second language was French.

The CHIJ was also an orphanage for girls as well as a home for discarded babies or foundlings usually left at the "small gate" often at the point of death. There was a dormitory for the boarders and a creche for the babies looked after by a team of dedicated sisters and nuns.

Chapel of The Convent of the Holy Infant Jesus now preserved.

From 1885 to 1903 CHIJ extended its services to help the sick in the General Hospital.

During the World War II (the Japanese Occupation) the Sisters and orphans left for Bahau, a settlement in Negeri Sembilan, Malaya. CHIJ suffered much damage during the Occupation. The windows of the Chapel were shattered and the stained glass group in the Lady Chapel was completely damaged and also two of the apsidal series encircling the high altar.

The Tiger Hall was used during the Japanese Occupation for instruction in Japanese.

After the return of the British in 1945, CHIJ was restarted and the Tiger Hall housed St Nicholas Girls' School.

In 1964 CHIJ was separated into a primary and a secondary School. By December 1983 CHIJ had to vacate its Victoria Street premises to give way for re-development. The beautiful Chapel is preserved and is now a National Monument leased out to be appropriately used.

CHIJ started functioning in its new premises at 626 Lorong 1 Toa Payoh and the official opening was on 17 August 1985 by the Vatican Ambassador to Singapore Archbishop Renato Martino. The Convent still maintains the spirit: "Simple in Virtue and Steadfast in Duty".

When Singaporeans look at the beautiful Chapel they will be reminded that CHIJ provided Catholic education for girls, an orphanage for girls and a creche for abandoned babies.

Stained glass of the Chapel

CALDWELL'S HOUSE

part of the Convent of the Holy Infant Jesus
Victoria Street

Catholic education for all girls.
A French Roman Catholic Institution: School, Chapel and Convent. The most famous of the Roman Catholic Girls Schools in Singapore.

H.C.Caldwell, Senior Sworn Clerk to the Magistrates built the house between 1840 and 1841. He owned the house until August 1852 when he sold it to Father J. M. Beurel, a French priest for 4,000 Spanish dollars. Father Beurel built the Convent of the Holy Infant Jesus in 1854.

G.D. Coleman, Singapore's first architect designed the house in neoclassical style. Caldwell's House has the hallmarks of Coleman's style.

The Convent of the Holy Infant Jesus moved to Toa Payoh and the Chapel has been leased to a private enterprise to retain the beautiful chapel and usage suitable to an old religious institution.

Caldwell's House (in the former Convent of Holy Infant Jesus) Victoria Street. Built between 1840 and 1841 for H. C. Caldwell by G. D. Coleman

ROMAN CATHOLIC CHURCH OF THE SACRED HEART

Tank Road

Once the Church with a large Chinese congregation

One of the most beautiful Churches in Singapore is the Church of the Sacred Heart built in 1906 by the Society of St Vincent de Paul.

This Church was built largely for a Chinese (Cantonese) congregation. The name of the Church is given in Chinese and so are most of the memorials in the Church.

A new Hammond organ was presented to the Church on 8 June 1941. Among the benefactors of the Church are A. Cashin, D. Pillay and A. Seth. The Church was renovated in January 1969 and the Parish Welfare Hall was established on 21 February 1971.

The stained glass windows add dignity to the facade and architecture.

Roman Catholic Church of the Sacred Heart, Tank Road largely with a Cantonese Congregation.

RAFFLES INSTITUTION

Bishan

(Old buildings at Bras Basah Road demolished and now occupied by Raffles City)
Oldest government School founded in 1823 by Sir Stamford Raffles.
Foresight and concern for education of the "natives" by a colonialist to set up a "native college" which became the Singapore Institution and later Raffles Institution.

When one passes Raffles City which houses the tallest hotels in the world, the Westin and the Stamford, one is reminded of the old Raffles Institution which stood on that site. Later after the demolition of old Raffles Institution, the school moved to Grange Road which was in an equally distinguished neighbourhood. Today Raffles Institution is in Bishan, a new satellite town and in the midst of Housing and Development Board (HDB) flats. It was from such neighbourhood that many students of Raffles Institution in Bras Basah Road and Grange Road came; now Raffles Institution is in the midst of the homes where most of our students come. Students of Raffles Institution are constantly reminded that when they become leaders in the professions they should not forget that they came largely from HDB flats.

"It is probably due to him (Raffles) more than to any other individual that education was begun in Singapore" (E. Wijeysingha). But before the Singapore Institution (Raffles Institution) was founded in 1823 there were a few Malay Schools, a small missionary school and three Chinese schools in Singapore.

Raffles' aim was to educate the local people by setting up a "native college" and he himself chose the site close to the government buildings and Churches. He launched a subscription to build the school and he made a personal donation of $2,000. The first President of the Singapore Institution was the Resident Lieutenant Colonel Farquhar and Reverend Morrison was the Vice-President. It is significant to note that Rev. Morrison, a Presbyterian Missionary who founded the Anglo-Chinese School in Malacca was also responsible for establishing Raffles Institution.

The school building was completed in 1827 at the site chosen by Raffles.

In September 1823 a sad decision was made by the East India Company to divert the funds of Singapore Institution to build a monument for Stamford Raffles who died in 1826 - a Town Hall and a Reading Room. Fortunately this did not materialise and plans to complete the school buildings were agreed upon. In 1834 Singapore Institution began to function as a school and in 1836 the School Committee decided to complete the buildings of the school as a

Raffles Institution (now at Bishan)
Oldest government and premier school founded by Sir Stamford Raffles in 1823. Old school buildings demolished and site now occupied by Raffles City.

A view of Raffles Institution at Grange Road after the school moved out of Bras Basah Road.

memorial to Stamford Raffles. In September 1839, the Singapore Free School moved from High Street to the Singapore Institution buildings. By 1841 both the wings of the Institution were completed.

The principal who contributed most to the Institution's growth and prominence was R.W. Hullet; he was the head for 36 years (1870-1906).

At the outbreak of the Pacific War in December 1941 Raffles Institution was requisitioned by the British forces. The Japanese used the Institution during their occupation of Singapore from 1942 to 1945. When the British returned to Singapore after the Japanese surrender in 1945 and the British Military Administration was set up, Raffles Institution functioned in St Joseph's Institution and Monk's Hill School. It returned to its own buildings in October 1946.

When the government decided to redevelop the City the old buildings at Bras Basah Road had to be demolished. Raffles Institution then moved to new buildings at Grange Road close to the residence of the American Ambassador in Singapore. Then Raffles Institution moved to its present site. It is still the premier school of Singapore that has produced both the Prime Ministers of Singapore: Mr Lee Kuan Yew and Mr Goh Chok Tong.

The motto of the school is "Auspicium Melioris Aevi": the Hope for a Better Age-for the School and the nation.

INSTITUTION HILL

River Valley
Raffles Institution once owned
Institution Hill

The Trustees of Raffles Institution once owned Institution HIll which comprised 28 acres of land. In December 1844 the Trustees sold the land to be used as a burial ground. The Free Press said that the sale was "to be deprecated" and it was called off. The Hill was bought by Adam Sykes and Mungo Johnston Martin in 1845 and finally it went into the hands of Dr Robert Little who lived on the Hill for 35 years.

On the Hill can be seen today several old houses in varying stages of neglect and decay. The River Valley Community Centre is at the foot of the Hill.

Decaying building on Institution Hill

TAO NAN SCHOOL

Armenian Street

This old school building
could be considered for
preservation by the
Preservation of Monuments Board
Chinese immigrants built schools to preserve their cultural identity and heritage.
The building will now form part of the National Museum.
The first school in Singapore to have Mandarin as the medium of instruction. Tan Kah Kee's contribution to education.

Tao Nan School was established by the Singapore Hokkien Association. The first school was set up in 1906 with an enrolment of 36 pupils in North Bridge Road in 'Siam House' - the former residence of Tan Kim Ching and the medium of instruction then was Hokkien. In 1910 the school moved to Armenian Street and the medium of instruction was changed to Mandarin, the first school in Singapore to do this.

Pupils in the early years wore white school uniforms, hats and had pigtails; many walked home and the well-to-do travelled in rickishaws. One of the pupils was Lee Kong Chian who became one of Singapore's great philanthropists and patrons of education.

One of the 110 founding members of the school was the great philanthropist and patron of education Tan Kah Kee who made millions from his business enterprises and spent as much on education for ordinary people. He donated large sums of money to Tao Nan School and other Chinese schools which included Chinese High School; he also donated money to English schools and this included $30,000 to Anglo-Chinese School in 1919 and $10,000 to Raffles College in 1929. The land for Tao Nan School was gift from Oei Tiong Ham.

Tan Kah Kee served Tao Nan School as President for 12 years and also as Administrator.

The enrolment of the School increased to 1300 and it was necessary to build a new school. In 1982 the new premises at Marine Parade were ready for occupation. The medium of instruction is now English. Pupils of all races now attend Tao Nan School.

"Tao Nan School was set up with higher ideals. The early Chinese immigrants recognised the value and importance of education. They saw it as a means for their children not only to earn a living but also to preserve their cultural identity and heritage. These ideals were expressed in collective efforts by community organisation and clan association to build schools to educate their young" (Mr Goh Chok Tong's message to Tao Nan School Eightieth Anniversary Commemorative Magazine 1906-1986).

Old Chung Hwa Girls' School, Bartley Road. First Chinese Girls' School in Singapore. Founded 1911. (New Premises Upper Serangoon).

Chinese High School, Bukit Timah Road. First Chinese Secondary School in Singapore founded by Tan Kah Kee, 21 March 1919. Bronze Statue of founder facing the field

Old Tao Nan School, Armenian Street
First School in Singapore to introduce Mandarin as the medium of instruction. Early Chinese immigrants set up their own schools to preserve their cultural identity and heritage.

Today Tao Nan School has achieved excellence in both academic and extra-curricular activities and the School has achieved distinction as it did at its inception.

MADRASAHS (Arabic Schools) - AL-JUNIED AND ALSAGOFF

Learning of Malay and Arabic is basic in inculcating Islamic values and culture to Malay pupils. Other than Malay Schools Madrasahs continued to serve Malays and Muslims in Singapore.

Even before Stamford Raffles landed in Singapore a few Koran schools (Madrasahs) functioned on the island. For Malay boys and girls it was absolutely necessary for them to be able to pray and read in Arabic. This was part of their basic education to learn Islamic values and culture which was an integral part of their education from earliest times. Graduates from these Koran schools also became religious teachers or "imams" (priests) in the Mosque.

Beginnings of Malay vernacular education in the Straits Settlements and later in the Malay States had their roots in these Madrasahs where a little Malay was also taught.

First formal instruction in Malay under the British administration was in August 1834 when the first Malay class of 12 boys was started in the Singapore Free School. When A. M. Skinner was appointed the first Inspector of Schools in 1871 he gave impetus to Malay education and two successful Malay Schools were established in Telok Blangah and Telok Seaga; classes were conducted up to primary six. In 1876 classes were opened in a residence belonging to the Sultan of Johore at the Istana Lama (old palace) at Telok Blangah. A Malay College was also started at Telok Blangah in 1878 but it was unfortunately closed in 1882.

The first Malay Girls' School was started in 1884 with 60 girls also at Telok Blangah; this was closed in 1887.

In the Lemon Report in 1919 the British government reiterated their policy: that government Malay vernacular schools "is the essential element in our education system."

British education policy in the Straits Settlements before World War II was: to provide free basic four years course in Malay and Malay Literature and later school leavers to join trade schools or pursue vocations in agriculture.

Madrasah Al-junied Main Building

Alsagoff Arab School 1912

The Madrasahs are still a feature of Malay education in Singapore. Private classes in the homes of religious teachers formed the foundation of the Madrasahs in the early 20th century largely by wealthy Arab families like the Alsagoffs and Aljunieds. Madrasah Aljunied in Victoria Street was founded in 1927 and Madrasah Alsagoff in 1912 in Jalan Sultan. Graduates of these Schools have served Singapore, Malaya and Brunei as religious teachers, teachers, priests, politicians, businessmen and social workers in the Malay and Muslim communities.

Today the Madrasah Al-Junied has pre-primary, primary, secondary and pre-univeristy classes. Both Arabic and English are the media of instruction. Students sit for the Cambridge Ordinary Level Examination and pre-university pupils are prepared to attend the University of Al Azhar in Egypt to become religious teachers and officials of the Mosque.

By 1941 the enrolment in registered schools in Singapore was: Malay Schools 5,800, Chinese Schools 38,000, Tamil Schools 1,000 and Trade Schools 300.

Formal Malay Schools continued to function after World War II and later when equality was given to all streams of education - Malay, Chinese, Tamil and English - choice was given to parents to select a stream, and a large number of Malay pupils opted for English Schools. This eventually led to the closure of Malay Schools but Malay pupils offer Malay as the Second Language in English Schools. They also continue to attend classes in Madrasahs before or after their regular school hours.

SAINT ANDREW'S SCHOOL

Woodsville
Serangoon Road

Contribution of the Anglican Mission to education; school started by Asians unlike other Mission and government schools in Singapore.

Anglican Chaplains like Rev R. S. Hutchings and Rev F. J. Darral played a significant role in setting up Government Free School. London Missionary Society had also established a number of good schools in the Straits Settlements. St Margaret's School the oldest Girls School was founded in 1842 by Mrs Dyer.

Anglican School for boys was first founded between 1850 and 1860 as a private school in Chin Chew Street, Chinatown by Sim Quee and Tye Kim. Later on 8 September 1862 it became St Andrew's School and functioned with Sim Quee as the first Headmaster. This is unique among Mission and Government schools in Singapore. The next year St Andrew's Church Mission took over the School and it moved to new premises in Upper Hokkien Street.

Though no financial support was given by the Church from 1866, Cheok Loy Fatt the new Headmaster managed the School which was popularly known as "Sekolah Loy Fatt". In the 1870s the School received government grants.

In 1872 the School moved to Victoria Street and the enrolment increased from 76 to 120 largely by the work of Rev W. H. Gomes the School's Superintendent but Cheok Loy Fatt was still the Headmaster. By 1873 there was the need for larger premises and government granted nearly 4 acres of land in Stamford Road at foot of Government Hill (Fort Canning) - today the site occupied by the National Museum. The School's Chapel was built first on 14 February 1875 and the school shifted from Victoria Street to hold classes in the Chapel. In 1878 the Missionary House was completed; in 1900 the Lower Elementary School Building was erected and 15 years later the School's Hall came into being.

When Rev Gomes died in 1902 Rev J. Romanis Lee who succeeded him was responsible for the modern characteristics of the School. Though new classrooms were added, St Andrew's was still a second grade School. In 1915 St Andrew's offered its first candidates for the Senior Cambridge Examination; previously the pupils went to Raffles Institution for secondary education.

St Andrew's Secondary School, Potong Pasir

Old St. Andrew's School, (now Primary School) Woodsville

St Andrew's introduced Boxing and Rugger; the School excelled in both games. This was largely due to teacher Rev Canon R. K. S. Adams in 1930 and 1933 respectively; he later served as Headmaster from 1934 to 1956.

By 1937 there was the need again to put up new buildings for the School. The government offered the Mission two sites: one at Tanjong Katong Road and the other at Serangoon Road near the old Serangoon Post Office. Both the sites proved unsuitable for the type of School buildings envisaged by the Mission.

In 1938 Woodsville Estate comprising 18.5 acres of land was purchased for $60,000. The new School buildings were completed and officially opened by S. W. Jones, the Officer Administering the Government, on 29 July 1940.

In 1940 Rev Canon D. D. Chelliah became Headmaster of the Upper School; previously he had served 26 years in the Anglo-ChineseSchool, Penang.

Japanese invasion began on 8 December 1941 when the Senior Cambridge Examinations were held in the School.

The School was damaged and most of its furniture was looted during the Japanese Occupation. Several of the staff died; some in Changi Gaol and others in the Siam Death Railway.

After the World War II St Andrew's was the first to be re-opened.

The new secondary School buildings and the Chapel are located in Potong Pasir. The foundation stone was laid by Rt Rev Dr Moses Tay Leng Koy, Bishop of Singapore, on 11 January 1986 and the buildings were completed on 31 July. The old buildings at Woodsville are occupied by the Primary School.

ST JOSEPH'S INSTITUTION

Bras Basah Road

Beginnings of the expansion of Roman Catholicism and Catholic education in Singapore

Site on which stood the first Roman Catholic Church in Singapore

St Joseph's Institution was founded by Father Jean-Marie Beurel who arrived in Singapore at the time when the Chinese were building the Thian Hock Keng Temple in Telok Ayer Street.

As early as 1833 the Catholics worshipped in a small chapel 20 metres by 10 metres in Bras Basah Road. Father Beurel during his 30 years of service to Singapore built the Church of the Good Shepherd, the St Joseph's Institution and the Convent of the Holy Infant Jesus. To meet the cost of these buildings and land he paid a proportion of his own personal income.

In 1847 Father Beurel wrote to his Queen Marie-Amelia for support for his projects in Singapore for both personnel and paintings.

The centre section of St Joseph's Institution was designed by Brother Lothaire and was opened in 1867 and the wings of the institution was planned by Brother Nain and built around 1900 but St Joseph's Institution was started in 1852 with 3 Brothers and the enrolment by 1900 had reached 426. The growth of the School was attributed to Brother Michael Noctor, the Governor of the Straits Settlements Sir John Anderson, Tan Jiak Kim and Charles Benedict Noin the priest of the Church of the Good Shepherd. The Institution did extremely well academically for in 1905 both the Queen's Scholarships were awarded to its students.

For the expansion of the Institution, money was raised from various sources and one who stands out was Tan Jiak Kim, a prominent resident and chairman of the appeal committee; he donated $14,000 in the first year of the appeal.

The staff comprised Brothers of different nationalities: in 1933 there were French, Germans, Chinese, Eurasians and a Bengali. It is interesting to note that when the Institution began students did not wear school uniforms; they wore a variety of attire or complete suits called "baju tutup".

During the Battle for Singapore all schools were closed in Singapore and St Joseph's Institution suffered from Japanese bombing - the centre of the inner courtyard and a classroom were hit. Miraculously there were no casualties. The Institution was also used by the military authorities as a hospital to receive military casualties. Forty-two classrooms were converted into wards and the Map Room into an operation theatre for amputation of

St Joseph's Institution
Founded 1852

Classroom Block

legs and arms to save the lives of the soldiers especially the survivors of the battleships, "Prince of Wales" and "Repulse" which were sunk in the South China Sea on 10 December 1941. At that time at St Joseph's Institution "the human had collapsed, the Divine shone."

During the Japanese Occupation (1942 - 1945) for a period, the Institution became temporary barracks for Japanese soldiers. Classes began under the new name of Bras Basah Boys's School which initially admitted boys from Standard VI to Standard IX but in May 1942 it was converted into a primary school. Classes were conducted on ethnic lines; separate classes were held for Chinese, Indian, Malay and mixed groups. Subjects taught included singing, gymnastics, drama, handicrafts, drawing, gardening and Japanese Language. Training classes for teachers were also conducted there.

St Joseph's Institution began to function normally after the return of the British in 1945. Between January and April 1946 Raffles Institution occupied the school premises in the afternoon while Raffles Institution was temporarily taken over by the British military authorities.

Today St Joseph's Institution occupies new buildings in Malcolm Road. The old St Joseph's Institution will be converted into an Arts Centre. The school today is an independent school but the spirit of the founder of this Institution still pervades it.

VIVEKANANDA AND SARADA DEVI TAMIL SCHOOLS

Norris Road

Several Tamil Schools were started by individuals, labour unions, religious institutions for Tamil children to study Tamil Language and Literature and sustain their Tamil culture and heritage in a foreign land.

"The gift of learning is the integrity of the soul which brings the conscience peace; the beauty of learning is the only true beauty." Naladiyar, a Tamil classic.

Tamil Schools emerged soon after Tamils who had emigrated from South India could bring their wives and children to the settlement of Singapore.

Early Tamil Schools were set up in shophouses in Tanjong Pagar, in Serangoon area and Potong Pasir. These were in fact small classes of pupils taught by a single teacher. The pupils learnt Tamil Language and Literature, the Hindu epics, Tamil values and culture. Hindu pupils also participated in their festivals and even learnt the "kolattam" dancing with two sticks.

Several Tamil Schools were established in the late 19th and early 20th centuries. The later schools were located near the British bases in Seletar, Sembawang and Changi where Tamils found employment.

Records show that the first formal education for Tamil children was started with 12 pupils in the medium of Tamil in August 1834 in the Singapore Free School. Unfortunately the class was discontinued in 1835 because of the lack of suitable text books. However, the class was revived in 1873. The British government established 2 Anglo-Tamil Schools in 1873 and 1876 where Tamil pupils learnt English through the medium of Tamil.

One of the earliest schools to be started by Christian Missions was the St Francis Xavier Malabar School in 1859 by the Roman Catholic Mission for the education of Tamil youth. Christopher Muruguppa Pillai School was opened in 1862. In 1887 the Methodist Church set up the Methodist Girls' School in Mount Sophia for Tamil girls and in 1913 another Tamil School was set up by the Methodist Mission.

Several private Tamil Schools were also started near Tamil workers' quarters. Those who belonged to the middle class sent their children to English Schools and attended Tamil classes after regular school hours. There were about 20 Tamil Schools managed by the workers, trade unionists, Indian Association and religious institutions by the 20th century. One

Site once occupied by a Tamil School in St. George's Road

Building once occupied by Vivekananda Boys' Tamil School and Sarada Devi Girls' Tamil School - Norris Road

individual who worked as a hospital assistant, Arumugam, founded the Kalaimagal Tamil School in Yiu Chu Kang. This School was taken over some time in 1960s by the Ramakrishna Mission which managed both the Vivekananda Tamil School for boys and the Sarada Devi Tamil School for girls in Norris Road. Others included Neelaambigai, Vasugi, Thangamani, Bharathidasan, Aravinda, Saraswati, Thandayuthapani, Valluvar, Avvaiyar, Nagamiah, Kamala Nehru Tamil Schools; these were distributed throughout the island where there were pockets of Tamils.

Before World War II, in Singapore, there were 4 Mission Tamil Schools, 14 private schools with an enrolment of about 1,000pupils.

During the Japanese Occupation a few Tamil Schools managed by labour unions were used for propaganda by the Indian Independence Movement.

After the end of World War II Tamil Schools were revived. Tamil leaders like K. Saragapany, editor of the "Tamil Murasu" (Tamil Daily) advocated Government support for Tamil Schools; government-aid was granted to 5 schools and St George's government Tamil School was established.

After 1955 greater recognition was given to all vernacular schools by the government; from 1959 equal treatment was accorded to all streams of education. Later Tamil parents preferred to send their children to English Schools and this move brought about the closure of all the Tamil medium schools in Singapore. The last to close was the Umar Pulavar Tamil School in Maxwell Road.

KADAYANULLUR STREET

TANJONG PAGAR
UMAR PULAVAR TAMIL LANGUAGE CENTRE
(predecessors were Umar Pulavar Tamil School and Umar Pulavar Tamil High School)

School started by the Kadayanullur Tamil Muslim community as early as 1926 when they formed the Muslim Improvement Club. Pioneers in Tamil education to sustain their cultural heritage, values and traditions.

Kadayanullur Street is named after the Tamil Muslims who migrated to Singapore from Kadayanullur, a town in South India. They settled in Tanjong Pagar.

The Kadayanullur Tamil Muslims in Chinatown were interested in educating their children in their mother tongue (Tamil) as it was imperative that they promote their cultural values. Tamil education started when Tamils began to settle down and brought their families from India to Singapore.

This community was a small one. Its members were petty shopkeepers, retailers, and office peons; they were either illiterate or had only a basic education but they realised the importance of Tamil education.

Early attempts to set up a Tamil School were unsuccessful but by 1936 a class of 26 pupils was started with one teacher who taught both English and Tamil; the school was located in Tras Street in Tanjong Pagar.

In 1946 Umar Pulavar Tamil School was established in a shophouse at 72 Tanjong Pagar Road. A new building was completed in 1950 and because of increased enrolment a Building Fund was started for bigger premises. In March 1960 the new building was completed and it became known as Umar Pulavar Tamil High School. The school functioned up to 1982. It closed when enrolment dropped because Tamil students could offer Tamil as their Second Language in English Schools. To remember the School the St George's Road Tamil Language Centre was renamed Umar Pulavar Tamil Language Centre.

Umar Pulavar Tamil Language Centre now in Serangoon Road (occupying former Beaty Secondary School) is a reminder of the keen interest shown by the Kadyanallur Tamil Muslims in Tamil education in Singapore. Umar Pulavar was a famous Tamil poet who lived in the 17th century and wrote the "Seerapuranam" and "Madhu Mozhi Malai". The title of "Pulavar" is given to a famous poet.

Umar Pulavar First Tamil Medium High School in Singapore was closed and name given to the Tamil Language Centre in Serangoon Road

The College of Medicine Building, Sepoy Lines previously the King Edward VII College of Medicine. Today the building houses the Ministry of Health Headquarters.

KING EDWARD VII COLLEGE OF MEDICINE

(Today College of Medicine Building)

Sepoy Lines

A symbol to reflect the concern of early Singaporeans for additional modern medical services for their fellowmen.

In September 1904 a petition was addressed by leading Chinese and non European Committee to the Governor of the Straits Settlements, Sir John Anderson, requesting that a Medical School be established in Singapore. It suggested that graduates of this School could be recruited into government service of the Straits Settlements, the Federated and non Federated Malay States as Assistant Surgeons or as General Practitioners.

The idea was mooted by Tan Jiak Kim, other Chinese leaders and the Principal Civil Medical Officer, Dr Maximilian F. Simon.

The Governor accepted the proposal and the Straits Settlements Legislative Council approved the project in June 1905. The government raised $71,000 for the Medical School which was established the same year. It was known as the Straits and Federated Malay States Medical School. It held its classes in the converted buildings of the old Female Lunatic Asylum at Sepoy Lines.

In 1911 a new building was added to the Medical School. It is still known as Tan Teck Guan Building, the cost of which was borne by Tan Chay Yan, a Chinese benefactor, in memory of his father.

Two years later the name of the School was changed to King Edward VII Medical School in recognition of a donation from King Edward VII Memorial Fund. In 1921 the School was renamed King Edward VII College of Medicine. It was officially opened in 1926.

The architect of King Edward VII College of Medicine was Major P.H. Keys who also designed Fullerton Building which housed the General Post Office as well as other government departments. The foundation stone of the College building was laid on 6 September 1923 and the new building was officially opened by the Governor, Sir Laurence Nunns Guillemard on 15 February 1926.

The building is reminiscent of classical Greek monuments like the Acropolis; behind the columns are sculptured timber doors; over the central doorway is a bas relief of a Roman eagle and on either side are bas reliefs depicting the teaching and practice of medicine.

In the College is a plaque which pays tribute to 12 medical students who died as a result of Japanese artillery fire on 14 February 1942, one day before British forces surrendered to the invading Japanese Imperial Army. Eleven students went to bury the student who had died from shrapnel wounds. They managed to find a trench which some British soldiers had evacuated. While they were deepening the trench a shell exploded in their midst. A grave that was to house one dead housed eleven more. It was through the obligations of friendship that they met with the accident that caused their death. The plaque commemorates those glorious eleven who risked their lives among others to provide medical attention to the hundreds wounded in the final days before the fall of Singapore to the Japanese. Fate had decided that they were not to be rewarded. A bond of friendship which brought a multi-racial group of Singaporeans and Malayans together: 5 Chinese, 4 Indians, 1 Malay and 1 Eurasian, ended in a bond of death. It speaks of the heroism and fortitude of most Singaporeans who survived the days of heavy artillery and air bombardment from the Japanese forces. During the month of February 1942 about 2000 refuges took shelter in the hall of the College.

In 1949 the College of Medicine and Raffles College in Bukit Timah became formally the University of Malaya. The Faculty of Medicine now functions in Kent Ridge as part of the National University of Singapore.

Renovated between November 1985 and June 1987 at a cost of $10 million, the College of Medicine houses today the Ministry of Health Headquarters, the Academy of Medicine, the Council of General Practitioners, a Library and an Exhibition Hall.

Governor Guillemard said when he opened the College in 1926:

"This building will be a source of pride not only to the architect and the College but to Singapore."

Today this holds true.

INSTITUTE OF EDUCATION

Bukit Timah

Originally Raffles College
and later University of Malaya, 1949
then University of Malaya -
Singapore Division and University
of Singapore and National University of Singapore
Raffles College for Arts and Science
founded because of clamour for
higher education; largest donors for
the building were Manasseh Meyer and
Oei Tiong Ham - two blocks named
after them

As a result of public demand the Colonial Government agreed to set up a College of Arts and Science as an institution of higher education.

The motion in the Straits Settlement Legislative Council to establish and maintain an institution for improved secondary education for both commercial and technical, supported by Dr Lim Boon Keng was introduced as early as January 1902 by Napier.

Raffles College was established in 1929 after the centenary of the founding of Singapore.

Students from Singapore and Malaya attended Raffles College which awarded diplomas to its graduates. Many graduates joined the civil service and the teaching profession. Prominent graduates included Mr Lee Kuan Yew and Dr Goh Keng Swee.

During the depression years (1930s) in Singapore and Malaya the enrolment of students of Raffles College was badly affected. During 1934 and 1935 there were only 80 students.

Before the Battle for Singapore in February, 1942 had begun thousands from the mainland fled into Singapore and many were billeted in hastily constructed dormitories in Raffles College. Raffles College later was used by the British forces and after the surrender Lieutenant-General Yamashita transferred his headquarters from the Ford Works Factory in Bukit Timah to Raffles College.

During the Japanese Occupation of Singapore (1942-45) the College was used by Japanese military personnel. When the British returned after the Japanese Surrender Raffles College re-opened in October 1946.

As a result of the Sir Alexander Carr-Saunders Report, King Edward VII College of Medicine and Raffles College were incorporated as the University of Malaya in October 1949. When Malaya achieved its independence in August 1957 it was renamed the University of Malaya Singapore Division and later the University of Singapore and finally the National University of Singapore.

When Kent Ridge was built all its Faculties occupied the new buildings. At present the Institute of Education and the Curriculum Development Institute of Singapore occupy the Bukit Timah Campus of Raffles College. The two buildings named after Oei Tiong Ham and Manasseh Meyer still stand with Oei Tiong Ham Hall completely renovated. Oei Tiong Ham and Manasseh Meyer donated $150,000 each towards the building - the largest donors.

The contribution of Manasseh Meyer to Singapore has already been mentioned. Oei Tiong Ham was the son of Oei Tjie Sien, a merchant of Java who owned large sugar plantations there and who was a partner in the Semarang Steamship Navigation Company. Oei Tiong Ham was a resident in Singapore. He owned the Heap Eng Moh Steamship Company at 22 Telok Ayer Street. Beside his donation to Raffles College, Oei Tiong Ham also donated the land to Tao Nan School on Armenian Street.

An old block of Raffles College now National Institution of Education, Bukit Timah Manessah Meyer Building, Raffles College-Manessah was a Jew, pioneer and philanthropist

NATIONAL LIBRARY

Stamford Road

Pioneers set up its predecessor the Raffles Library and today it is a very modern National Library with branches.

Those pioneers of Singapore who were interested in setting up a public library met in 1844; however, the proposal dates back to 1823 when the idea of the Singapore Institution (Raffles Institution) was mooted. Raffles Institution was selected to establish a small collection of books that could be borrowed for a small fee by the early residents of the settlement. The headmaster was both the librarian and secretary of the Library Committee.

Later the public library was transferred to the Town Hall (Victoria Memorial Hall). The government eventually took over the library and named it the Raffles Library and by 1837 it had 392 volumes. In 1876 the Raffles Library was re-located in the Raffles Institution and thence to the Raffles Museum building. In 1920 J. Johnson was appointed as the first qualified librarian and in 1923 a Junior Library was added to the main Library which was then subordinate to the Raffles Museum; it was only in June 1882 that both became separate public institutions.

Soon after the British Surrender on 15 February 1942 Governor Sir Shenton Thomas requested the Japanese military authorities to preserve the scientific and historic collections especially those in the Museum and Botanic Gardens. Singapore was fortunate to have had Professor Tanakadate, a vulcanologist and geologist from Tohoku Imperial University of Sendai as Director of the Museum and Library. He and E.J. Corner, Assistant Director of the Botanic Gardens both saved the Museum artefacts and the records in the Library. Corner himself secretly removed even the newspapers to the Botanic Gardens during the Japanese Occupation. Records from the Raffles College, Raffles Girls' School, Raffles Institution, Colonial Secretary's Office and Government House (most were damaged buildings and offices) were mostly preserved through their joint effort.

During the Japanese Occupation the general library was used mainly by Europeans, Germans, Irish, Czechs, Dutch and Eurasians employed by the Japanese Department of Information.

The Raffles Library re-opened to the public on 1 December 1945 after the return of the British to Singapore.

The present building in Stamford Road was a project of the Labour Front government. In 1958 the National Library was officially established. In 1960 the Yang di Pertuan Negara, Inche Yusof bin Ishak, officially opened the new premises of the National Library on 12 November 1960. The site of the National Library was previously occupied by the old St Andrew's Chapel and the British Council building.

The National Library officially opened by Inche Yusof bin Ishak, the Yang di Pertuan Negara in 1960, Stamford Road.

Today the National Library represents the growth of the Republic of Singapore. The Library is computerised and has a very large collection of reference materials, books, newspapers and audio- visual aid equipment. There is also a special section on South- East Asia and books are in English, Chinese, Malay and Tamil - the official languages of the Republic. There are also branches of the Library in different parts of the island. The Library is also constantly updated.

The National Library is one of the few libraries in the world to combine the functions of a public and national library. Promotion and outreach include lectures, film shows, plays, exhibitions, forums and debates. It has also sponsored the formation of a variety of clubs for children.

LONG SHAN SI

Race Course Road

One of our oldest Buddhist Temples

The original Long Shan Si was in Anping District in Fukien. Its Abbot Chun Wu came to Singapore carrying with him an urn and a statue of Kuan Yin. He bought a plot of land in Race Course Road and built a small temple there; it was made up of huts and in one of them he had the altar of Kuan Yin.

In 1926 new buildings were built from funds raised by devotees and renovations were made in 1930, 1962 and 1970.

Statues of Sakyamuni Buddha, Kuan Yin and other Bodhisattvas are placed in the main hall. The other deities, the Sword Brothers of the Three Kingdoms and the Goddess of Birth are placed near the main altar. Also near the main altar are statues of Confucius and Cheng Huang.

The main hall of the Temple resembles a Chinese palace. The roof is a traditional one with a blazing pearl and dancing dragons on the gables.

This Temple attracts a large number of devotees during festivals and the road in front of it is normally congested on those days.

Years ago when the author visited the Temple with members of the History Association of Singapore the Chief Abbot took us on a guided tour of the Temple. He also gave us an excellent vegetarian meal and later he brought out from a wooden chest a number of Chinese antique porcelain pieces which were donated to the Temple by grateful devotees.

Long Shan Si, an old Buddhist Temple, Race Course Road.

SHUANG LIN TEMPLE

(Siong-Lim-Si)
Kim Keat Road, Toa Payoh
(This Temple was gazetted a national monument on 17 October 1980)

The oldest Buddhist Temple in Singapore - reflects our cultural heritage and the large number of Buddhists in early Singapore.

Shuang Lin Temple is the oldest Buddhist Temple in Singapore. The full name Lin Shuang Siong Lim Shen Si means the Twin Grove of the Lotus Mountain Buddhist Temple. This Temple is the second largest in this part of the world and was built between 1902 and 1908 at a cost of about $500,000 in the swampy Balestier Plain. A wall plaque in the Temple has the year 1904. The funds were largely raised by Low Kim Pong, a general trader and Yeo Poon Seng both wealthy Hokkien merchants and community leaders.

Inside the Temple are the deities of Rain and Air and the Spirits of Evil and God. There are also idols of the Buddha from Siam and a very beautiful Goddess of Mercy. In the interior are pictures of hell and heaven and these depict how human beings can attain Nirvana - the state of non-existence and perfect bliss.

There are three sections to the Temple. In front is Tien Wang Palace where the Buddhist Maitreya is worshipped and in the rear is Wei To who battles against evil. There is a courtyard, a Drum Tower and a Bell Tower. Near the Drum Tower is the altar of Bodhidharma and opposite this is the altar of the Majestic Guardian Spirits. The main altar is for Shakyamuni Buddha.

It is said that 12 members of a Seow family sailed from China (1892-98) to visit various Buddhist countries. They arrived in Singapore and with the help of Low Kim Pong built Shuang Lin.

Tien Wang Palace, section of Shuang Lin Temple

Shang Lin Temple - oldest Buddhist Temple in Singapore

GUAN YIN TANG

2 Telok Blangah Drive

Another Temple to sustain our cultural heritage.

Guan Yin Tang was built in 1880 by a Taoist by the name of Wong Guan Teck who hailed from Hainan. The hill site was selected because it stood between the sea and a hill at its rear.

The roof has a blazing pearl and two dancing dragons symbolising strength and power of the deities. A hall was built in 1892.

Altars for Buddha, Guan Yin, the Monkey God, the Gods of War and Literature and the Goddess of Birth are found in the Temple. Idols found in other altars include those of the Sun God and Wei Tuo, the military Bodhisattva.

In the 19th and early 20th century the Temple must have been a distinct land mark overlooking the sea when there were no high rise buildings in front as well as in the rear. However, its significance, its cultural and historical heritage and spirituality is still strong for its devotees in the neighbourhood and elsewhere.

Guan Yin Tang Temple
Telok Blangah Drive

LITTLE INDIA

Serangoon Road

An early settlement of the Indians; earliest was Tanjong Pagar.

In November 1822 Stamford Raffles wrote to the Town Committee about "the proper allotment of the Native division of the town..." About the Chuliah Kampong (Indian village) Raffles wrote: "advantage of allotting a separate division for the town class of Chuliahs (Indians) up the Singapore river, and this will of course be done with a due consideration of their expected numbers, and the necessity of their residence being in the vicinity of the place where their services are most likely to be called for."

Nairaina Pillay, a Tamil accompanied Raffles to Singapore in May 1819 and the Tamil later invited other Tamils in Penang to join him in Singapore. The earliest Tamil Mosques are found in Telok Ayer Street and South Bridge Road where the oldest Hindu Temple is also located. Upper Cross Street was known as "Kampong of the Indians" by the Chinese; the Malays referred to it as "Kampong Susu" and the Tamils "Pal Kampong" both meaning "Milk Kampong" because there were Indian milk vendors. Kadayanallur community from South India settled in Tanjong Pagar. The earliest Tamil School was also located in Chinatown. Near Raffles Place are Chulia Street and Market Street where the Chettiars (money lenders) had their office and residence. A large number of Indians were employed in Keppel Harbour, Dockyard and the Railways; they all lived in Tanjong Pagar. The original Little India was therefore Tanjong Pagar.

The Indian convicts in Bencoolen were transferred to Singapore in 1825 and their re-settlement was in Bras Basah. All classes of the Indian society were among the convicts; these included Benares "Brahmanas", Sikh and Dogra "ksatriyas", Chettiars, Bengali and Parsi financiers and untouchables from different parts of India.

By 1822 Serangoon Road was already planned and in 1828 it was marked on a map by Lieutenant Jackson.

Serangoon area was an attraction to settlers because of the presence of rivers and where gambier, nutmeg, coconuts and even rice were grown. When agriculture failed, cattle raising became the most important occupation of the Indians because of abundant water and grass; Serangoon was also near the main roads. Another attraction was the Race Course.

Those who settled in Serangoon area came from India in the latter part of the 19th century long after Indians had settled in Tanjong Pagar.

Besides cattle rearing and related activities, wheat-grinding, sesame oil presses, rattan works and pineapple preserving factories became an economic feature of Serangoon area. At one time cattle raising was dominated by J. R. Belilios (Bellios Lane is named after him), a Venetian Jew. Adolph Landau and L. C. Joffie set up business as Pineapple Merchants. Pineapple skins, sesame and wheat husks became fodder for cattle.

Other than rearing cows and buffaloes for the dairy trade, bulls and buffaloes were used for drawing bullock-carts - the chief cargo transport vehicles in the 19th century. Cattle and sheep were also imported for slaughter-houses which were located in Syed Alwi and Sungei Roads. H. Desker (Desker Road named after him) and his family ran a profitable abattoir there. Tamil Muslims were also engaged in this business.

Horses were used to draw carriages and many were in the stables in Race Course Road as race horses.

In the 19th century Peranakan India from Malacca settled in Serangoon area.

Other communities also settled there; these included Chinese and Baweanese (Indonesians); the former grew vegetable gardens in the Lavender and Balestier areas and the Peranakan Indian lived in Kampong Kapor. The Baweanese were employed as horse trainers at the Race Course,

Quaint Building in Little India - where Singaporeans of diverse ethnic origins live.

carriage and bullock-cart drivers, syces and gardeners; they lived in "pondoks" (lodging houses). Peranakan Chinese built their distinctive houses in Petain Road and the Straits Chinese Methodist Church is located in Kampong Kapur.

Indians from different parts of their homeland settled in certain sections of Serangoon area; South Indian Muslims, Bengali Hindus, Tamils and Telegus had their own localities. The Tamil area stretched as far as Potong Pasir. These enclaves were largely due for security in a foreign land.

Serangoon area has one of the oldest Mosques, the Abdul Gaffoor Mosque (in Mayo Road) and three of the oldest Hindu Temples: the Veeramakaliamman, the Srinivasa Perumal and the Vadapathirakaliamman. There are also three old Buddhist Temples in Race Course Road.

In the first decades of the 20th century Serangoon area was the centre of Indian migration. The opening of the Naval Base, Seletar and Changi Air Bases brought in an influx of Indians particularly Tamils and Malayalees near these bases.

During the 1930s Serangoon was gradually transformed into a residential and commercial one. The early years saw the male dormitories where both employers and employees lived above their working place. It was communal living of about 25 persons who belonged to the same caste and occupation.

Farrer Park
Singapore's First Race Course

Certain areas were transferred to Chinese migrants who redeveloped them. What is known today as Little India became mostly an Indian-Hindu commercial area.

Just before the Japanese invasion of Malaya in December 1941 many Indian men sent their wives and children back to India and those who remained behind suffered along with other communities from Japanese bombing and artillery fire and under Japanese Occupation.

After the return of the British in 1945 Serangoon area remained very much an Indian settlement with quaint Indian shops and even with the few male dormitories of the 19th century.

Little India is a tourist attraction; there are a variety of Indian shops and businesses; these include garland makers, cloth merchants, gold smiths, costume jewellers, provision stores and restaurants. Little India contributes its Indianess to enrich our multi-cultural Republic of Singapore.

The vast majority of Indians now live in high-rise buildings in a multi-racial environment.

Old Abdul Gaffoor Mosque
Mayo Road, Little India

ABDUL GAFOOR MOSQUE

41 Dunlop Street.

Old Mosque in a predominantly Hindu Tamil Settlement in Serangoon Road
Gazetted as a national monument on 13 July 1979

The original Mosque known as Shaik Abdul Gapore Mosque was a wooden structure built by Shaik Abdul Gafoor Shaik Hyder in 1859 on a land originally belonged to the Parsi Curjetsee Framroj. Abdul Gafoor was then the Chief Tamil clerk with the legal firm of Khory and Bridys.

By 1884 the old Mosque had already become a land mark in early Singapore.

In 1887 as Trustee of the Mosque, Abdul Gafoor applied to the government to erect a new Mosque. He raised the necessary funds from the rentals for the shophouses and sheds he had built nearby.

The present Mosque was completed in 1907. It is of brick with beautiful coloured glass cupola which are supported by pillars of the Roman/Saracen style. Its elaborate ornamental touches are not found in modern Mosques of Singapore which lack the old world charm of Abdul Gafoor Mosque.

The Mosque and the burial ground at Race Course Road also belonged to Shaik Abdul Gafoor; the burial ground was closed by the Municipality on 31 March 1921.

The Abdul Gafoor Mosque reminds Singaporeans of the early Indians especially the Tamils in Serangoon Road. Hindu Temples are close by and so is the Roman Catholic Church, Lady of Lourdes at Ophir Road which catered for the spiritual needs of the South Indian(Tamil) Catholics. Chinese, Malays, Indonesians, Eurasians and Indians still live in peace and harmony in Serangoon and Jalan Besar as they did in the early years in Singapore.

CHITTY ROAD

off Kampong Kapur

One of the colonies of Chitty Melaka (Chitty means merchant) or Peranakan India - the counterparts of the Peranakan Chinese - the Babas and Nonyas

The Peranakan India
are part of our
Indian community
and descendants of the early South Indian merchants who
inter-married with the Malays
of Melaka. They speak Malay, wear
Baba attire and jewellery and
cook Nonya food but most are staunch Hindus.

In "A Nonya Mosaic" Gwee Thiam Hock writes:

> *"... the Indian Babas who except for their Hindu religion, are similar to us in many respects. A majority of them cannot converse in their mother tongue, and their food, their cakes, their ladies' mode of dress and their favourite pastimes are similar to ours."*

South Indian merchants had from the first millennium A.D. traded with South-East Asia and the Malayan coast especially with Melaka after its foundation about 1402.

South Indian merchants travelled to Melaka and remained in Melaka for some months to wait for the change of monsoons to take them home to India. Many settled in Melaka and married Malay women. Through these marriages was evolved the Peranakan India, the Indian Babas and Nonyas. Many early Chinese traders married local Malays and Peranakan India.

Peranakan India lost contact with their homeland particularly after the Dutch occupation of Melaka in 1641 because of the Dutch monopoly of the Melaka trade. The Peranakan India then became permanent settlers in Melaka.

During the periods when Melaka was ruled by Malay Sultans, later by the Portuguese (1511 - 1641) and the Dutch (1641 - 1824) the Peranakan India and earlier as South Indian merchants had occupied a prominent position in Melaka society and were wealthy merchants. One Naina Chitty even was conferred the office of the Bendahara by the Portuguese.

The Peranakan India despite the political power of the Melaka Sultanate and the onslaught of Christianity by the Portuguese and the Dutch remained staunch in their Hindu faith and tradition. They carried Hindu classical names. However they were influenced by Chinese and Malay traditions in their attire, their food, their cakes and favourite pastimes, and their jewellery. After their Hindu classical wedding ceremony the Peranakan India would join in the "Dondang Sayang". They would play Chinese "cherki" cards during their leisure and social occasions.

There is a small Peranakan India community in Singapore. Some members are professionals; a few are in the Police Force and the Singapore Armed Forces, and several are in the teaching and legal professions.

The Peranakan India migrated to Singapore from Melaka in the 19th century and settled in Selegie Road, Race Course Road, Chitty Road and Serangoon Road. Today they are widely distributed over the island.

They are a community proud of their culture. Occasionally they visit Melaka. The Peranakan India there live on their own land in Gadja Berang. The oldest Hindu Temple in Singapore and Malaysia is in Melaka built by the Peranakan India; it is known as Sri Poyyatha Vinayagar Moorthy Temple built in 1781.

Chitty Road - formerly a colony of Peranakan India (Indian Babas and Nonyas)

OUR LADY OF LOURDES

OPHIR ROAD

Originally the Indian Roman Catholic Church in Singapore

"The Church that stands as evidence of the staunch faith of the early Indian Roman Catholics most of whom came from French Pondicherry in South India in Singapore is the Our Lady of Lourdes, situated in an unobtrusive way at 50 Ophir Road along the Expressway that passes above the MRT." It was erected in an area generally occupied by the early Indians largely Tamils, close to Serangoon area (Little India).

As there was the need to cater for the spiritual needs of the Indian Roman Catholics not only in Singapore but also in South Johore that this Church was built in 1888 in the mould of the Basilica at Lourdes, France, by Father Joachim Alexander Marie Meneuvrier. He was the first missionary exclusively in charge of the Indian Catholics in Singapore. His successor who spent 34 years in this Church was Father Louis Burghoffer. Both these priests are fondly remembered by the parishioners of the Church in two brass tablets in the Church.

It is significant that a Tamil school was set up next to the Church to cater for the children of the parishioners.

During the Japanese invasion of Singapore two bombs fell on the premises of the Church. Miraculously the Church was untouched. The parish school and the presbytery suffered much damage; the second storey of the parsonage was blown off.

The Japanese military temporarily occupied the Church during their occupation of Singapore.

It was in 1974 that the Church authorities decided that this Church "should become a parish on territorial basis, embracing and serving everyone irrespective of race and language."

The Church reflects Gothic architecture. The trimmings, pointed arches, spires, flying buttresses and the sixteen slender steel pillars were all imported from Paris. The stained glass windows depicting the fifteen mysteries of the Most Holy Rosary and the electric bells playing the tune of "Ave Maria" were installed to coincide with the Centenary of the Apparitions in 1858 at Lourdes. Inside the Church is the unique grotto with the celestial shrine of the Lady.

Other buildings of historical interest erected by French priests include churches at Bukit Timah and Serangoon, the Good Shepherd Cathedral, the Church of Saint Peter and Paul, the Convent of the Holy Infant Jesus and Saint Joseph's Institution.

Lady of Lourdes Roman Catholic Church, Ophir Road (established for South Indian Roman Catholics)

KERAMAT HABIB NOR BIN MOHAMED AL-HABSHI

Palmer Road
(This Keramat is ear-marked to be preserved as a national monument)

Habib Nor was born in Penang. He settled in Singapore in 1819.

He was revered as a holy man and credited with supernatural powers; he could be present in more than one place at the same time. Habib Nor showed compassion to the poor and it is said that he would pick up coins from money-changers and distribute them to the poor with no protests from the money-changers. He loved the company of children and was quite often seen surrounded by them.

The holy man died in July 1866 and the tombstone was built by Syed Mohamed bin Ahmad Alsagoff about 1890. The keramat is maintained by the Alsagoff family.

Keramat Habib Nor Bin Mohamed Al-Habshi
Palmer Road

P GOVINDASAMY PILLAI KALYANAMANDABAM

Serangoon Road

Built by
Singapore's Tamil pioneer
businessman and philanthropist
who believed in investing in Singapore and
settling here.

P. Govdindasamy Pillai built this Wedding Hall. It was officially opened by Inche Yusof bin Ishak, the Yang di Pertuan Negara. Govindasamy Pillai paid for the Raja Gopuram (Main Gateway) of the Sri Srinivasa Perumal Temple adjacent to the Hall and donated the land on which the Ramakrishna Mission stands at Bartley Road.

Govindasamy Pillai came to Singapore in the early 1900s when he was about 17 years old. After being unemployed for some time he secured a job in a provision shop. Later he started his own business. He built his own house first in Cambpell Lane and later in Race Course Road; he had other landed property as well.

Govindasamy Pillai led a frugal life, saved money and gave generously to charities - temples and schools.

Just before the outbreak of the Pacific War in December 1941 he left for South India leaving his business in the hands of a relative. He returned to Singapore after the Japanese surrender.

He was a founder member of the Indian Chamber of Commerce and the Ramakrishna Mission; he built the Temple and the library. He donated a room to the Mount Alvernia Hospital and contributed to the University of Malaya Fund.

When he died in 1980 at the age of 93 an Indian community leader commented: "The Indian community will mourn the loss of a grand patriarch of old whose like Singapore will not see again." Govindasamy Pillai's guiding principle was to share what he had with the poor and under-privileged. He strongly advocated the principle that Indians should invest in Singapore and settle here.

Govindasamy Pillai J.P. BBM Wedding Hall Serangoon Road

THANDAYUTHAPANI TEMPLE

Murugan Temple
15A Tank Road

A Temple built by the elite and
wealthy pioneer community known as the
Chettiars - who are bankers
and property owners; commonly called money lenders; they
loaned money to small entrepreneurs
they are staunch devotees of the deity Murugan.
Contributed to the economic prosperity of early Singapore and
the Republic of Singapore.

The Chettiars are Tamils who originated from South India and migrated to Singapore in the early 19th century to become "bankers" here. They bought landed property in Tank Road and River Valley Road. Names of roads named after Chettiars are still seen there: Muthuraman Chetty Road, Arnasalem Chetty Road. Others include Meyappa Chettiar Road in Potong Pasir. Most of their offices were and some still are in Market Street.

Such a large number of Tamil businessmen lived in a street close to Raffles Place that the Colonial government named the street Chulia Street which means the Street of the Indians. Devout worshippers of the deity Thandayuthapani or Murugan the Chettiars have built two temples in Singapore, one in Tank Road, and the other in Kreta Ayer. In every Chettiar community there is a Murugan shrine or Temple.

The Thandayuthapani Temple in Tank Road was built in April 1859 and has been renovated periodically. The main tower or "Rajagopuram" is new and was consecrated on 24 November 1983. A wedding hall adjoining the Temple was completed at the same time.

The temple is Saivite, that is, it is dedicated to Shiva one of the Hindu Trinity and Hindus over the centuries have looked upon their deities as constituting a family: Shiva as father, Parvathi as mother, elder son is Ganesha and the younger is Murugan who depicts the five senses and the searching mind. Murugan carries a "vale" a long spear to symbolise Murugan as the destroyer of all evil forces.

The major festival held annually in this Temple is Thaipusam when "kavadis" are carried by devotees of Murugan. "Kavadis" are in various forms. Elaborate ones contain skewers that pierce the bodies of the devotees and needles that pierce their tongue or cheeks. The devotees fast and abstain from sensual pleasure in a test of their resolve to seek self-perfection. Devotees carry "kavadis" to fulfill an oath taken and as a penance. For Hindus none can absolve their sins except the sinners themselves.

Devotees who carry "kavadis" begin their journey from the Vishnu Temple in Serangoon Road and end in the Thandayuthapani Temple where the skewers are removed.

Before World War II the Chettiar community celebrated Thaipusam with fireworks at the Esplanade.

The Chettiars were bankers in early Singapore. Businessmen, merchants and traders who needed capital borrowed from these Chettiars because regular banks would not lend them the money. People of all ethnic groups borrowed from the Chettiars. One major difference between established banks in early Singapore and the Chettiars was this: the Chettiars loaned money without any collateral. In this sense the Chettiars have made a valuable contribution to the economy of Singapore.

Thandayuthapani Temple (Murugan Temple), Tank Road, Built by pioneers of the wealthy Chettiar community - local bankers who gave finance to many local traders and merchants in early Singapore. Locally called money-lenders.

HONG SAN SEE TEMPLE

31 Mohamed Sultan Road
off River Valley Road.

Centre for early immigrants from Nan Ann Town in Fukien Province and a house of worship

This Temple was gazetted as a national monument on 10 November 1979

The original Hon San See Temple was erected in 1829 on Tras Street in Tanjong Pagar. It was used as a gathering place for immigrants from Nan Ann Town in Fukien Province. It is an example of an early Chinese organisation which assisted Chinese to settle in Singapore.

The present Temple in Mohamed Sultan Road was built between 1908 and 1912 at a cost of $56,000. It replaced the Temple at Tras Street when the government took over the land for a road-widening project.The land on which the Temple now stands was bought from Tomlinson, an Englishman.

The Temple was built by Lim Law, a well-known building contractor who had helped to erect Victoria Memorial Hall and other buildings around Empress Place.

Architecturally it is a syncretic Temple, that is, it is a blend of elements of Taoism with Buddhism. The building has a classical Chinese roof and elaborately carved granite pillars. The most admirable features of the Temple are the exquisite carvings of wood.

Two major repairs were undertaken in 1934 and 1962.

It is interesting to note the location of the Temple. It is in the midst of several warehouses and a few roads named after Indians e.g. Muthuraman Chetty Road and Kanisha Marican Road which played a significant role in early Singapore and still does. The most prominent of the Nan Ann community was Dato Lee Kong Chian. The Temple is still owned and managed by the Nan Ann Huay Kwan.

Hong San See Temple, a special feature are the beautiful wood carvings with gold leaf.

SRI SRINIVASA PERUMAL TEMPLE

397 Serangoon Road

Serangoon area is one of the early settlements of the Indians; Hindus met, worshipped and sustained their cultural heritage in the Temple. This is the only Vishnu Temple in Singapore.

This Temple was gazetted as a national monument on 10 November 1978

Sri Narasimha Perumal (Vishnu) Temple was founded in the 1860s by Narasimhaloo Naidu whose family deity was Narasimha. Narasimhaloo Naidu was a wealthy person and endowed some of his landed property to the Temple; he had bought the land from the government for 21 rupees and 3 annas. The Temple's name was changed to Sri Srinivasa Perumal for it was wrongly believed that it was named after its founder.

Hindu residents in the neighbourhood added a hall to the original structure. There was a large pond beside the Temple and many male Hindus bathed here; it was closed in the 1920s and a small well took its place.

The government took over the administration of the two Hindu Temples, the Sri Mariamman Temple in South Bridge Road and the Sri Srinivasa Perumal Temple and incorporated them under the Hindu and Mohamedan Board in 1905.

In the 1960s the Sri Srinivasa Perumal Temple was renovated and the Temple Committee brought a new statue from India. Further renovations were carried out in the 1960s and the "Kopuram" (Main Tower) (expenses met by P.Govindasamy Pillay) was added. In 1990 further renovations were being made.

An important aspect of the Vaishnavite (worshippers of Vishnu) religion is the worship of "avatars" (incarnations). "It is the belief that the divine nature becomes incarnate in animal or human form in order to conquer an evil being, to arrest the growth of unrighteousness, or to induce men to reform their lives". Vishnu's work is to put right what he sees as the great wrong done to humanity.

The number of "avataras" of Vishnu varied but by the eighth century the number had been stabilised as ten. The first five "avataras" are clearly mythological; the next three are heroic; the ninth is an effort to assimilate Buddhism into Vaishnavism and the last is eschatological. The ten are as follows:

1. Matsya. Vishnu appeared as a fish to rescue Manu Vaivasvata (the Hindu Noah) from the Flood, to recover the Vedas (ancient Hindu scriptures) which were stolen by a demon and to instruct Manu in the Vedas.

2. Kurma. Things were in chaos after the Flood; the divine beings discovered that the nectar of immortality had been lost and was at the bottom of the ocean. The divine beings decided to churn the ocean to bring up the chalice which contained the nectar. Vishnu volunteered to transform himself into a tortoise to use his back as a pivot for the gigantic churning stick.

3. Varaha. The demon king Hiranyasha once dragged the earth to the bottom of the ocean; Vishnu assumed the form of a boar, killed the demon and raised the earth from the ocean's depths.

4. Narasimha. When Hiranyaksha had died his twin Hiranyaksasipu ascended the throne of the demons. His tyranny threatened the divine beings, men and animals. Because the demon was given a boon that he could not be killed either by man or beast, Vishnu took the form a man-lion and slew him.

5. Vamana. According to a myth, the demon Bali took control of the three worlds and to regain the worlds Vishnu assumed the form of a dwarf and begged that he be allowed as much land as he could cover in three steps. Bali agreed. Vishnu then assumed giant proportions and took two strides to cover earth and heaven; Vishnu however did not take the third step, and left the underworld to Bali.

6. Parashurama. "Rama of the Axe" is Vishnu incarnated to deliver the Brahmins from the tyranny of the Kshatriyas.

Sri Srinivasa Perumal Temple, Serangoon Road

Lord Vishnu at the entrance to the Temple

7. Rama. Vishnu was born as Rama, the hero of the "Ramayana" to slay the powerful king Ravana of Lanka.

8. Krishna. This is the most popular of the "avatars"; Vishnu becomes Krishna of the "Bhagavata Gita" (the scriptures) and of the "Bhagavata Purana".

9. Buddha. It is the belief that Buddha is an "avatar" of Vishnu.

10. Kalki. Kalki is the name of the incarnation yet to come in this Kali Yuga (period of time). Vishnu will appear on the earth to restore its purity and "Kalki" (white horse) signifies the steed upon which he will ride.

Vishnu is the forgiver of sins and gratifier of all one's wishes and guide to the path of virtues; he is love embodied, a righteous judge sees that good triumphs over injustice and evil. In Hindu mythology it was Vishnu as the benefactor of man cleared the earth of a multitude of giants and monsters. To come to earth to see that good triumphs over evil he becomes an "avatar". The earth then becomes his home. In a family the husband and father (householder) is regarded as Vishnu for he is the compassionate sustainer, benevolent provider, a resourceful and amiable protector.

Hindus believe in the brotherhood of all creatures on earth under the fatherhood of God. Lakshimi, Vishnu's consort, enriches and brightens lives by inspiring man to turn despair to resourcefulness; she is also the goddess of beauty and wealth; gold symbolises her.

Sri Veeramakaliamman Temple, Serangoon Road

SRI VEERAMAKALIAMMAN TEMPLE

141 Serangoon Road

*One of the oldest Hindu Temples in
Singapore and the oldest in Serangoon;
Tamil pioneer workers built
the shrine of Veeramakaliamman, the powerful
goddess to protect them in a foreign land;
it was also the centre of early Indian
sociocultural activities in the area.*

One of the earliest localities where Indians, particularly Tamils, settled was Kampong Kapor (Lime Village) Buffalo Village or New Kampong. In 1835 the early Tamils built a shrine for Veeramakaliamman, the powerful goddess who destroys evil and protects her devotees. Perhaps the Tamils who worked in the lime kilns initiated the building of the shrine, or those involved in cattle-raising activities.

By the end of the 19th century a wooden Temple had replaced the shrine and gradually more rooms were added to the building. A statue of the goddess was shipped from South India in 1908. By 1938 other deities were added to the Temple and this included Lord Murugan and Lord Ganesha. In 1938 a chariot was purchased. Renovations and additions were made in 1953 and in 1987 a "Koburam" (Gateway) was erected.

The Sri Veeramakaliamman Temple reflects the deep faith the Tamil Hindus have in their religion and Veeramakaliamman - the Mother Goddess; it is a centre for their sociocultural activities. The Tamils always believe: never to live in a country without a place of worship.

During the Japanese invasion of Singapore many devotees took refuge in the Temple.

Today the Temple not only caters for the Hindus in Singapore but it has also become the meeting place of many Hindu tourists from India and workers from Tamil Nadu.

VADAPATHIRAKALIAMMAN TEMPLE

Serangoon Road

The Temple was founded as a small shrine by Tamil Hindu residents of Potong Pasir; they wanted the protection of Mother Goddess and sustain their cultural heritage; it was developed under B. Govindasamy Chettiar, pioneer labour contractor to the Port of Singapore, philanthropist and Indian community leader.

In the early 20th century the Tamil Hindus of Potong Pasir under the leadership of Rengasamy Murier, Murugaiyan, Samiappan and Vairappan Thevar built a small hut as a Temple in Upper Serangoon Road and later it was handed to B. Govindasamy Chettiar, the pioneer labour contractor to the Port of Singapore to manage the Temple. He developed it and later it was his nephew and son-in- law S.L. Perumal who at his own expense built the present Temple.

Vadapathirakaliamman is the same deity as Sri Mariamman; Veeramakaliamman refers to an attribute of the Mother Goddess. Vadapathirakaliamman means the pure as fire protective Motherly spirit from the North.

B. Govindasamy Chettiar came to Singapore from South India (Madras) at the age of 16 in 1905. He initially partnered with Mohammed Yusof and later solely managed the Indian Labour Company and supplied the stevedores, lightermen, wharf workers, lascars and dockyard workers to the Harbour Board. Govdindasamy Chettiar employed 3,500 Indian workers and had also Chinese gangs working for him in the port. He recruited the labourers from India and they were paid as daily-rated men.

The offices of Govindasamy Chettiar were where the present Gate 2, opposite the old Customs Building in Keppel Road is located. Adjoining the offices were the quarters for some of his staff. There was also a large kitchen which never stopped functioning as free meals were supplied day and night. Free meals were served to all those who worked in the port as well as those who lived outside it. All were fed and none was turned off. The common saying was "if you want a free meal go to Govindasamy Chettiar's "kottai" (shed).

Govindasamy Chettiar donated freely to charities and Temple funds; he helped to complete the renovations of the Sri Mariamman Temple and served as a trustee of this Temple for many years.

If anybody came to him for any assistance, financial or otherwise he never refused them. His philosophy was: "Oh, I am getting the men to work for me; their sweat is our money and therefore they deserve financial aid when they ask for it".

Sri Vadapathira kaliamman Temple, Serangoon Road

Site once occupied by offices of Govindasamy Chettiar, Indian pioneer and contractor to the Harbour Board.

Govindasamy Chettiar continued to work during the Japanese Occupation when the Syonan Koun Kaisha ran the port.

In 1948 the Singapore Harbour Board decided to discontinue the system of contract labour to the port and all the labourers were employed by the Board. This broke the heart of Govindasamy Chettiar.

After a short illness he died on 6 April 1948 at the age of 59. Hundreds of all races attended his funeral - the funeral of an Indian community leader who was charitable to all races and an understanding and kind employer.

Before his death he requested his nephew and son-in-law the late S.L. Perumal to build a new main tower the "Rajakopuram" and other additions to the Vadapathirakaliamman Temple. S. L. Perumal agreed and kept his word. When Hindu devotees worship here they feel the sanctity of this house of worship - which was started by Hindu devotees from Potong Pasir to sustain their cultural heritage.

The Deity Vadapathira kaliamman

THE RAILWAY STATION

Keppel Road

Reflection of Singapore's economic prosperity and link with Malaya (Singapore's hinterland) in the early years

In 1902 the main railway station was at Tank Road. Eight trains ran daily to Woodlands Station; from there a steam ferry took passengers across the Straits of Johore to Johore Bahru from 1903. A train would travel from Tank Road, along Orchard Road and over an overhead bridge to Cuppage Road; it then cut through Emerald Hill to Monk's Hill Estate and on to Newton Circus and Bukit Timah Road Station.

From there it proceeded straight across the plain towards Bukit Timah Hill. Winding round the foot of the hill, the train glided through gambier, pepper and pineapple plantations past Bukit Panjang Station to Kranji and thence to Woodlands.

Malayan Railway Station Keppel Road

Between 1906 and 1907 an extension line was laid to link Pulau Saigon, People's Park, Duxton Hill and Alexandra Barracks.

For the railway link between Singapore and Johore Bahru across the Straits of Johore, land was sold by the Singapore government to the Federated Malay States for $4,136,000. Work on a Causeway was begun in 1919 and the railway link was open for traffic in 1923. This linked the Malayan hinterland to Singapore.

Keppel Railway Station was completed in 1932 after three years of construction by the Federated Malay States (formed in 1896, a loose union of Perak, Selangor, Negri Sembilan and Pahang).

Keppel Railway Station was officially opened by Governor Sir Cecil Clementi Smith in 1932. The dignified building in classical style was influenced by Eliel Saarinen's Helsenki Station. The facade has four heroic figures representing Commerce, Agriculture, Industry and Shipping.

Opening the Railway Station the Governor said it would be "a terminus of world importance." His words became a reality.

Old Railway Station (demolished), Tank Road

SUN YAT SEN VILLA

Tai Gin Road off Balestier Road

Singapore - headquarters of Dr Sun Yat Sen for his Campaigns to overthrow the Manchu dynasty.

Sun Yat Sen was born on 12 November 1866 in the province of Kwantung. He studied in a High School in Honolulu and graduated as a doctor in 1892 from the University of Hong Kong.

Sun Yat Sen Villa is situated at 12 Tai Gin Road. It became the Headquarters of Dr Sun Yat Sen for his campaign against the Manchus. Some of his military operations were planned in the Villa. He made 9 visits to Singapore and stayed at the Villa on three occasions.

The land occupied by the Villa was previously a sugar plantation owned by the first American Consul to Singapore. The Villa was formerly known as Bin Chan House owned by a Cantonese businessman. In 1937 Lee Kong Chian and Tan Ean Kian pooled their wealth and acquired the Villa.

Dr Sun Yat Sen founded the Society for Rebuilding China (Hsing Chung-hui) in Canton in 1894; its aim was to topple the Manchu Dynasty.

Dr Sun first visited Singapore in 1900 and during his stay here he travelled to the Malay States, Penang and Malacca to get support for his cause and raise money for the campaign. He visited Singapore again in 1905 and during his third visit in 1906 he founded the Singapore Branch of the Tung Ming Hui. The Villa became his headquarters for South-east Asia. He also set up branches in Malaya.

Dr Sun was in the United States where he remained until the revolution succeeded. As a result of the revolution, the Kuomintang was formed on 13 August 1912; it was a fusion of 5 societies including the Tung Ming Hui. Dr Sun became the President of the Republic of China. In 1913 the Singapore Branch of the Kuomintang was registered and one of its members was the eminent Dr Lim Boon Keng.

Dr Sun Yat Sen died at the age of 59. He is recognised as a great reformer.

In 1942 the Japanese converted the Villa into a military camp. After the Japanese Surrender in 1945 renovations were carried out and the Villa became the branch office of the Kuomintang until 1951. Later it fell into disuse and after 15 years, on the centenary of Dr Sun Yat Sen's birthday, it was restored for the fourth time by the Singapore Chinese Chamber of Commerce and Industry.

The Villa is architecturally classified as a colonial bungalow - a mixture of East and West - blending the Palladian style in Europe with Chinese and Malay influences.

Dr Sun Yat Sen Villa where Dr. Sun Yat Sen planned some of his campaigns to overthrow the Manchu Dynasty

Sun Yat Sen Villa, Statue of Dr Sun Yat Sen, President, Republic of China.
Used Villa as headquarters.

The Chinese in Singapore before the outbreak of the Pacific War in 1941 were broadly classified as supporters of the Kuomintang, the Chinese Communist Party and the Peranakan Chinese who had largely settled in Singapore and were generally English speaking. Some of the Peranakan Chinese were supporters of Kuomintang cause like Dr Lim Boon Keng, an acknowledged Chinese community leader in Singapore.

On the ground floor of the Villa are displayed photographs of and documents on Dr Sun Yat Sen and his revolutionary colleagues. On the first floor are photographs and newspaper cuttings of the Japanese invasion of Malaya and Singapore and the Occupation years. In glass cases around the room which is also a library are artefacts collected from graves of victims of Japanese torture during the three and half years of Syonan (Singapore). These gruesome reminders include jewellery, dentures and even stethoscopes of doctors!

A sub-committee of the Singapore Chinese Chamber of Commerce and Industry manages the Villa. It is open to the public. There is no admission fee.

RAFFLES HOTEL

A symbol of British Colonial ambience but built by Armenian pioneers
The Hotel was gazetted as a national monument on 6 March 1987

Built in the old French Renaissance style, Raffles Hotel is one of the most famous hotels in the world; it richly deserves this distinction. Royalty from Europe, Thailand, Japan, the Middle- East and Malaya and writers like Rudyard Kipling, Somerset Maugham and Noel Coward and other distinguished personalities including film stars have some time or other occupied rooms in this Hotel.

During the Colonial era the Hotel was a symbol of colonialism for Europeans patronised it and natives were discreetly excluded. The curry tiffin, the bar, the dinners and the balls exemplified their gracious living. Even when Asian couples rarely had the chance to take to the dance floor European men while dancing deliberately stepped on the Asian men's feet!

When complaints were made to the manager the explanation given was that it was a private Hotel and it could not be prevented. Things got better after 1930.

Surprising it were not the British who established this Hotel. Three Armenian brothers: Tigran, Aviet and Arshak established the Hotel which opened on 18 November 1896. The Sarkies brothers who came from Julfa (Turkey) built Raffles Hotel in Singapore, the Eastern in Penang and the Strand in Rangoon.

The Hotel was built in Beach Road because it was the area assigned by Raffles for Europeans. Further it was just at the edge of the sea. In fact, during high tide sea water used to seep into the Hotel and special steps at the entrance were built to prevent this. On the site of the Hotel once stood the fine bungalow of W.R. George. Behind the Hotel were gharries-carriages drawn by one pony and led by a groom.

When there were no available rooms in Raffles Hotel the first and second floors of Stamford House nearby were used as an annex.

Raffles Hotel was famous for its curry tiffin (in fact the hotel began as a "tiffin-house" within a private residence), the buffet lunch in its Palm Court, the internationally known long bar and the Singapore Sling (the cocktail) and for its dinners and ballroom.

The early rickishaw riders always fought for the Raffles Hotel pitch; the two groups that fought were the Heng-wha and the Hockcha.

There is an interesting episode about how a tiger escaped from a show and sought refuge under the table in the Billiards Room and Mr C. Phillips the headmaster (from 1916-21) of Raffles Institution across the road rushed out of his office with his rifle to shoot down the animal before it did any harm to the occupants. Indeed, he was a principal of an independent school.

Raffles Hotel

Many official functions, dinners and balls were held in the Hotel and these continued right up to the outbreak of the Pacific War and the Japanese invasion of Malaya. During the Battle for Singapore the Hotel was overcrowded with European families who escaped from Malaya. Some of the most expensive silver ware were buried in the garden of the Hotel just before the British Surrender.

During the Japanese Occupation (1942-45) Raffles Hotel was used by the Japanese Imperial Army Headquarters for the Transport and Supplies Section and as rooms for senior Japanese officers. Occasional functions were organised in the Hotel to entertain visiting senior Japanese military officers. During those years the main entrance was shifted from the front to the side. The Hotel was then known as Syonan Hotel.

As soon as it became known that Japan had surrendered some Japanese military officers in the Hotel committed suicide in true Japanese Samurai spirit and code. British prisoners of war from Changi Gaol were transferred to Raffles Hotel after the surrender before they were sent home to Britain. Raffles Hotel soon became a transit point for allied army personnel from Singapore, Java, Sumatra as well as those rescued from internment camps and the islands of the East Indies.

In 1946 Raffles Hotel began to function without much of its past glory and it took some time to regain its pre-war status. Various organisations and clubs booked Raffles Hotel for their annual dinner and dance. The author remembers those days when he was a student teacher and General Secretary of the Singapore Teachers' Training Association organising dinners there. After the dinners the student teachers rushed to eat their Eastern meals outside the Hotel because there was not much to eat inside and the menu was printed in French!

Raffles Hotel is now under renovations and should be completed by September 1991; it should after this look very much what it was when it was first built. The main entrance would be shifted to the front to its original place. Special features would include a collection of historical memorabilia which would be displayed in Raffles Museum in the Hotel and Jubilee Hall - a Victorian theatre to bring back the colonial ambience.

Raffles Hotel is indeed an architectural rarity built in the French Renaissance style.

ORANJIE BUILDING - STAMFORD HOUSE

Stamford Road

Built for firm Whiteaway Laidlaw and upper floors as annex to Raffles Hotel and later Orange Hotel

Stamford House was built by architects Swan and MacLaren in 1900 for the firm of Whiteaway Laidlaw and Co. Seth Paul called the building Oranjie Building and Whiteaway Laidlaw carried on their business there until 1910. Raffles Hotel because of a shortage of rooms took over two top floors as an annex for some years. In 1933 Seth's daughter Mrs Theodora Van Hein renovated the building and converted it to become the Orange Hotel. In February 1942 a number of survivors of the "Prince of Wales" and the "Repulse" were housed in this Hotel.

During the Japanese Occupation the building was used as a hotel. After World War II rooms were rented and the ground floor used as shops. In 1963 the building was sold to Basco Enterprises Private Limited. It named the building Stamford House.

Stamford House is under renovations. The exterior will retain its original facade.

Next to Oranjie Building stood the Sailors' Home (Shaw Building and Capitol Theatre).

Stamford House, previously Oranjie Building

ALBERT STREET

Original place where Hindus held their fire-walking ceremony; tourist attraction in the early years.

Until the 1970s Albert Street was famous for its Chinese restaurants, bars, medicine shops, and food stalls and a great tourist attraction. In the early 19th century Hindus held their fire- walking ceremony in Albert Street before it became a regular ritual at Sri Mariamman Temple in South Bridge Road. Tamils in Singapore used to call Albert Street the "Street for Fire-walking". As a large number of Tamils lived in Serangoon Road it was natural that this ceremony was held in their neighbourhood.

Today Albert Street is deserted and all night life has disappeared. It is hoped that with redevelopment Albert Corner will again spring to life. However it will not recapture the charm and quaint atmosphere of the past.

Old Albert Street
site of early fire-walking ceremony.

SINGAPORE CEYLON TAMILS' ASSOCIATION

NEW PREMISES IN THE SRI SENPAGA
VINAYAGAR TEMPLE
Ceylon Road (old one was at Handy Road)

> *Ceylon Tamils as early as 1909 formed as Association to look after their interest, sustain their culture and identity.*
> *Ceylon Tamils have contributed to the growth of Singapore particularly in the civil service and professions; they helped to convert the jungles and swamps into a new world.*

Prime Minister Mr Lee Kuan Yew wrote in his Foreword (dated 18 December 1967) to the book, "A Hundred Years of Ceylonese in Malaysia and Singapore (1867-1967)" by S. Durai Raja Singam:

> *Our Ceylonese citizens like the other citizens of migrant stock, have made a distinctive contribution towards the enrichment and growth of Singapore, as they have towards the modernisation of Malaysia and Singapore during the past hundred years. Their forefathers emigrated and sweated and toiled to build a new world out of virgin jungle and swamp so that their descendants could live in dignity and equality; not on sufferance but as of right because they sweated and toiled to build their new homeland.*

In the same book Mr S. Rajaratnam, former Senior Minister of Singapore gave the following message:

> *They (Ceylon Tamils) have contributed substantively towards the development of railways, public works, schools hospitals and other departments of administration without which modernisation would have been impossible.*

If we today boast of one of the soundest
administrations in this part of the world,
it is an inheritance handed down to us,
by among others, the Ceylonese who helped
to create it.

It is difficult to establish when the first group of Ceylon Tamils emigrated to Singapore but it is evident that they came here after the control of the Straits Settlements was transferred from the India Office to the Colonial Office in 1867.

Ceylon was ruled by the Portuguese (1597-1656), the Dutch (1656-1796)and finally British who assumed control of that island after Dutch occupation. It became a British Crown Colony in 1802. British officials served in both Ceylon and the Straits Settlements; even some of the Governors served both these Colonies.

Ceylon Tamils from the peninsula of Jaffna (in the north of the island) in the 19th century underwent compulsory education for about 3 years; they learnt Tamil, English and other subjects in the Jaffna College (American managed) Hindu College and elsewhere. These English educated Ceylon Tamils found employment under the British in Ceylon. The British officials found the Ceylon Tamils responsible, loyal, efficient and employees with integrity. When some of these British Colonial officials were transferred to Singapore they offered employment to Ceylon Tamils who were prepared to emigrate. Other Ceylon Tamils emigrated on their own free will in the 1870s and found employment in government service as surveyors, engineers, hospital assistants (called dressers), doctors, teachers, and clerks in the civil service, railways and postal department.

Many of these pioneers came from the District of Vaddukotai because they were either educated in Jaffna College or Hindu College. One of the earliest of the pioneers was Murugasu Vaithilingam Pillai who perhaps came to Singapore about 1870, and was an overseer of roads and a philanthropist. V. Murugesan Pillai emigrated about 1876 and served the Singapore Municipality for 21 years; he was also the leader of the Hindu community for about 10 years. About the same year Mudaliar Annamalai Pillai arrived in Singapore and worked as a surveyor and rose to become Surveyor-General. He was responsible for surveying many areas of Singapore and opened up modern roads and lanes. He owned several large areas of land and travelled in a horse-carriage drawn by 4 horses. This became the envy of many. Dr James Muthiah Handy was one the earliest medical practitioners who set up St Mary's Clinic. The nephew of Mudaliar Annamalai Pillai was I. Mudaliar Nagalingam, a clerk with the legal firm of Donaldson and Birkinshaw; he was a philanthropist who helped anyone who turned to him for assistance, irrespective of his racial origin. There was Saravanamuthu Ampalavanar an employee of the Municipality for 34 years. H. M. Hoisington a graduate of Cambridge University taught mathematics at Anglo-Chinese School. Dr C.

Subrahmanyam was one of the earliest graduates of the King Edward VII College of Medicine; he won several scholarships and in his final year won the Gold Medal for outstanding results. He served as Senior Pathologist in the Singapore General Hospital and later as Professor of Pathology in the College of Medicine. There were several other prominent pioneers from Jaffna. Some were Christian missionaries who served the local Churches like Rev. S Weerakathy Underwood.

In 1909 the leaders of the Ceylon Tamil community decided that they form an association to look after their interest, to organise literary, cultural and sporting activities for their members. A meeting was convened by S. Muthuthamby on 16 October 1909 and the decision was taken to establish the Ceylon Tamils' Association which was registered on 26 July 1910. J. Henry Ponnampalam became its first President. By 1911 it was felt that the Association should have its own building. Dr J.M. Handy donated a piece of land in what is today Handy Road opposite Cathay Cinema. Three trustees for the Association were elected; they were H. M. Hoisington, K. Thambyrajah and S. Muthucumaru the contractor who put up the building. The foundation stone was laid on 22 May 1915. After completion the opening ceremony was performed on 31 March 1916 by the eminent Dr Lim Boon Keng member of the Straits Settlements Legislative Council and a leader of the Chinese community.

Singapore Ceylon Tamil's Association occupies a room in the Senpaga Vinayagar Temple, Ceylon Road

The Association organised social, literary, cultural and sporting activities. Sports were held in the Association's piece of land in Balestier Plain where was a cricket pitch and a modest pavilion. The Association lost this field at the end of World War II.

The Association submitted memoranda on various subjects to the government: these included appeals for higher education, increase of number of members for the Municipal Council and the legislature, for the setting up of a Hindu Advisory Board and public holidays for Deepavali and Hindu New Year.

The Association building was damaged during the Japanese invasion of Singapore but was repaired after the war by money advanced by Dr P. Thillainathan.

The Association's building was taken over by government for re-development and the Association now occupies a room within the premises of Sri Senpaga Vinayagar Temple in Ceylon Road.

The Ceylon Tamils' Association is still an active body. Ceylon Tamils continue to make their valuable contribution in the social and cultural spheres in our Republic. Many members of this community still serve the various professions as judges, lawyers, doctors, teachers, professors, in the armed forces, police force and the civil service.

One sad feature of the Association today is the absence of Christian Ceylon Tamils in its membership. They played a vital role in the founding of the Association and served it with distinction in the past.

Sri Senpaga Vinayagar Temple, Ceylon Road

SRI SENPAGA VINAYAGAR TEMPLE

Ceylon Road, Katong

The Temple was a meeting place for Singapore Ceylon Tamils to sustain their cultural heritage, their identity and values in the 19th century; their descendants continue to do so.

Before a Temple was erected on the site in Ceylon Road a small shrine was put up by Ethirnayagam Pillay and several Tamil labourers. They placed an image of Vinayagar under a Senpaga (Chempaka) tree. This gave the name Senpaga Vinayagar to the deity.

Vinayagar is a facet of the manifestation of the Divine reality which blessed the wandering man with wisdom to develop good judgment. Worship of this deity brings harmony to the home, relations, friends and business associates. He is the patron of the Arts and Science and brings culture, creativity and religion into one's life; Vinayagar is also the personification of material existence and represents abundance and fertility of the earth. Before any ceremony and cultural performance this deity is invoked to seek his blessings and protection for the success of the occasion. Vinayagar is the spirit that assists the souls in their evolution towards maturity, perfection and purity. He is the embodiment of love, hope and compassion; he with affection forgives failings of human beings who vow to correct their shortcomings.

E. Pillay, S. Muthusamy, Rengasamy, K. Vallipuram and V. Subramaniam were appointed to collect funds to build a Temple and four others: S. Muthucumaru, I. Mudaliar Nagalingam, Dr, K. Kramathiapathy and Dr S. Nagalingam among others donated sums of money towards the building fund. A Temple with a wooden roof was erected and the image of Vinayagar was consecrated there.

From 1923 the Temple's Committee of Management was elected at the Annual General Meeting of the Singapore Ceylon Tamils" Association. In November 1924 under the leadership of S. Muthucumaru decision was taken to build a new Temple with ancillary buildings. By May 1926 the plans had been completed and the chief sculptor arrived from Jaffna, Ceylon, to commence work.

Many Ceylon Tamils donated towards the building fund and S. Muthucumaru paid for the main shrine, the "Moolasthanam". Other major donors included S. Thillaipalam, Dr N. Moorthathamby, Dr K. Thambipillai, I. Mudaliar Nagalingam, K. Paramoo, M. Velupillai, Kanapathipillai, V. Subramaniam and K. Nadarajah.

On 3 February 1930 the consecration ceremony was held followed by rituals and prayers. In June 1939 the priest's quarters and a school were completed; these were officially opened in December the same year. On 22 January 1941 during the Japanese invasion of Singapore a bomb fell near the Temple and parts of the buildings were severely damaged. It was through the personal efforts of Dr P. Thillainathan that repairs were carried out and normal activities of the Temple were resumed.

In 1949 renovations were made to the Temple. Major renovations including the erection of the Main Gateway, the "Maha Gopuram", the Cultural Hall were completed in November 1989 largely through the inspiration and driving force of S. M. Vasagar who served with distinction as President of the Temple Committee for several years.

The Temple and the Singapore Ceylon Tamils' Association continue to serve the Ceylon Tamils and other Hindus. The Temple is still a meeting place of the Ceylon Tamils helping them sustain their cultural heritage, values and traditions which their ancestors brought to Singapore in the 19th century.

Vinayagar - the main deity in the Temple.

SRI KRISHNAN TEMPLE

152 Waterloo Street

V Pakirisamy Pillai, Indian pioneer, community leader and philanthropist developed this Temple. Temple originated to cater for Hindus in the neighourhood bounded by Bras Basah Road, Victoria Street and Albert Street; it was started by Hanuman Beem Singh in 1870 and later managed by his son Humna Somapah, and Joognee Ammal. V. Pakirisamy Pillai took over from February 1935.

There was a large Hindu community in the neighbourhood bounded by Bras Basah Road, Victoria Street and Albert Street. In 1870 Hanuman Beem Singh set up a shrine for Lord Krishna under a banyan tree in Waterloo Street. As its congregation of Hindus grew so did the Temple. When Beem Singh was too old to manage the Temple he passed it on to his son Humna Somapah who was a landed proprietor. In 1904 Joognee Ammal took over the management. She built the main shrine. In February 1935 she requested V. Pakirisamy Pillai to manage the Temple. Pillai built the Hall and the walls of the Temple and dedicated them to the memory of his mother Alamayloo Ammal. When Pillai died in May 1984 his son P. Sivaraman took over the management and was responsible for major renovations to the Temple in 1989.

V. Pakirisamy Pillai's father Koona Vayloo Pillai was a rich Tamil pioneer who died at the age of 75 in 1931. Pakirisamy Pillai and his brother V. Narayanasamy Pillai inherited their father's estate. Pakirisamy Pillai was born in December 1894 in Cairnhill Road where Khee Fatt School once stood. After completing his education at Anglo-Chinese School he became the Chief Court Clerk of the law firm of Allen and Gledhill for about 25 years. His home was 109 Bideford Road. He devoted much of his time to community service particularly in religious activities. He served as Chairman of the four main Hindu Temples' Committees of Management and in 1948 he entered politics. He served as a City Councillor from the late 1940s to early 1950s. He became a Justice of the Peace in 1946. He was a recipient of the Coronation Medal and bestowed with the Most Excellent Order of the British Empire in 1952. For his services to Singapore he was awarded the Singapore Certificate of Honour and in 1970 the President of the Republic of Singapore bestowed upon him the Bintang Bakti Masharakat (BBM) for his many years of social and community work.

V. Pakirisamy Pillai was a generous and religious man. He died in May 1984 at the age of 89.

Sri Krishnan Temple

THE KWONG WAI SHIU HOSPITAL

Serangoon Road
(occupying the former site of
Tan Tock Seng Hospital in the Balestier Plain)

A fine example of a hospital founded to serve the Cantonese community in 1910 now serves patients of all ethnic groups in Singapore truly reflecting our development towards nationhood.

Kwong Wai Shiu was established in 1910 to serve the Cantonese community in Singapore. In a hall in the administration section of the Hospital the photographs of the founders of the Hospital are prominently displayed.

In the past Kwong Wai Shiu only admitted Cantonese as in-patients. It was at an extraordinary meeting on 11 March 1973 that the constitution of the Hospital was amended to admit in-patients from all ethnic groups. On 15 June 1974 the new policy came into force.

Today Kwong Wai Shiu is a modern hospital comprising 14 blocks 8 of them wards for 425 patients. Three of the blocks which can be easily recognised by their architecture were built for the old Tan Tock Seng Hospital. The foundation stone for the new building was laid on 13 December 1959 by Leung Yun Chee.

Today there are 4 medical officers, 2 Chinese physicians and 150 nurses and other employees.

Kwong Wai Shiu is a fine example of a communal hospital opening its doors to all communities in a multi-racial and multi-cultural country. Truly this is a reflection of our evolvement towards nationhood.

An old ward of Tan Tock Seng hospital now part of the Kwong Wai Shui Hospital

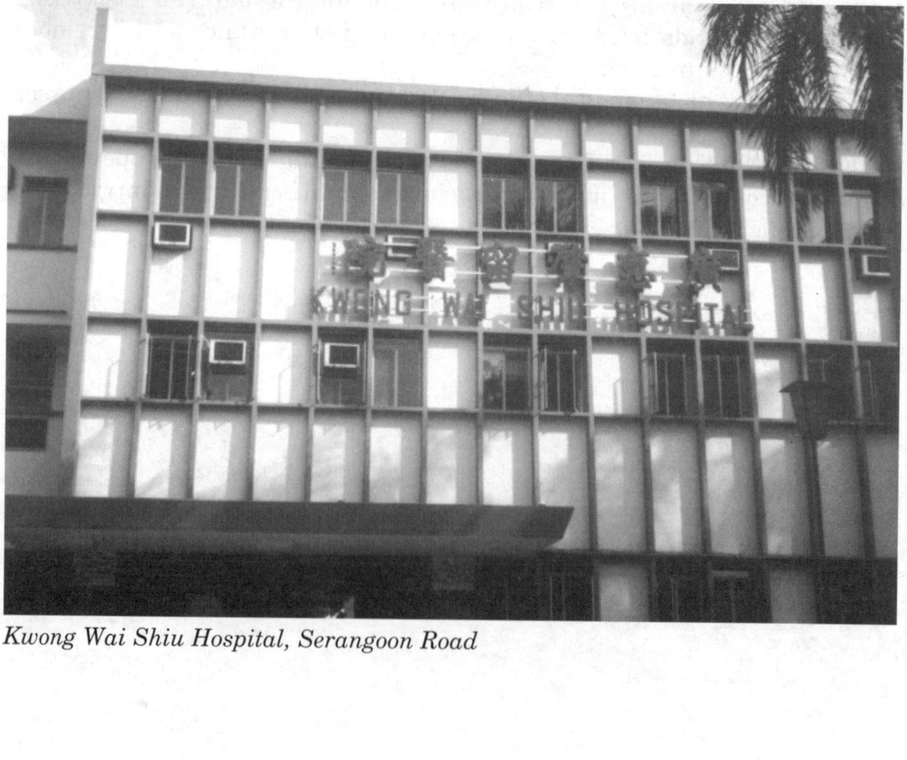

Kwong Wai Shiu Hospital, Serangoon Road

HADJA FATIMAH MOSQUE

Beach Road

Hadja Fatimah was a very wealthy Malay business woman and a charitable one in Singapore.
The "Leaning Tower" of Singapore

It was gazetted as a national monument on 6 July 1973.

Hadja Fatimah came from a well-known family in Malacca. She married a Bugis prince who unfortunately died when she was still young.

Hadja Fatimah was a very wealthy business woman. She carried on a large lucrative trade and owned many vessels and prahus. She also had good connections with several Rajahs from Celebes, the homeland of her husband.

Hadja Fatimah was a charitable lady. She built a house in Java Road in Kampong Glam where glam trees grew. They were used to make medicinal oil and for caulking boats. The house was unfortunately attacked twice by robbers and also set on fire. When the house was attacked and burnt the second time, she abandoned it and built the Hadja Fatimah Mosque on the present site and another house for her family. She died at the ripe old age of 98.

In the early years of Singapore an Arab merchant Abdul Rahman Alsagoff settled in Singapore. He travelled widely and died in Grisseh in Java. His son Syed Ahamd bin Abdul Rahman Alsagoff married Raja Siti, the daughter of Hadja Fatimah; he was a rich trader and owned several steamers and sailing vessels. After his death he was buried behind the Hadja Fatimah Mosque.

In Java Road several houses were built for the poor by the Alsagoff family. Twice every year large feasts were held there and thousands attended them including Muslims of all ranks and classes. One of the feasts was held on the anniversary of the death of Hadja Fatimah.

The Hadja Fatimah Mosque was built between 1845 and 1846; the minaret and ancillary buildings were probably erected by J.T. Thomas. the government surveyor (1841-1853). The main Mosque was rebuilt in the 1930s by Malay artisans trained by the French contractor Bossard Mopin to the designs of Chung and Wong. It is not true that the minaret was designed based on the steeple of the old St Andrew's Church which was demolished and replaced by the St Andrew's Cathedral.

Hadja Fatimah Mosque, Beach Road

The Hadja Fatimah Mosque displays a hybrid of architectural types. It is a walled square enclosure with a domed main prayer hall, a bathing area and a school. The central minaret, the ritual washing area, and the two flanking houses are European in style. Many Chinese features in the windows and woodwork are easily recognisable. The Mosque has a universal flavour. At the back of the Mosque are a number of old tombstones.

After Hadja Fatimah's death she was buried in a special chamber at the rear of the Mosque; her tombstone as well as her daughter's stand side by side in the well carpeted chamber.

Tombstones of Hadja Fatimah and daughter Raja Siti

JALAN EUNOS MALAY SETTLEMENT

Kampong Eunos
Changi Road

Muhammad Eunos Abdullah, Chairman "Kesatuan Melayu Singapura" (Singapore Malay Union) - origins of Malay nationalism in Singapore.

Muhammad Eunos Abdullah was born in Singapore in 1876. He was the son of a Minangkabau merchant from Sumatra. He studied in Raffles Institution in 1893 and later worked in the office of the Master Attendant, Singapore Harbour. In 1907 he became the editor of the Malay paper "Utusan Melayu"; he was a social worker and was the first Malay to become a Justice of the Peace in 1922. The other outstanding Malay then was Dr Abdul Samad, the first Malay doctor in Singapore.

The first signs of Malay nationalism appeared in the founding of "Kesatuan Melayu Singapura" (Singapore Malay Union), a quasi political organisation formed in 1926 by Muhammad Eunos Abdullah, its first President. The main objectives of the Singapore Malay Union were to promote Malay progress, higher and technical education among Malays and interest in politics. Membership of the union was restricted to Malays; Arabs and Indian Muslims were excluded from it. It could be said that the Singapore Malay Union was the predecessor to the United Malay Nationalist Organisation in Singapore.

Muhammad Eunos Abdullah who was a member of the Straits Settlements Legislative Council made an appeal in 1927 to the government requesting that a plot of land should be reserved for a "Malay Kampong" where Malays could lead a Malay way of life. The government gave its approval and a sum of $700,000 was granted to the Singapore Malay Union to buy 600 acres of land. This eventually became known as Kampong Eunos or Kampong Melayu.

Later similar Malay kampongs were established in other parts of Singapore; these were Kampong West Coast (Pasir Panjang), Kampong Sembawang and Kampong Ayer Gemuroh.

In the early 1930s the government decided to build Kallang Civil Airport. It became necessary to resettle the Malays of Kallang Village in Kampong Melayu.

In Singapore Government Gazette, (1950) "the occupation of land (Malay Settlement, Jalan Eunos) Rules 1950" said:

The right of occupancy of all allotment in the Settlement will be granted only to

> *male members of the Malay race who habitually speak the Malay language, profess the Muslim religion and conform to Malay customs, and who have been born in the Colony of Singapore or the Federation of Malaya provided always that preference will be given to applicants born in the Colony of Singapore.*

It was also specified that those with substantive salaries or wages unlikely to exceed $100 per mensem were eligible for the right of occupancy.

Later as a result of rapid urban redevelopment, priority had to be given to programmes like public housing, urban renewal and industrialisation and it was inevitable these Malay Settlements had to be discontinued.

Today Singaporeans irrespective of their ethnic background live as neighbours in Housing and Development Board flats - another feature of our evolution towards nationhood.

Jalan Eunos Malay Settlement - now Malays live in multi-racial high rise buildings. Silat Federation's office here.

MANMATHA KARUNESHVARAR TEMPLE

226 Kallang Road

Temple started by Hindu workers in the Gas Depot nearby and later managed by trustees and finally V. Pakirisamy and his brother Narayanasamy.

The Manmatha Karuneshvarar Temple was established soon after the Municipal Gasworks or depot was set up in Kallang Road. The large number of Hindu employees started a shrine and installed the main deity to seek its protection as well as to sustain their Hindu traditions and values.

Though there were not many Hindus in Kallang and Kampong Bugis the Hindu employees of the Gas Depot had living quarters close to the Depot and so they built the shrine. At that time Indians were concentrated in Tanjong Pagar and Serangoon area.

It was only in 1909, the site, an area of 8255 square feet, was granted on government lease for 99 years made in favour of four persons: Soona Veloo Vendir, Nagalingam Kathirayson, Annamalai Mecappa Komarasamy and Veerapatra Mudaliar. When these died, V. Pakirisamy and his brother Narayanasany built the present Temple in 1937 at the request of the Hindu devotees. After the consecration ceremony in August 1937 a Committee of Management was formed with A.V. Irullappa Pillay, a foreman of the Municipal Gas Works, as chairman. In March 1973 three trustees were appointed by the Chief Justice of Singapore; they were V. Pakirisamy, V. Narayanasamy and Balakrishna Murugase Thirunalam.

Further renovations were carried out in 1974 and the sons of V. Pakirisamy are now managing the Temple.

Manmatha Karuneshvarar Temple, Kallang Road next to Gas Works whose early employees established this Temple

Quarters of Gas Works' employees next to the Temple

The Chinese Chamber of Commerce Building, Hill Street
Built in 1964 on the site of the classical house of Wee Ah Hood (1828-1875
pioneer and pepper king.

THE CHINESE CHAMBER OF COMMERCE BUILDING

Hill Street

A symbol of the contribution of Chinese merchants to the social, cultural and economic prosperity of Singapore from the earliest times to the present day.

The foundation stone of the present building which houses the Chinese Chamber of Commerce and Industry was laid by Dato Lee Kong Chian on 15 September 1962 and officially opened by Mr Lee Kuan Yew, the Prime Minister, on 20 September, 1964.

The architecture of the building is a mix of Chinese and Western. There are two dragon murals at the entrance to the building.

The old building which stood on the present site was the house of the pepper king Wee Ah Hood (1828-1875). It was built as a classical Chinese house and was leased to the Chinese Chamber of Commerce which was established in 1906. The pioneers who set this up included Seah Liang Seah, Tan Jiak Kim, Tan Yong Siak, Tan Keong Siak and Goh Siew Tin. At its inception the Chamber functioned from a room in the Thong Chai Medical Association in Wayang Street.

The Chinese government in Peking promoted the setting up of a commercial organisation in Singapore. In 1906 the Chinese Consul-General formed the Chinese Commercial Association. In 1917 the name of this Association was changed to the Singapore Chinese Chamber of Commerce.

The Singapore Chinese Chamber of Commerce building symbolises the entrepreneurship and farsightedness of the Chinese and their contribution towards the prosperity of Singapore.

HILL STREET POLICE STATION

Today the building is known as the Hill Street Building

The first high rise building in Singapore and symbolises the modernising of the Singapore Police Force. Opposite stood the Old Ice House of Hoo Ah Kay (Whampoa)

Hill Street Police Station is the first high rise building in Singapore. It symbolises the modernisation of Singapore's Police Force in the early 20th century.

The building now houses the Archives, Oral History Department and Offices of the Official Assignee and the Film Censor. It was previously the site of the old Assembly Rooms.

The building which was both the Hill Street Police station as well barracks for the police personnel was erected in 1934. It was occupied in 1935 and renamed for a while as Silver Jubilee Building to commemorate the 25th anniversary of the reign of King George V. Public Works Department Architect F.Dorrington designed this building.

Opposite Hill Street Police Station was Whampoa's Ice House in Boat Quay, now demolished for redevelopment. The Ice House was erected in 1854 by Whampoa (popularly called Hoo Ah Kay). He imported ice from the United States of America. He was also a Counsel for Russia, China and Japan and the first Singaporean to be appointed a Member of the Straits Settlements Legislative Council. His residence, Whampoa House, in Serangoon Road was demolished.

Whampoa was a Singapore pioneer. Whampoa Road and Whampoa Secondary School were named after him.

Hill Street Building, Singapore's first high rise building.

TANGLIN BARRACKS

Minden Road

> *Tanglin Barracks*
> *former British Military Headquarters*
> *and second Headquarters, Ministry of*
> *Defence, Singapore (the first were the*
> *Upper Barracks, Pearl's Hill); a symbol of our*
> *independence.*

In the early years the area occupied by Tanglin Barracks comprised 1600 acres of a nutmeg plantation owned by William W. Willans; Ho Ah Kuay (Whampoe) also had a plantation there.

It was after the Indian Mutiny in 1857 that intensified efforts were made to build new forts or reinforce old ones. There was the fear that Sepoys in Singapore might also mutiny.

It was necessary to increase the number of British troops in the Settlement and Tanglin Barracks were built to accommodate them. The original building was built in 1868 a year after the control of the Straits Settlements was transferred from the India Office to that of the Colonial Office and became a Crown Colony. The attap barracks were erected by Colonel George Chancellor Collyer, the Chief Engineer of the Straits Settlements; he also carried out the defence works at Fort Canning.

The first British troops to occupy the Barracks were the 80th Foot Staffordshire Volunteers in 1872.

While Fort Canning became the Military Headquarters for Singapore Base District, Tanglin Barracks was the Headquarters for the Far East Land Forces.

Lieutenant General Gordon Bennett, the Australian Commander used Tanglin Barracks as his military headquarters before the British Surrender on 15 February 1942. Gordon Bennett escaped from Singapore leaving his troops behind to become prisoners of war under the Japanese.

The British established their military headquarters at Tanglin Barracks after the Japanese Occupation. They remained there until 1971 when they handed Tanglin Barracks to the Singapore Government.

When Singapore formed the Singapore Armed Forces soon after separation from Malaysia, the Ministry of Interior and Defence set up its headquarters in Pearl's Hill. Later the Ministry of Defence moved its headquarters to Tanglin Barracks with the Central Manpower Base (transferred from Kallang) next to it. It was at the Tanglin Barracks that the author worked as Head, Education Department as well as Public Relations Officer for the Ministry of Defence.

Now the Tanglin Barracks have been vacated. The Ministry of Defence has moved to new buildings in Gombak and the Central Manpower Base to Depot Road.

Tanglin Barracks
British headquarters for Far East Land Forces. Previous headquarters of Ministry of Defence, Singapore

THE LABRADOR BATTERY

(now the Labrador Park Pasir Panjang)

One of the Batteries for defence of Singapore

Labrador Park was one of nine sites where British forces set up their batteries for the defence of Singapore. This strategy was based on the belief that invasion of Singapore would not come from the north. These batteries would fire shells against naval invaders to Singapore.

The Labrador Battery included two six-inch 37-ton guns which were installed in 1938. These guns could fire 102 lb shells almost 10 miles.

In addition to these two guns there were searchlights to beam at enemy battleships.

In February 1942 these guns were traversed almost 180 degrees to fire upon the advancing Japanese Imperial Forces on Pasir Panjang Road towards Alexandra Road. However, they were not effective against land forces because of their very flat trajectory.

What we see today in Labrador Park are only the gun positions and not the guns. However, these remind Singaporeans that wrong military strategy can lead to disaster. Winston Churchill called the fall of Singapore "the greatest disaster to British arms which our history records".

Labrador Battery Emplacement
Pasir Panjang (now Labrador Park)

Gun Emplacement

ST GEORGE'S CHURCH

Minden Road
off Napier Road

LICH GATE in front of the Church was built by British prisoners of war during Japanese Occupation of Singapore

Gazetted as a national monument on 10 November 1978

The British Army in Singapore required a new Church in Tanglin Barracks to replace the old one built in 1884.

Captain Stanbury of the Royal Engineers began work on the new Church in 1910 and the total cost of the building was £2,000. St George's Church was completed in 1913.

The exterior of St George's Church is austere with its red bricks with minimal white decoration. The simple cross is conspicuous. The interior is of brickwork and has stained glass windows. Just before the British surrendered to the Japanese in February 1942, the original stained glass was buried somewhere in the Church grounds and was never recovered after the Japanese Surrender.

During the Japanese Occupation, the Japanese used the Church as an ammunition dump.

After the return of the British a re-dedication ceremony was held on 10 November 1946. On 29 June 1947 Field Marshall Montgomery on his visit to Singapore read the lesson at the morning prayer.

Tanglin Barracks became the headquarters of the Singapore Ministry of Defence until it moved to its present site at Gombak. St George's Church continues its regular worship services. Today at the annex in the rear of the Church functions a kindergarten.

When the British Army withdrew in 1971, St George's Church became a civilian Church.

The original Lich Gate (the replica is in front of the Church) was built in December 1942 by British prisoners of war of the 18th Division at Changi Camp and it was placed at the camp cemetery. After the war the graves were resited in the Commonwealth War Cemetery in Kranji and the Gate was removed and taken to St George's Church. With the British Army's withdrawal from Singapore, the Lich Gate was dismantled and shipped to Britain. A replica, the present one, was erected and dedicated on 2 December 1984 to commemorate the centenary of the building of the first St George's Church.

St George's Church and the replica Lich Gate in front of the Church, Minden Road

FORT SILOSO, SENTOSA

Grim reminder to Singaporeans of the need for total defence of Singapore - lack of this brought the greatest military disaster in the history of the British Empire in 1942.
Blakang Mati was the old name of Sentosa, south of Singapore.

After the opening of the Suez Canal in 1869 Singapore's trade with the rest of the world increased. It was not only a port but also a coaling station for steamships. There was therefore the necessity to fortify the port. After a report was submitted by a British Officer, Major Edward Lake of the Madras Engineers, it was decided to fortify Sentosa with gun batteries in Mt Siloso and Mt Serapong in the 1880s and to have a clear field of fire for its guns. The hills of Blakang Mati and uneven terrain were cleared. Extensions to the fortifications were made in the 1890s and 1930s to meet possible threats to Singapore.

In the 1880s there were 7 inch RML guns and two 64 pounders; electro magnetic mines were also laid across the narrow Straits and the electricity for them was supplied by an underground power house. In the 1890s five 10 inch guns were installed and the power house was extended to provide electricity to operate these guns. During the 1930s further additions were made; these included a twin 6 pounder, quick-firing anti-torpedo boat guns, five search-lights, a Director Tower, an Operational Tower, two machine-guns and two twin Lewis anti-aircraft machine-guns.

Close to the Control Tower is the site from where a powerful searchlight beamed across the Straits at the besieged house (in Alexandra) of the British Commander of the mutinous 5th Light Infantry on 15th and 16th February 1915. The search-light prevented the mutineers from attacking the house under cover of darkness.

The Fort was manned by the Singapore Artillery Corps and the British Royal Artillery.

The Japanese Imperial Army began its invasion of Malaya on 8th December 1941 and by 31 January, 1942 the entire Malaya Peninsula had fallen into their hands. The invasion of Singapore began on 8 February 1942 and Fort Siloso also came under Japanese attack. A Japanese supply ship was sunk by the Fort's guns in February 1942. The heavy calibre guns were swung 180 degrees to fire over the island on Japanese positions and against the Japanese when they advanced on the city from Tengah Airfield. The guns were also used to demolish the oil tanks in Pulau Bukom and Pulai Sebarok when the fall of Singapore was imminent.

Fort Siloso, Sentosa

A Search light which beamed across the Straits at Alexandra during Mutiny of 1915.

During the Japanese Occupation of Singapore (1942-1945) Fort Siloso was used as a prisoners-of-war camp.

When the British returned to Singapore after the Japanese Surrender in September 1945, Fort Siloso was occupied by the Royal Navy in 1946 and its guns were manned by the 1st Malay Coast Battery and the Royal Artillery which was eventually disbanded and the Gurkha Detachments took over.

During the undeclared war by Indonesia against Malaysia and Singapore was part of it (1963-1965) Fort Siloso was used by the 10th Gurkha Rifles to prevent Indonesian saboteurs landing on Blakang Mati and Keppel Harbour.

Fort Siloso became a Catholic retreat for British forces until the island was given up by the British in 1967 and taken over by the Singapore Armed Forces.

Today Fort Siloso has become the repository for the various coast guns of Singapore, a gun museum and a permanent exhibition of its history.

Fort Siloso is a grim reminder to Singapore of the fall of Singapore to the Japanese and the need for the Republic of Singapore to have a strong and viable Singapore Armed Forces and Civil Defence.

A Gun at Sentosa

TANJONG KATONG FORT

The Tanjong Katong Fort which does not exist today stretched from the present Fort Road, Meyer Road and as far as Arthur Road and included the site now occupied by Katong Park. The old fort was demolished after World War I to make way for the present Park.

The walls of the Fort were five foot high and had a moat all round with a wooden drawbridge. There were also tunnels leading in different directions; the face of the Fort was directed towards the sea.

Tanjong Katong Fort,
now Katong Park

STRAITS SETTLEMENTS VOLUNTEER CORPS' DRILL HALL

Beach Road

Volunteer Corps of 19th Century origins of our People's Defence Force -
an integral part of the Singapore Armed Forces

Before the Pacific War the local defence forces included four battalions of the Straits Settlements Volunteer Corps (SSVC) led by British Officers. A small civil defence force was formed in 1939 as part of the Passive Defence Services; these included air raid precautions services, a Medical Auxiliary Unit, transport, demolition, debris as well as burial squads.

The first Volunteer Corps was formed in 1854 and was called the Singapore Volunteer Rifle Corps. It had the support of the Governor Colonel W.J. Butterworth. The Second Corps was established in 1857 and the Third Corps, the Artillery Corps, was formed in 1888 after the disbandment of the Second Corps. By 1921 there were three units: the Singapore Volunteer Rifles, the Singapore Volunteer Engineers and the Singapore Volunteer Infantry. Eventually they were amalgamated as the Straits Settlements Volunteer Force under one commandant, who was also the Officer Commanding the Singapore Volunteer Corps (SVC).

The idea of a volunteer Corps was first mooted in 1846 after the Chinese riots and it was meant primarily for internal security. There was also the Crimean War. After a public meeting in July 1854 it was decided to form a Volunteer Corps in Singapore and the Governor became its first Colonel and the first Commandant Captain (later Colonel and Colonial Secretary) Ronald Macpherson.

The volunteer movement gained impetus after the Indian Mutiny, the Boxer Revolution in China, and the South African War.

The headquarters of the Singapore Volunteer Artillery Corps was in the Town Hall because there was no Drill Hall. Gun drills were held in Fort Siloso and later at Fort Tanjong Katong.

In 1889 two Maxim guns were publicly subscribed for; Chinese merchants like Cheang Hong Lim (donated $2500) and other donors included the Sultan Abu Bakar of Johore, members of the general Chinese community, the Arab, Malay and Chettiar communities also subscribed towards the cost.

In 1890 the first Volunteer Drill Hall was erected on the site previously occupied by Fort Fullerton. It was built by the executive engineer Major McCallum, the SVC Commandant. This building lasted for 43 years on this site and later removed to SVC Headquarters in Beach Road; it was finally demolished in 1933 when a new building took its place.

In 1894 a cyclist detachment was introduced as a unit of the SVC. In 1901 Tan Jiak Kim, a leading Chinese businessman strongly advocated that the Straits Chinese British Association should offer its services for the defence of the Colony. Lord Onslow, the Under-Secretary of State for the Colonies approved the formation of a Chinese Company of the Singapore Volunteer Infantry. The Company was formed in November 1901. Dr Lim Boon Keng, Song Ong Siang, and Tan Soo Bin joined the Company and Tan Soo Bin (son of the Tan Jiak Kim) had the honour of being promoted to the rank of Major. Seven members of this Company were part of the contingent which represented the Straits Settlements at the Coronation of King Edward VII in 1902 in London.

The Volunteer Cadet Movement was also started for boys in Raffles Institution, St Joseph's Institution and the Anglo-Chinese School. Most of these boy cadets were Eurasians and Chinese.

Owing to the growth of the Chinese Company a new volunteer club was built in May 1907 at the end of Beach Road with a central meeting hall, a bar and a billiards room. The earlier club was at Waterloo Street.

Until January 1908 the Drill Hall for the Chinese Company was the Old

Straits Settlements Volunteer Corps Headquarters, Beach Road Now People's Defence Force Camp.

Gaol in Bras Basah Road before it moved to Beach Road but the Eurasian Company continued to operate from the Gaol until its disbandment in 1909 but it was reformed in July 1918.

In 1910 a Malay Company was inaugurated by the Governor and the Old Gaol in Bras Basah was offered to them as their headquarters; the Company began with 40 Malay volunteers and by 1911 it had grown to 120. From 1910 to 1932 the "F" Malaya Company's headquarters was still at the Old Gaol.

The Eurasian Volunteer Headquarters opened at the SVC headquarters at Beach Road in February 1927. On 8 March 1932 the Governor Sir Cecil Clementi laid the foundation stone of the new headquarters after the old Drill Hall was demolished. On 4 March 1933 the Governor officially opened the new SSVF Headquarters at Beach Road.

The Straits Settlements Volunteer Air Force was formed in 1936 and the Straits Settlements Royal Naval Volunteer Reserve "Panglima" in 1937.

Volunteers by 1940 had become auxiliary units of the Singapore Defence Force and fought against the Japanese in the Battle for Singapore.

At the end of World War II the Volunteer Force was disbanded and in 1948 it was re-formed and recruitment began in 1949. In 1952 by the National Service Ordnance the SVC became the Singapore Military Forces. After Singapore's separation from Malaysia and Singapore became an independent and sovereign Republic on 9 August 1965 the People's Defence Force (PDF) was formed and a large part-time volunteer citizens joined the PDF.

Today the PDF is an integral part of the Singapore Armed Forces.

CHIN KANG HUI-KUAN

27 Bukit Pasoh Road

The headquarters of the Mobilisation Council Chung Kuo Council (China National Council) formed by the Chinese in Singapore to help in defence of Singapore against Japan

As the Japanese Imperial Army advanced southwards across the Malay Peninsula the pro-Communists, the pro-Kuomintang and the Straits Chinese set aside their differences to help the British defend Singapore. A deputation of Chinese leaders met the Governor, Sir Shenton Thomas to offer their services to the country. On 31 December 1941 the Chung Kuo Council (China National Council) was formed under the leadership of the philanthropist Tan Kah Kee; the headquarters of this Council was at 27 Bukit Pasoh Road.

There was enthusiastic response from the Chinese community to help in the defence of Singapore. The Council mobilised a labour force to man essential services and to construct defence works. Lim Bo Seng became head of the Labour Services - he provided thousands of labourers for the British war effort.

The Council also approached the Governor to form a Chinese Military Force. Eventually the government agreed to form a Singapore Chinese Anti-Japanese Volunteer Battalion - the Dalforce under Lt Colonel John Dalley. The Chinese recruits went through a 10-day crash training programme. They were equipped with all sorts of weapons and provided uniforms. The British also released communists from prison and with agreement with Lai Teck, the Secretary-General of the Malayan Communist Party, organised and trained communists for guerrilla warfare against the Japanese. One hundred and sixty-five men were trained in special guerilla schools and these eventually became the nucleus of the Malayan People's Anti-Japanese Army.

The Communist recruits came from all walks of life; there were College boys, even rickishaw pullers. The young and the old joined this Force.

The initial strength of the Chinese Dalforce was 2000 and they were allotted to different commanders on the island. One Company of these Chinese volunteers was assigned to a sector around Kranji where the initial assault of the Japanese forces was expected. Some of these men were given the task of patrolling the mangrove swamps as scouts to detect possible Japanese infiltrators.

The Chinese force dug in the mangrove swamps and despite the heavy Japanese shelling these volunteers were amazingly cheerful.

Chin Kang Hui-Kuan, Bukit Pasoh

After the Japanese had landed on the beach the Chinese fought the enemy with shot guns and sporting rifles. When their supply of 7 rounds of ammunition had exhausted they resorted to fierce hand to hand combat. Finally the entire Company fell to the enemy. Only one British Officer and five other ranks escaped.

Another Company of the Chinese Dalforce fought a similar heroic battle at Kent Ridge, Pasir Panjang.

The Chinese volunteer force proved their mettle in the Battle for Singapore.

SINGAPORE GENERAL HOSPITAL

Outram Road

Courage, loyalty and service are the hallmarks of our doctors, nursing and other staff of our hospitals particularly during the Battle for Singapore and the Japanese Occupation.

Today it reflects the high standard of medical services provided by the Republic.

The first General Hospital was built in 1882 on the present site to meet especially the needs of the sea-faring population of Singapore. The Hospital was staffed by both nuns and nurses until the new Hospital buildings were completed in 1926. A lunatic asylum and a Medical School were also in the same locality.

When Singapore was a Colony the Chief Medical Officer, the Matron, Sisters and Consultant Surgeons, were all British while the Asians held subordinate positions. Before World War II because of the shortage of beds in the General Hospital many patients requiring admission had to be turned off.

The clock-tower block was then restricted for first class patients, the middle block for children and babies and the lower floors were for third class patients.

The courage, loyalty and service of the medical staff especially the doctors and nursing staff were seen during the Japanese invasion of Malaya and the Battle for Singapore. The first casualties of Japanese bombing were admitted at the Hospital which was the main civilian Hospital on 8 December 1941 when Singapore was first bombed. By 15 February 1942 there were about 3400 patients in the General Hospital.

Throughout the Malayan Campaign and the Battle for Singapore all medical staff. doctors, nurses, attendants and "amahs" (female attendants) continued to work harmoniously and did their best for the patients though shells from Japanese artillery fell all around them.

In the old Brebner House built in 1923 as a Nurses' Hostel was a plaque which read:

To the Nurses of Singapore And Malaya Commemorating
Their courage And loyalty And their Patient kindness
To the internees Of Singapore 1942-45
In deep gratitude from the Patients of Singapore Hospitals And their friends.

The names of the 129 nurses who worked during the Japanese Occupation in the internees' wards of the General Hospital, the hospitals of Kandang Kerbau, Tan Tock Seng, Middleton and the Mental Hospital were recorded on the plaque.

New wards - Singapore General Hospital

Clock Tower, Bowyer Block

Near the former Norris Block of the General Hospital beside Hospital Drive is a common grave. The tombstone has a simple wooden cross and the inscription on the tombstone reads:

> *Beneath this cross lie 107 British soldiers and 300 civilians of many races who perished in captivity in February 1942. The soldiers are commemorated by name at Kranji War Cemetery.*

Immediately after the British Surrender on 15 February 1942 the Japanese Imperial Army gave orders to the authorities of the Singapore General Hospital to evacuate the Hospital within 24 hours. More than 1000 civilian patients who could walk were sent back to their homes. Other civilian patients were transferred to the mental asylum while the military wounded were sent to various other places. The Hospital was then occupied by the wounded Japanese soldiers.

Hospital blocks were named after those medical staff who were killed by Japanese bombing - they were Margaret Brebner, Dr. D.J. Bowyer and Dr. Victor H. Norris. Margaret Brebner, the Matron of the General Hospital, was ordered to leave Singapore; she reluctantly did so but the ship on which she travelled was bombed by the Japanese. Dr Bowyer who was Chief Medical Officer was tortured to death by the Japanese and Dr Norris was killed by a bomb at the Kandang Kerbau Maternity Hospital.

The Singapore General Hospital is perhaps the most modern one in South-East Asia and is fully air-conditioned. It has now been privatised and is managed by the Singapore General Hospital Private Limited.

Common grave at Hospital Drive - for 107 British soldiers and 300 civilians

ADMIRALTY HOUSE

Canberra Road
Sembawang

Historic building where senior military commanders held meetings after the Japanese invasion of Malaya.

The Admiralty House was the venue of several meetings of Senior Military Commanders and officers soon after the Japanese invasion of Malaya on 8 December 1941.

Today it is a Club House whose members include Singapore Armed Forces personnel.

Old Admiralty House, Old Nelson Road. Important meetings held here by British military officers after Japanese advance into Malaya.

OLD KALLANG AIRPORT

The first civil airport;
The last operational Royal Air Force Base before British Surrender to the Japanese;
The first Central Manpower Base, Singapore Armed Forces;
presently the headquarters of the People's Association.

The first aeroplane landed in Singapore in 1911 in Farrer Park which became a regular stop between England and Australia.

Seaplane bases at Sembawang and Royal Air Force Seletar were completed in 1920s; decision was taken in 1930s to build a civilian airport at Kallang.

In Kallang the kampongs (villages) were relocated for the construction of the grass runway and the terminal building.

On 21 November 1935 a flight of Hawker Ospreys from the aircraft carrier "H.M.S. Hermes" landed on the unfinished airfield - the first planes to land on Kallang Airport. It is interesting to note that "H.M.S. Hermes" was in the Indian Ocean during the Japanese invasion of Malaya in 1941 and could have taken the place of "H.M.S. Indomitable" the escorting aircarft of the "Prince of Wales" and the "Repulse" and which ran aground in Kingston harbour in the West Indies and therefore could not get to Singapore.

The "H.M.S. Hermes" could have been diverted to the Malayan waters. This might have altered the course of events of the Malayan Campaign.

In 1936 the terminal building was completed and in 1937 the hangars. Governor Sir Shenton Thomas officially opened the airport in June 1937 and after his address a signal rocket was fired indicating that the civil airport was open. By end of 1937 the Kallang Airport was fully operational and civil aircraft carried out daily flights to Kuala Lumpur, Ipoh and Penang; the aircraft also conveyed special postal services.

During World War II Kallang Airport was used as a military airbase and planes carried out bombing missions against the invading Japanese military forces. The Japanese bombed the airport three or four times a day and made fresh bomb craters which made it possible to use only one strip of the runway (700 yards long).

The air defence of Singapore ended on 9 February 1942 and the last of the 8 "Hurricanes" flew to Palembang, Sumatra. On 11 February 1942 the Fighter Aircraft Operations Room at the Kallang Airport was abandoned and the Senior Radio Officer, Flight Lieutenant Carter, destroyed all the secret papers on the performance of British radar - a secret at that point of time to the Germans, Italians and the Japanese.

Before the British Surrender to the Japanese on 15 February 1942 the final British perimeter included the Kallang Airport.

During the Japanese Occupation the Japanese used the Kallang Air Base.

The Kallang Airport became operational soon after the return of the British to Singapore in 1945 and the airfield was initially used by the Royal Air Force transport aircraft and later it was restored as a civil airport.

The only air disaster in Singapore occurred on 13 March 1954 when a BOAC Constellation crashed as it approached the runway. A total of 32 passengers and 2 crew members died in that disaster.

It became clear by 1948 that the Kallang civil Airport was not adequate for the increased air traffic; the development of the Airport was limited because it was close to the harbour and built-up areas. Decision was taken to build a new airport in Paya Lebar. The new airport was officially opened on 20 August 1955 and the Kallang Civil Airport was closed to air traffic the next day.

In March 1956 six British Members of Parliament visited Singapore to assess Singapore's ability to deal with internal security. A mass rally was organised on 18 March 1956 at the old runway at Kallang to demonstrate the people's desire for independence. There was a crowd of 25,000 carrying

Headquarters People's Association
previously Old Kallang Airport and first Central Manpower Base, Ministry of Defence.

various banners and slogans. Mr David Marshall, the Chief Minister, the British Parliamentarians and other members of the Singapore Legislative Assembly were on a stage erected for them. The rally turned into a riot. The Chief Minister appealed to the crowd to restrain themselves; Mr Lee Kuan Yew also addressed the gathering to remain calm. Those on the stage made a dash to the old terminal building. About 50 persons including 20 policemen were injured in the melee that followed.

Britain was convinced that the Colony was not capable of dealing with internal security.

In 1959 the People's Action Party came into power and Mr Lee Kuan Yew became Singapore's first Prime Minister and Singapore became independent in 1963 by joining Malaysia.

Singapore was separated from Malaysia and became an independent Republic of Singapore on 9 August 1965. The Singapore Armed Forces were being formed. The old Kallang Civil Airport became the first Central Manpower Base which eventually moved out to Holland Road and finally to its present location at Depot Road.

The People's Association was officially inaugurated by the Prime Minister Mr Lee Kuan Yew at the old terminal building of the Kallang Civil Airport on 20 August 1960. The headquarters of the People's Association is still located here and it organises and promotes group participation in social, cultural, educational and sporting activities and also youth leadership training courses. During its inception the People's Association was also the second line of defence against the communists.

The National Stadium, the Kallang Theatre and other sporting facilities now occupy the former runway of the old Kallang Civil Airport.

SINGAPORE-JOHORE CAUSEWAY

Link between Singapore and Malaysia

Symbol of close relationship between Singapore and Malaya. One time Malaya hinterland to Singapore.

Work on the Singapore-Johore Causeway began in 1919. It was officially opened by the Governor and High Commissioner Sir Laurence Guillemard on 28 June 1924. The Causeway was opened to goods trains on 17 September 1923. Passenger trains began to operate between Singapore and Malaya from 1 October 1923.

The Causeway linked Singapore with Malaya. Rubber, tin, palm oil, and copra were transported to Singapore which right up to the 1960s depended on entrepot trade.

As soon as the retreating British forces had withdrawn into Singapore a 70 foot-wide gap in the Causeway was blown off on 31 January 1942. The Japanese invasion of Singapore began on 8 February 1942 and within a few days the Causeway was repaired and it became operational for the invading Japanese troops.

The Causeway today is a symbol of the close relationship between Singapore and Malaysia.

Singapore - Johore Causeway

SWISS CLUB ROAD

Fierce battle in the Swiss Club area
Swiss Club housed the Royal Australian Medical Corps
During battle for Singapore final phase
General Matsui set up his headquarters in
Bukit Tinggi Hill and directed operations
End of 1943 Japanese took over Swiss Club
and became the residence of the Commander
of the Japanese military unit

There was fierce fighting between Japanese forces under Lieutenant General Matsui, Commander of the 5th Division and British forces in the vicinity of the Swiss Club and Bukit Tinggi where Matsui set up his Divisional Headquarters and conducted the final operations in the Battle for Singapore.

Once occupied by Japanese General during Battle for Singapore

The Swiss Club had housed the Royal Australian Medical Corps. During the Malayan campaign the Club was used by the Royal Air Force as a rest camp.

Before the British Surrender on 15 February 1942 the Australians vacated the building to move towards the final perimeter around Singapore Town.

By the end of 1943 the Japanese military authorities took over the Swiss Club and it became the residence of the Commander of the Butai, a Japanese military unit.

The Swiss Club was established in 1871. It was then known as the Swiss Rifle Shooting Club of Singapore and had its premises off Balestier Road. Later in 1910 the Club moved to Bukit Timah and in 1925 to Bukit Tinggi.

Though Switzerland remained a neutral country in World War II, the Swiss in Singapore did voluntary services as Air Raid Precaution Wardens and served in the auxiliary medical services and bomb disposal squads.

FULLERTON BUILDING

Singapore's General Post Office

Singapore Club occupied the top floor before World War II - Governor Sir Shenton Thomas and Lady Thomas occupied rooms here before British surrender to Japanese

Named after Robert Fullerton Governor of Straits Settlements (1824-30); he saved Central and South Malaya from Siamese domination; two important treaties: the Anglo-Dutch Treaty 1824 and Anglo-Siamese Treaty 1826 were signed when he was Governor.

In 1874 the old post office moved from the South Bank of the Singapore River near Empress Place to Fort Fullerton, the present site of Fullerton Building. The Exchange Building built between 1865-70 also stood on the site of Fort Fullerton. Before the completion of Fullerton Building, Mansfield Office (later Ocean Building) was used as the General Post Office.

When Fullerton Building was completed in 1928 it housed the Exchange, the Chamber of Commerce and the Singapore Club. The building was designed by Keyes and Bowdeswell in French Renaissance style.

Fullerton Building was named after Robert Fullerton, the first Governor of the Straits Settlements (1824-1830). He is remembered for preventing the expansion of Siamese influence into Central and South Malaya in the 19th century; he signed the important Anglo-Siamese Treaty in 1826. Robert Fullerton was also responsible for the Naning War; he claimed Naning near Malacca as British territory. This war cost the British government £100,000 and made Britain reluctant to intervene in the Malay States until 1874.

The Anglo-Dutch Treaty (1824) which created a British and a Dutch sphere of influence in the East Indies was drawn up during Fullerton's tenure of office. Fullerton claimed that if Britain was to retain Singapore under this Treaty the islands south of Singapore, Rhio and Lingga, should be part of Singapore. His claim was based on the historical fact that the old Malay Empire included Pahang, Johore, Rhio and Lingga. The Directors of the East India Company in London did not pursue Fullerton's claim. A ruler of this old empire is buried in Telok Blangah in the old dignified cemetery beside Keppel Road opposite the Puma Flour Mill; next to it is the Temenggong's Mosque - the property of the Johore Government.

In 1828 Fullerton had proposed that Malacca should be capital of the Straits Settlements. He said Malacca was an ancient capital with a more healthy climate and more centrally located resources for defence.

Fullerton Building named after Robert Fullerton the first Governor, Straits Settlements (1824-1830)

Fullerton building in 1941 housed various Government departments which included Agriculture, Fisheries and Forest departments.

In February 1942 Government House was under constant artillery fire and aerial bombardment. It received several direct hits. Governor Sir Shenton Thomas and Lady Thomas decided to move out of Government House into the Singapore Club which occupied the top floor of Fullerton Building. Singapore Club was first established at Cecil Street, an exclusive European Club and in 1928 occupied the top floor of Fullerton Building; there the Club had dining rooms, billiard and card rooms and sleeping accommodation. On 13 February 1942 the Governor and his wife occupied two rooms there which were safer, "quieter and cooler".

It was while driving from Government House to Fullerton Building that the Governor became fully aware of the damage to buildings and roads caused by Japanese bombs.

During the last days before the British Surrender Fullerton Building was converted into a hospital with make-shift operation theatres to receive hundreds of wounded British soldiers. Conditions were shocking. Patients had to sleep on floor landings and corridors which were stacked with bodies of the dead waiting to be buried.

It was at the Singapore Club that General Percival informed the Governor of the decision of the military to surrender. From Fullerton Building Governor Shenton Thomas drove to the Broadcasting Station to make his final broadcast and to announce the military surrender of the British.

Today Fullerton Building houses a very modern and efficient General Post Office, the Income Tax Department and other government offices. The Singapore Club functions elsewhere in the City.

TYERSALL

Japanese Air Force - indiscriminate bombing - Battle for Singapore

At Tyersall was located the Indian Military Base Hospital in the north-west of the town. The hospital was clearly marked with a large red cross to indicate its purpose; it was actually a cluster of huts where the wounded Indian troops were warded.

A squadron of Japanese bombers dropped incendiary bombs on the hospital on 11 February 1942 and the whole cluster of huts was turned into a raging inferno. All the 700 patients of the casualty packed wards were burnt to death.

Tyersall

ALEXANDRA HOSPITAL

(previously Alexandra Military Hospital)

Japanese massacred British military personnel both patients and staff of Hospital on 14 February 1942 before British Surrender

Alexandra Military Hospital, Singapore, was meant for British military personnel from British Malaya, Singapore and the Far East. On 15 September 1971 the British handed the hospital to the Singapore Government. It is now called Alexandra Hospital.

On 14 February 1942 Japanese Imperial Forces advanced through Kent Ridge down Pasir Panjang Road to Alexandra Military Hospital. The British retreated west through the Hospital. They set up machine guns on the first and second floors to cover their retreat. A lieutenant carried a Red Cross brassard and a white flag to meet the Japanese. The Japanese killed him.

Alexandra Hospital where Japanese soldiers massacred British patients and staff in February 1942

Among the patients in the Hospital were a four Company force nicknamed the Plymouth Argylls who were survivors of the "Prince of Wales" and "Repulse" which were sunk by Japanese torpedo bombers off the coast of Kuantan, Pahang, on 10 December 1941.

Japanese troops rushed into the wards and operation theatres and bayoneted a total of 250 patients and staff members. Before they could repeat their brutalities in other wards, an officer ordered them to assemble in the Hospital grounds. The troops, however, removed about 400 patients and staff and locked them up in a staff bungalow nearby. Next day these people were taken out in small groups and shot. The bodies were buried in a mass grave.

Walter Salmon of the Royal Signals wounded by a mortar bomb was hospitalised on the top floor and had come to the canteen. He sat there a stunned witness of the abominable spectacle.

On 15 February when Yamashita heard of the massacre in the Hospital, he went round the beds of the remaining patients and saluted them; he apologised profusely for the shocking conduct of his soldiers. He brought some crates of canned fruit and opened them with his bayonet and served the fruit to the patients.

Later when he learnt that some Japanese soldiers were looting the Hospital he ordered them to be executed.

After the Japanese Surrender in 1945 a book was kept in the Hospital. It contained the names of the victims who were massacred by the Japanese. The present location of the book is not known.

FORD MOTOR WORKS

(Now Bridgestone Factory)

Bukit Timah Road
Site of the formal surrender of
the British forces to the Japanese
Imperial Army - 15 February 1942
Also first car assembly plant in South East Asia

In October 1941 Ford Motor Works moved into new premises in Bukit Timah from Anson Road where its factory was first established in 1926. It was the first motor-car assembly plant in South East Asia.

In the final phase of the Battle for Singapore Lieutenant-General Yamashita moved his headquarters from Johore Bahru Sultan's Palace to Ford Motor Works.

It was here that Lieutenant-General Percival, Commander of the British Forces surrendered unconditionally to Yamashita on 15 February 1942. The British delegation led by Lieutenant-General Percival included Brigadier Torrance (General Staff) Brigadier Newbiggings (Chief Administrator), and Major Wilde of 43 Light Infantry (the interpreter). The formal surrender document was signed in the Board Room. The Board Room is still there but the table at which both the British and Japanese delegations sat is in the Canberra War Museum, Australia.

General Yamashita's 25th Army began its invasion of Malaya and Singapore when his forces landed in Kota Bahru (Kelantan, North-East Malaya), Singora and Patani (South-East of Thailand) in the morning of 8 December 1941. On the same day Singapore was bombed by the Japanese Air Force.

The invasion was an expected one and the points at which the Japanese forces landed were anticipated by the British.

As early as 1937 Major-General W. Dhobie, General Officer Commanding (GOC) Malaya (1935-1939), had stressed that it was imperative that the British forces should defend in depth and hold the whole of Malaya. Defence of Singapore meant the defence of the mainland (Malaya).

As a result of this military strategy the British had formulated two secret plans; one was codenamed "Operation Matador" and the other "Operation Krohcol". The former was a pre-emptive move: the British were to move into Thailand and forestall the expected Japanese landings in Singora and Patani. This operation was to be activated even without approval from the Thai government. The latter ("Operation Krohcol) was to stop the Japanese inside Thailand.

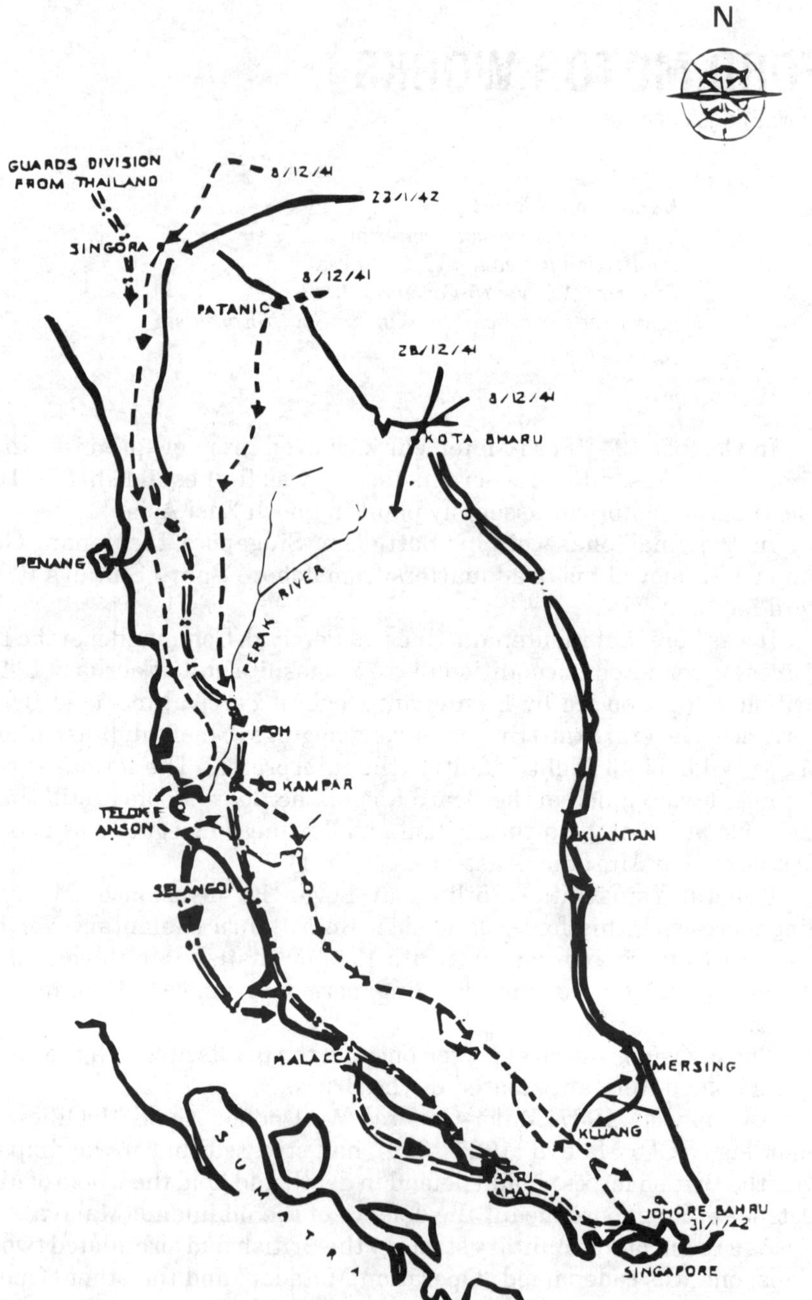

JAPANESE INVASION OF MALAYA

Air Chief Marshal Sir Robert Brooke-Popham, the Commander-in-Chief, hesitated to launch "Operation Matador" even as late as 7 December 1941. Eventually when the operation was implemented after the Japanese landings it proved disastrous against the ferocious onslaught by the invading forces. "Operation Krohcol" was also a failure because it could not check the Japanese advance into Malaya.

The arrival of two British warships "HMS Prince of Wales" and "HMS Repulse" in Singapore on 2 December 1941 boosted the morale of the British forces, the government of Singapore and its people. It was a tragedy that the escorting aircraft carrier "HMS Indomitable" ran aground in Kingston harbour, West Indies and did not escort these two ships. Another aircraft carrier "HMS Hermes" which was operating in the Indian Ocean was unfortunately not diverted to Singapore.

To intercept the Japanese landings in Singora and Patani "Prince of Wales and "Repulse" and their escorting vessels left Singapore on 8 December 1941. They had no air cover. On 10 December 1941 off the coast of Kuantan (Pahang) both the ships were sunk by Japanese torpedo bombers based in Saigon.

In December 1941 the British had about 100,000 troops but no tanks; the Japanese forces numbered only half the British strength but had tanks. After the first day's fighting the Royal Air Force had ceased to be an effective force; the Japanese Air Force therefore ruled the skies over Malaya and Singapore.

Despite stiff resistance by the British ground forces and several major battles, the Japanese 25th Army advanced rapidly on three-pronged direction - southwards down the Malay Peninsula to Johore Bahru. The Japanese 18th Division Commanded by Lieutenant-General R Mutaguchi raced down the East coast to Johore Bahru while the 5th Division under Lieutenant-General T. Matsui and the Imperial Guards Division commanded by Lieutenant-General T. Nishimura fought their way along the West coast and Central Malaya to Johore Bahru. The Japanese used unorthodox tactics by seaborne infiltration to get behind British lines and also to cut off the retreating forces in the West. By 25 January 1942 the British commanders realised that the retreat to the Fortress of Singapore was inevitable. Rear guard delaying action was taken for their forces to withdraw into Singapore. By the morning of 31 January all the British troops had crossed into Singapore except the Indian 22 Brigade stragglers who were still on the mainland. At 8.15 a.m. on that day Indian sappers blasted a seventy-foot gap in the Causeway linking the island of Singapore with Johore.

General Yamashita moved his headquarters from Kluang (Johore) to the tower ("a glass enclosed operations room") in the Sultan's palace in Bukit Serene in Johore Bahru. From the tower he could see the defences of Singapore; it was here he finalised his plans for the invasion of Singapore - the "invincible fortress of the East."

First landing of Japanese Troops in this area (North-West Singapore)

Mangrove Swamp in North-West Singapore defended by Australian troops. Japanese iinfiltrated between defence positions.

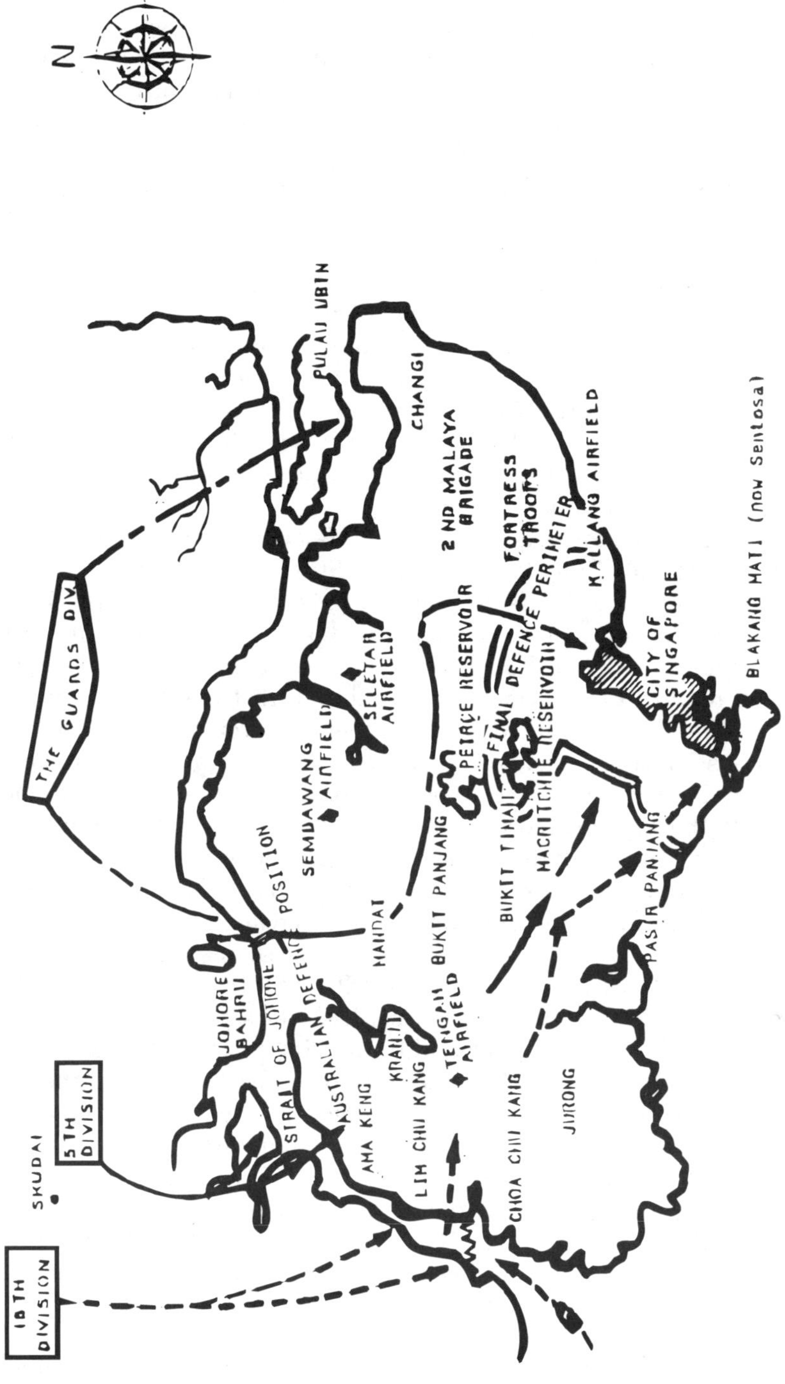

BATTLE FOR SINGAPORE

"The truth of the matter is: the Singapore guns were not pointing the wrong way..." (Ong Chit Chung) and by 19 January 1942 the British Chiefs of Staff were told tnat "full preparations should be made to use fortress guns against landward attack". The various Batteries on the island could traverse 180 degrees and could hit targets at a maximum range of 36,300 yards. The guns could reach parts of South-West coast of Johore and also targets in Singapore. These guns were only supplied with 1200 armour piercing rounds against ships and not high explosives for land targets. Those explosive rounds that were ordered never reached Singapore which did have the range tables necessary for their efficient use. Guns however did fire landward at Japanese targets in Johore and Singapore but they were only flat trajectories which just created craters and caused no harm to ground troops. The four, 6" guns at Siloso Battery and Labrador Battery, were particularly active against the Japanese in the Western sector of Singapore.

General Percival's plan in February 1942 was to divide the island for its defence into three sectors: the Southern sector, the Northern sector and the Western sector with a Central reserve.

The Southern sector was assigned to Major-General Keith Simmons with his 1st and 2nd Malay Regiments, the Straits Settlement Volunteers, the Fortress troops and the fixed defences. This sector included the Jurong River, Keppel Harbour, Blakang Mati (Sentosa), Pulau Brani and Pulau Bukom. Lieutenant-General Sir Lewis Heath took charge of the Northern sector with his 3rd Corps comprising Indian 11th Division, British 18th Division and the Indian 9th Division. This sector stretched from Changi to the Naval Base and the airfields of Sembawang and Seletar. The Commander of the Australian Imperial Force, Major-General Gordon Bennett was placed in charge of the Western sector defended by the Australian 22nd, 27th infantry brigades and Indian 44th brigade. This sector included the Jurong River and most of the Western shoreline, Tengah Airfield and Bukit Timah trunk road. General Bennett it became clear would face the initial onslaught of the Japanese forces. The General Reserve was assigned to Brigadier A. C. Paris who would take command of Indian 12th infantry brigade. This sector included the vital MacRitchie and Peirce Reservoirs and the food, fuel and ammunition dumps especially around Bukit Timah Race Course.

On Sunday 1 February 1942 General Percival broadcast from the radio station at Caldecott Hill a pessimistic message to the residents of Singapore. He said, "Today we stand beleaguered in our island fortress; our task is to hold this fortress until help can come, as assuredly it will come." He believed that Singapore could sustain a three-month siege by the Japanese.

The demolition of the Naval Base, the flooding of the dockyard and sinking it was an admission of defeat and this affected the morale of the British troops and the civilians even before the Japanese invasion of Singapore.

General Percival transferred his headquarters from Fort Canning to Sime Road to be closer to the battle ground.

Ford Motor Works, Bukit Timah Road, site where British signed surrender document, 15 February 1942, Now Bridgestone Warehouse.

Machine-gun bunker - entrance to Sime Road
still stands today opposite the golf course - a grim reminder to Singaporeans.

General Yamashita's strategy for his invasion of Singapore was initially to land his forces on the North-West of the island using the 5th and 18th Divisions whilst the Imperial Guards Division would create a feint in Changi in the East to give the impression that the Japanese initial attack would come from that direction.

General Yamashita's objectives were to initially occupy Tengah Airfield, then Bukit Panjang Village, Mandai and Nee Soon and cut off the British forces around the Naval Base at Sembawang; the next target was Bukit Timah and then on to Seletar, Peirce and MacRitchie Reservoirs. The General believed that once the Reservoirs were in Japanese hands the British forces would surrender and the task of attacking Singapore Town would not arise.

General Bennett's Western sector was the most difficult to defend because of the mangrove swamps, inland creeks and heavy jungle which made it extremely difficult for placing obstacles; further, battalion posts were yards apart with the terrain in between. This was ideal for Japanese infiltration. Though hurried fortifications were in place with available materials, the defence here was considerably weak.

Japanese intelligence unit which swam across the Straits of Johore was able to map out accurately British troop deployment and artillery positions. From the tall Johore government building and one man balloons above the Straits, the Japanese were also able to study the British defence preparations and direct bombing and artillery fire on to them.

By 4 February Japanese artillery fire from Johore hit Tengah, Seletar and Sembawang Airfields which had to be abandoned and the remaining serviceable aircraft were flown out to Kallang Civil Airport. The fuel tanks in the Naval Base also came under fire.

The Imperial Guards Division on 5 February with very little British resistance occupied Pulau Ubin in the East. Japanese artillery also hit several targets in the Town as well as Government House on this day.

On 6 February General Yamashita in his previous headquarters in Kluang had already given his general orders to his generals for the attack on Singapore before moving his headquarters to the Sultan's palace in Bukit Serene.

British intelligence officers returning from Johore reported the concentration of Japanese troops in the North-West and that the invasion of Singapore was imminent from that direction.

On the morning of 8 February the Japanese concentrated their heavy artillery fire and bombing on the North-West sector held by the Australians and wrecked havoc on British defences. As a result, communication was cut off between the forward and rear command posts. The Australians retaliated with artillery fire on the Japanese well camouflaged assembly points in the Skudai and Melayu Rivers, North-West of Singapore. At 8.00 p.m. that night after intensive Japanese artillery fire at the North-West coastline of Singapore, came the first wave of 4,000 Japanese troops in various craft across the

Straits of Johore; they were from the 5th and 18th Divisions. The Australians repulsed the first wave. Many Japanese soldiers were bogged down, many stranded, drowned and machine-gunned. Other waves of Japanese troops soon followed. Fierce fighting ensued with heavy casualties on both sides. Soon after, the invaders had landed on the beach. By midnight the Japanese 5th Division had established a wedge between the Australian 27th and 22nd brigades. This Division took Tengah Airfield on the afternoon of 9 February despite fierce Australian resistance. The Japanese advanced through Choa Chu Kang and Jurong towards Pasir Panjang. The 18th Division occupying Ama Keng Village after bitter street fighting, advanced down Lim Chu Kang Road towards Bukit Timah.

At midnight on 9 February General Percival after studying the situation of his forces issued secret instructions to General Bennett, General Simmons and General Heath on their final perimeter in the event this became necessary. The orders were to hold a perimeter including Kallang Airport, MacRitchie and Peirce Reservoirs and the Bukit Timah depot areas.

The imperial Guards Division joined the main battle on 10 February with a thrust across the Straits of Johore against the Australian 27th brigade. The first wave, the Kobayashi infantry regiment, suffered heavy casualties when flaming oil accidentally engulfed them; the oil had gushed from the fuel tanks demolished earlier. General Nishimura, the commander, sought General Yamashita's approval to call off his regiment's attack in view of the debacle but General Yamashita insisted that his plan should be executed.

Successive waves of this regiment overpowered the Australians who took a heavy toll of Japanese lives with their mortars and machine guns. The Japanese then moved towards Kranji by Bukit Timah Road and then to Mandai, Bukit Panjang, Ulu Pandan and Farrer Road. The Imperial Guards also took the Naval Base.

On the same day through a serious misunderstanding of the emergency orders of General Percival, the Australians began withdrawing down Woodlands Road and the British tragically therefore lost the vital Woodlands high ground overlooking the Causeway and the key to the Northern defences. The Japanese forces were pleasantly surprised at this move!

Brigadier Taylor of 22nd Australian brigade also mistaking General Percival's emergency orders gave instructions to his troops to move out to the Singapore perimeter. This had serious repercussions which ultimately led to the abandonment of the Jurong-Kranji line.

General Sir Archibald Wavell, the British Commander-in-Chief, flew into Singapore on 10 February for a meeting with his senior commanders in General Bennett's headquarters in Holland Road. Japanese aircraft made a direct hit on the headquarters; this was an example of the excellent intelligence of Japanese agents inSingapore. Miraculously all the commanders escaped unscathed.

On the same day the Japanese deployed their tanks for the first time in the Battle for Singapore and pushed towards Choa Chu Kang to Bukit Panjang Village junction with Bukit Timah Road. The Imperial Guards now had advanced towards MacRitchie and Peirce Reservoirs. At the same time the 5th Division pushed its way towards Race Course where the supply depots were located. In the meantime the Causeway had been repaired and Japanese supplies were moving quickly into Singapore.

On 11 February General Yamashita in his new headquarters in Tengah Airfield ordered that letters in communication tubes with red and white ribbons be dropped on British lines with the message that the British cease hostilities. One of these letters was handed to General Percival.

The Japanese troops advancing along Jurong Road reached Bukit Timah Village and the vital British food, fuel and massive ammunition dumps fell into Japanese hands. On the same day General Percival in Sime Road headquarters heard the sound of machine gun fire near the golf course. He shifted his headquarters to the underground bunkers at Fort Canning. The Indian Military Base Hospital at Tyersall was also bombed on this day and 700 wounded Indian soldiers were burnt to death.

The Imperial Guards Division were now advancing towards MacRitchie Reservoir, Lornie Road, Adam Road and Farrer Road areas. The Japanese forces were nearing the outskirts of the Town where thousands of Army deserters, stragglers were finding protection in large commercial and public buildings from the incessant Japanese bombing and artillery fire.

The Guards backed by their tanks were nearing Nee Soon Village held by British and Indian units on 12 February. On this day General Percival in his bunker in Fort Canning made the decision to withdraw all his forces to the final 28 mile long perimeter - Kallang Airfield, Thomson Village, MacRitchie Reservoir, Adam, Farrer, Holland and Buona Vista Roads and the south coast. Government House this day came under intensive mortar and artillery fire.

General Yamashita read intelligence reports of the final stand of the British at the new perimeter and was concerned whether with lack of men and ammunition he could sustain a protracted street fighting in the Town. He therefore ordered the 18th Division to take Alexandra Barracks through Pasir Panjang and Ayer Rajah and the Imperial Guards to attack the Northern perimeter defences.

The 56th regiment of the Japanese 18th Division moved to the Pasir Panjang Ridge on 13 February through the "Gap" on Buona Vista Road. Below the Ridge the Japanese 14th regiment sent its tanks along Ayer Rajah Road.

The Ridge was a key sector and it was held by the 2nd Loyals, the 1st Malay Regiment and a Dalforce of Chinese released from Changi Gaol where they were held as suspected communists.

Bloody battles were fought for the control of the Ridge and they were some of fiercest during the Battle for Singapore. It lasted 48 hours. Both the

Malays and the Chinese fought ferocious hand to hand combat and many were bayoneted. The locals proved without doubt the mettle they were made of. The "C" Company of the 1st Malay Regiment fought to the last man. During these battles the British artillery positioned in the harbour opened fire on the Japanese.

On 13 February Governor Shenton Thomas and Lady Thomas moved out of Government House to Singapore Club in Fullerton Building. On their route they witnessed the havoc Japanese bombing and artillery fire had caused on the buildings, roads and human life.

In the bunker at Fort Canning, General Percival held an emergency conference with his senior military commanders. He suggested to them that a counter-offensive should be mounted to which all his officers said was not feasible because of the demoralised and exhausted troops. General Percival signalled General Wavell (in Java) who replied that the fight should continue.

The Japanese on 14 February advanced through Pasir Panjang and Ayer Rajah Road towards Alexandra Barracks. In the afternoon the Japanese troops swarmed into Alexandra Military Hospital and bayoneted about 200 patients, surgeons and staff - a massacre. General Percival this day informed the Governor of the critical military and water situation.

On Sunday 15 February General Percival in his bunker proposed to his senior commanders that they should either recapture MacRitchie Reservoir and the food depots in Bukit Timah or surrender. His commanders unanimously agreed that a counter-attack was impossible. Then General Percival decided on the inevitable - to surrender.

A white flag was flown over the Broadcasting Station at Caldecott Hill and a delegation was sent to General Yamashita's headquarters in Ford Motor Works in Bukit Timah but the Japanese General wanted General Percival to present himself personally. General Percival, two staff officers and an interpreter left the bunkers at Fort Canning and arrived at the Ford Motor Works at 5.15 p.m. The British signed the unconditional surrender document and all hostilities ceased that night.

THE CHANGI MURALS

ST LUKE'S CHAPEL, CHANGI

Faith, hope and inspiration in captivity.

St Luke's Chapel is in one of the military barracks in Changi.

Originally it was part of a prisoner of war hospital. It was Rev. F.H. Stallard who managed to receive the approval of the Japanese military authorities to convert a dysentery ward into a Chapel where prisoners could pray and reflect.

The prisoners of war rallied round Rev Stallard to decorate the Chapel. One was Bombardier Stanley Warren, a member of the No. 15 Field Regiment, who was recovering from serious injuries in the hospital.

Warren painted life-size murals on the walls of the Chapel drawing inspiration from the New Testament. It was Rev F. Chambers, Stallard's

St Luke's Chapel as it is today in Changi Barracks.

successor, who requested Warren to paint the murals. Only five murals were painted and what remain today are about 75 per cent of the work.

For many years the murals were hidden in the Chapel which had been converted into a store-room and the walls repainted. Fortunately later they were discovered by the Singapore Armed Forces when the store-room was redecorated.

Warren returned specially to Singapore in 1963 to restore the murals that remained. In July 1982 Warren came again to Singapore to complete the restoration.

The murals are a source of inspiration to Singaporeans of what can be achieved through faith and inspiration even under extreme conditions.

Changi Mural

CHANGI GAOL

Symbol of fortitude, courage and inventiveness of the of the prisoners of war during the Japanese occupation. Singaporeans outside its walls displayed similar qualities.

Two days after the British surrendered to the Japanese at Ford Motor Works in Bukit Timah, the Japanese military authorities ordered all civilians of European origin to assemble on the Padang on 17 February 1942 at 10.30 a.m. These civilians were allowed to carry their personal belongings and asked to march about 15 miles to Changi Gaol. Those who were too old or sick to walk were provided transport. It was a long column led by Sir Shenton Thomas, Governor of Singapore. On their route they maintained their morale by singing: "There'll always be an England."

Changi Gaol was built in 1936 to accommodate 600 prisoners (24 cells were reserved for Europeans) but in February 1942 about 3,500 civilian men, women and children were cramped within its walls. There were 400 women and they were placed in a separate female wing.

Governor Sir Shenton Thomas occupied a separate cell and on 21 July 1942 he was moved to Formosa and then to Manchuria where he remained until the Japanese Surrender in 1945.

In May 1944 all civilians were transferred to Sime Road. Changi Gaol was then occupied by prisoners of war from Selarang Barracks and those who returned from the "Death" Thai Railways. There was a total of 12,000 prisoners; 5,000 were accommodated inside the Gaol and the rest in the attap sheds built by the prisoners themselves within the prison walls.

Both civilian and military personnel were highly inventive. They improvised various types of equipment, tools and other items which were absolutely necessary for their survival. They survived because of their fortitude, their indomitable spirit and faith in God.

The prisoners set up the "University of Changi" where qualified persons lectured on subjects like Engineering, Science, Agriculture, Law, Medicine and Languages. There was also a Play House where even Shakespearean plays were staged. Crude workshops were established where paper was made from pounded grass, water and potash; latex from rubber trees nearby was coagulated with urine (there was no formic or acetic acid) to produce soles for shoes and for patching up clothes; wood and odd metal were used to make artificial legs for amputee prisoners. Sea water was boiled to make salt; tapioca, potatoes and vegetables were grown in the field outside the prison walls. Doctors provided treatment without resorting to anaethetics.

Religion became the most powerful unifying force and primitive Churches were built. A replica of one of them is Changi Chapel outside the walls and Worship Services are still held there on Sundays.

Changi Museum next to Changi Chapel has copies of artefacts, sketches, photographs and other memorabilia and is open to the public free of charge. Of special interest are the photographs taken secretly with his camera by George Aspinall.

The "Changi Murals" in St Luke's Chapel in Changi Camp are excellent examples of what men under extreme suffering and deprivation can achieve through fortitude, faith and inspiration.

Singaporeans outside Changi Gaol were no less inventive. Through fortitude, faith and inventiveness they survived, three and a half years of terror.

Changi Gaol housed hundreds of British prisoners of war and internees.

THE CHANGI PRISON CHAPEL

THE CHANGI PRISON MUSEUM

Symbol of hope, faith, courage, fortitude and perseverance of man under Japanese captivity

Changi Prison Chapel that stands opposite Changi Gaol is a replica of the Chapel built by the prisoners of war who were held in Changi Gaol during the Japanese Occupation from 1942 to 1945. The original Chapel was dismantled after the war and reassembled in Australia.

Changi Prison Chapel is a symbol of man's faith in God under extreme deprivation. Numerous prisoners of war worshipped regularly in this Chapel. Several other Chapels were built but most were destroyed by the Japanese.

It was because of the overwhelming interest shown by ex-prisoners of war, their relatives friends and the general public in Singapore that the Singapore Tourist Promotion Board and the Singapore Prison Service jointly built the replica of this Chapel.

Next to the Chapel is the Changi Prison Museum which contains an excellent collection of drawings, sketches and photographs by the prisoners of war depicting life inside Changi Prison during the Japanese Occupation.

Together Changi Prison Chapel and Changi Prison Museum are memorials to the prisoners of war and their wartime experiences.

Today regular worship services are conducted in Changi Prison Chapel on Sunday evenings.

The Chapel and the Museum are open to the public. There is no admission charge.

Changi Prison Chapel replica of Chapel built by prisoners of war

Changi Prison Museum houses artefacts of prisoners of war

"SYONAN (SINGAPORE) MEMORIAL TO THE SPIRITS OF THE LOYAL SOLDIERS"

The "Chureito"
Lorong Sesuai
off Bukit Timah Road

135 concrete steps in Bukit Batok are another grim reminder of the Japanese occupation of Singapore

Five hundred Australian prisoners of War from the Royal Australian Artillery and Anti-Tank Units marched daily from Sime Road and Adam Park to Bukit Batok to build the memorial to the Japanese soldiers who died in the Malayan Campaign.

Lieutenant-General Yamashita mooted the idea of a memorial and the site at Bukit Timah was chosen because the fiercest battle in Singapore was fought there. The Australian suggestion of a memorial to British soldiers who died during the Battle for Singapore was accepted by Yamashita. A wooden cross 10 feet high was erected by the Japanese Engineering Company near the Japanese Memorial.

The Japanese Memorial, the "Chureito", was a cylindrical wooden pylon forty feet high, the top of which was encased in a brass cone. It stood on two tiers of earth and cement. The ashes of the Japanese forces who died at the battle in Bukit Timah were buried there.

The Japanese Memorial was officially unveiled at 11 a.m. on 11 September 2602 (1942) and religious ceremonies were conducted according to Shinto rites.

The Memorial Cross to British soldiers was unveiled and Lieutenant-Colonel McEachern addressed the gathering of British prisoners of war.

Leaders of the four main communities in Singapore witnessed the unveiling ceremony: they were Dr Lim Boon Keng (for the Chinese), S.C.Goho (for the Indians), Ibrahim bin Hj Yusof (for the Malays) and Dr C.J.Paglar (for the Eurasians).

A small shrine was erected by the Japanese soldiers.

Immediately after the Japanese Surrender and the return of the British forces in 1945, the Japanese Memorial and the shrine were both demolished. David Nelson in his book "The Story of Changi Singapore" writes: "It is a pity the relieving troops (British) felt obliged to destroy a memorial "torri" erected to the Nipponese Army on a hillock at Bukit Timah in memory of the fallen. Friend or foe, each was serving his country."

Today only the 135 concrete steps which led to the Japanese Memorial remain but they remind Singaporeans of a nightmare of three and a half years of Japanese Occupation.

A Drawing of the "Chureito" Lorong Sesuai demolished by British soldiers in 1945.

135 steps that led to the Japanese Memorial

CATHAY BUILDING

Site of old bakery; Cathay Building headquarters of Admiral Lord Louis Mountbatten, Supreme Commander, South-east Asia Command in 1945 and Singapore's first skyscraper.

Cathay Building stood on the site of an old bakery and Victorian building managed by Teo Ho Lye and Louis Molteni from Poland. Moulteni came to Singapore in the 1880s and started his confectionery.

The Victorian building was demolished in 1934 and the land sold to the Loke family.

Cathay Building designed by Frank Brewer was completed in 1939. It became Singapore's first skyscraper and second multi-storey building; the first was the High Street Police Station. The building housed the Cathay Cinema which exists today but the hotel was converted into an office complex.

Opposite Cathay building is Dhoby Ghaut (Ghaut is of Indian origin; one meaning is a stair-case) referring to the terraced rocks upon which the Indian dhobies in the early years washed the clothes for their customers. They used water from a stream Sungei Bras Basah which flowed along Bras Basah Road.

In early 1941 Colonel Alan Ferguson Warren of the Royal Marines came to Singapore to train guerillas to infiltrate into Malaya. He made Cathay Building the headquarters of the Special Operations Executive (SOE) Orient Mission and a base for his operations.

In February 1942 before the British surrendered to the Japanese, Cathay was one of the buildings where hundreds of British army deserters sought refuge from constant Japanese aerial and artillery bombardment. The Field Survey Company also used the roof of Cathay Building to spot enemy guns. On 9th February 1942 crowds gathered at Cathay for the official evacuation from Singapore.

The local staff employed in Cathay Building remained loyal and brave and continued working each day despite the bombing of their homes and families members being killed. It was just before the British surrender that they were paid off and sent home.

Lt General Percival on his way to meet Lt General Yamashita, flew a large Union Jack atop Cathay Building to indicate that he (Percival) had agreed to a ceasefire. The unconditional British surrender took place at Ford Motor Works in Bukit Timah on 15 February 1942.

Old Singaporeans would remember that soon after the British Surrender the Japanese military authorities beheaded looters. In front of Cathay Building were heads of 5 persons who had been beheaded and the gruesome spectacle was a prelude to what was to come.

During the Japanese Occupation Cathay Building was used as one of the Japanese military establishments.

Admiral Lord Louis Mountbatten, Supreme Commander, South-east Asia Command (SEAC) arrived in Singapore in September 1945 to accept the surrender of the Japanese. He established his headquarters in Cathay Building and hoisted the national flags of the Allies - Britain, United States of America, China, France and the Netherlands. Mountbatten promulgated from Radio Malaya functioning in Cathay Building the implementation of the British Military Administration which lasted until 31 March 1946 when civil government was restored. On 1 April 1946 Singapore was separated from Penang and Malacca and the 9 Malay States to become a separate Colony of Singapore. The Malay States, Penang and Malacca became the Malayan Union.

Cathay Building Singapore's first skyscraper.

KRANJI WAR MEMORIAL

Upper Bukit Timah Road

Resting place for many of the Allied Soldiers including Singaporeans who died defending Singapore, Malaya and neighbouring lands and seas.

The Memorial designed like an aerofoil with 12 broad columns and the inscription in the main memorial reads:

1939-1945
On the walls of this Memorial are recorded
the names of twenty-four thousand soldiers and airmen
of many races united in service to the British Crown
who gave their lives in Malaya and neighbouring lands and seas and in
the air over Southern and Eastern Asia and the Pacific
But to whom the fortune of war
denied the customary rites
accorded to their comrades in death

THEY DIED FOR ALL FREE MEN

Kranji War Memorial

The memorial gives the names of all Singaporeans and Malayans who died in the Malayan Campaign and Battle for Singapore. They include those who served in the Straits Settlements Volunteer Force, the Local Defence Corp the Dalforce and the Malay Regiments.

There are other memorials to those who died in the Malayan Campaign.

The following Prayer is recited every year on 11 November:

FAR EAST PRISONER OF WAR PRAYER

And we that are left
grown old with the years
remembering the heartache,
the pain and the tears;
hoping and praying
that never again man will sink
to such sorrow and shame.
The price that was paid
we will always remember
every day, every month
not just in November.

There are 4498 graves each marked with a head stone. The names of all those who died are recorded in a Register maintained by the custodian in the United Kingdom. The graves are maintained by the War Graves Commission, Maidenhead, England.

Tomb of Inche Yusof bin Ishak
First President, Republic of Singapore. Died on 23 November 1970.

Tomb of Dr Benjamin Henry Sheares second President, Republic of Singapore, died on 12 May 1981.

KRANJI STATE CEMETERY

Inche Yusof bin Ishak succeeded Sir William Goode (the last of the Colonial Governors and first Yang di Pertuan Negara) as Yang di Pertuan Negara (Head of State) from 1959 to 1965. He retained the same title when Singapore was part of the Federation of Malaysia in 1963. When Singapore was separated from Malaysia in August 1965 Inche Yusof bin Ishak became the first President of the Republic of Singapore.

Inche Yusof bin Ishak died on 23 November 1970. His body lay in state at City Hall for the people to pay their final respects to their President. His hearse was driven by a military vehicle and he was buried with full state honours at Kranji State Cemetery.

Dr Benjamin Henry Sheares succeeded Inche Yusof bin Ishak as the second President of the Republic of Singapore on 2 January 1971. He died on 12 May 1981 and the people paid their last respects to their President at the Istana. He was succeeded by Mr C.V. Devan Nair who became the third President of the Republic on 24 October 1981.

THE CENOTAPH

Connaught Drive

Memorial to those who died in two World Wars

The Cenotaph was constructed as a memorial to those who died in World War I (1914 - 1918), later to include those who perished during the Second World War (1939 - 1945).

The memorial was designed by the well-known architect, Denis Santry of Swan and MacLaren. The foundation stone was laid on 15 November 1920 by the Governor of the Straits Settlements, Sir Laurence Nunns Guillemard. It was unveiled on 31 March 1922 by the Prince of Wales (later Duke of Windsor and King Edward VIII) during his tour of Malaya, India, Australia and New Zealand. He was accompanied by young Mountbatten later the Earl of Burma who landed in Singapore in September 1945 as Supreme Commander, South-east Asia Command, to receive the surrender of the Japanese at City Hall almost directly opposite the Cenotaph.

The Cenotaph Connaught Drive. Memorial to those who died in World War I (1914-18) and World War II (1939-45)

LIM BO SENG MEMORIAL

Esplanade

A memorial to a Singapore hero and martyr.

Major-General Lim Bo Seng was one of Singapore's heroes and a martyr of World War II. The pagoda-like structure at the Esplanade was erected as a tribute to him.

The pagoda is of marble with a solid bronze roof and is guarded by four bronze lions.

Lim Bo Seng (alias Tan Choon Lim) was born in China on 27 April 1909. He came to Singapore when he was sixteen years old. He studied at Raffles Institution where he passed his Senior Cambridge Examination in 1928 and later at the University of Hong Kong. After his graduation he joined his father's construction company.

The company had built some of Singapore's historical buildings including the Victoria Memorial Hall and Parliament House.

After the Japanese invasion of China in 1937 Lim Bo Seng raised funds to support the Chinese war effort. Because of his anti-Japanese activities the British government at one time considered banishing him from Singapore and Malaya. Before the Japanese invasion of Malaya and Singapore Lim Bo Seng recruited workers to prepare for the urgent defence of Singapore; his men also assisted in blowing up the Causeway when British forces retreated from Malaya to Singapore.

Lim Bo Seng was advised by the British to leave Singapore for China when it was apparent that Singapore would fall to the Japanese in 1942. He, however, returned to Malaya in 1943 in a British submarine to join the underground resistance movement in Malaya. Later he went to Ipoh, the capital of Perak, to direct guerilla operations against the Japanese. The Japanese Military Police (the Kempetai) captured him in March 1944. He died on 29 June 1944 at the age of 34 after three months of Japanese torture at Batu Bajah Jail where he stubbornly refused to betray his comrades. He was buried in a shallow grave behind the prison.

When the British returned to Malaya in 1945 his body was brought to Singapore. He was buried with military honours at MacRitchie Reservoir on 13 January 1946. A Memorial Service was held at the steps of the Municipal Building (City Hall). The memorial at MacRitchie Reservoir was erected on 27 June 1952 by the Lim Bo Seng Memorial Committee.

Later, a more befitting monument was erected. A sum of Hong Kong $85,000 was raised to erect the pagoda at the Esplanade. It was officially unveiled in 1954.

Lim Bo Seng Memorial Esplanade A memorial to a Singapore's hero and martyr.

JAPANESE CEMETERY PARK

Chuan Hoe Avenue

Ashes of Field Marshal Count Terauchi - Commander Japanese Southern Army - are buried here among those of other Japanese military personnel.

Japanese prisoners of war cleared the cemetery immediately after the Japanese Surrender.

Tombstones were erected for various categories of Japanese who had been cremated and their ashes buried in this Cemetery. One inscription in Japanese on a tombstone reads: "In memory of the souls of the Labour Force comprising Army and Navy Personnel who died in Singapore between September 1945 and April 1947." Under this tombstone are the ashes of more than 10,000 Japanese Prisoners of War. Two small pillars mark the site where the ashes of the 135 Japanese war criminals who were tried and sentenced to death lie along with the ashes of another 79. Ashes of those who committed suicide and those of women who were courtesans of Japanese soldiers during the Occupation are also buried there.

Field Marshal Count Terauchi was Commander of the Japanese Southern Army in Saigon. After the British Surrender in February 1942 Terauchi occupied Government House (Istana).

In September 1945 Terauchi was too ill to surrender personally to Lord Louis Mountbattten, Supreme Commander, South-east Asia Command, at Municipal Building (City Hall). Terauchi, however, sent his sword.

Terauchi was placed under house arrest in Johore Bahru where he died in 1946. He was cremated and his ashes were buried in this Japanese Cemetery Park.

A prominent tombstone has been erected where his ashes have been buried. Fresh flowers are always placed in front of Terauchi's tombstone.

The Japanese Cemetery Park

Tomb where ashes of Field Marshal Count Terauchi are buried.

A MEMORIAL FOR CIVILIAN VICTIMS

A Memorial for civilian victims killed during the Japanese occupation of Singapore (Syonan) 15 February 1942 to 18 August 1945
A grim reminder to Singaporeans of what can happen to a conquered people

In 1962 some of the remains of Chinese massacred by the Japanese soon after their conquest of Singapore were exhumed in various parts of Singapore. These included Pasir Puteh, Changi, Yio Chu Kang, Jalan Kayu, Jurong, Telok Ayer, Kranji and Siglap. Official figures give the number of victims to 6,000 but the estimated number could have been between 25,000 to 50,000.

On 21 February 1942 the Japanese Army carried out an identification and interrogation of Chinese youth (ages between 18 and 50) - an Operation "Sook Cheng" (to purge or eliminate).

Chinese youths were dragged out of their homes and ordered to register at "Sook Cheng" Centres, in Jalan Besar, Arab Street, Tanjong Pagar, Geylang and Paya Lebar. At these centres which were in open spaces with no water, masked men identified those whom they regarded were anti-Japanese.

Chinese youths had joined the British to fight the Japanese in the Battle for Singapore. Under Tan Kah Kee, the Chinese National Council for Mobilisation (Chung Kuo Council) was formed and hundreds of Chinese youths were trained in the use of various types of weapons to fight the Japanese; also hundreds of youths suspected of being communists in Changi Gaol were released by the Governor for the same purpose. These youths joined Colonel Dally's Force 136. At Kranji and Kent Ridge they fought ferocious battles including hand to hand combat against the invading Japanese. Many died heroic deaths and many escaped to join Force 136 in Malaya to continue their struggle against the Japanese as guerillas during the Japanese occupation years.

Many Chinese donated money to the China War Relief Fund operated by the Kuomintang government for its war against the Japanese in China; these donors were to be identified as well. There were other categories of Chinese whom the Japanese regarded as anti-Japanese or undesirables. Japanese agents in Singapore under British rule maintained a book containing the names of anti-Japanese Chinese.

All those identified as "undesirable" by the Japanese at Sook Cheng centres were loaded on military trucks and driven away to be massacred. Others not under this classification were stamped on their clothing or body as "cleared" and allowed to return home. Many were rearrested and executed.

Memorial for Civilian Victims during Japanese Occupation of Singapore 1942-1945
Reminder to Singaporeans of what can happen to a conquered people.

The Japanese exacted $50 million from the Chinese in Singapore, Penang, Malacca and the Malay States as a "token of atonement" for supporting the Kuomintang with funds to fight the Japanese and for their "past hostility to Japan." The $50 million were apportioned between Singapore and Malaya. Many Chinese had to sell their property and others had to use their savings to meet the demand of the Japanese. Singapore Chinese raised $10 million, the other $40 million was borne by Malayan Chinese. Singapore raised its $10 million but the Malayan Chinese managed to raise only $18 millions. The Japanese authorities ordered that the rest of $22 million be met by a loan repayable within a year from the Yokohama Specie Bank. The cheque for $50 million was handed to Lieutenant-General Yamashita by Dr Lim Boon Keng Chairman, Overseas Chinese Association, at a ceremony in Fullerton Building.

After the Japanese Surrender, the Japanese government gave the Singapore government a grant of $25 million and a loan of $25 million, repayable on liberal terms as "atonement for atrocities" committed by the Japanese during their occupation of Singapore.

It was decided to build a memorial to remember the civilians killed by the Japanese during the occupation. The Singapore government offered 4½ acres of land and met half of the cost of $750,000 to erect the memorial. The Singapore Chinese Chamber of Commerce and the people of Singapore contributed the rest.

The Prime Minister, Mr Lee Kuan Yew, turned the sod on the site on 15 June 1963 witnessed by members of the diplomatic corps and community leaders.

The Memorial is 222 feet high and remains of some unknown victims are buried at the base of the Memorial.

On 15 Februaryt 1967 the Prime Minister Mr Lee Kuan Yew officially unveiled the Memorial.

This Memorial is a grim reminder to Singaporeans of what can happen to a conquered people. Total Defence becomes meaningful to Singaporeans.

Bibliography

Abadi Kenangan, *Geylang Serai Down Memory Lane*, Heinemann Asia, Singapore National Archives, Singapore 1956

Allen, Louis, *Singapore 1941-1942*, MPH Distributors (S) Pte Ltd, Singapore 1977

Archives and Oral History Department, Singapore, *The land transport of Singapore from earliest times to the present* (revised edition) Singapore 1984.

Archives and Oral History Department, Singapore, *Serangoon Road - a pictorial history*, Singapore, 1983

Beamish, Jane and Ferguson, Jane, *A History of Singapore Architecture - The Making of a City*, Graham Brash, Singapore 1985

Bowden, Tim, *Changi Photographer George Aspinall's Record of Captivity*, Australian Broadcasting Corporation, Sydney, 1984

Braddell, Roland, *The Lights of Singapore*, Kuala Lumpur 1982

Buckley, Charles Burton, *An Anecdotal History of Old Times in Singapore*, Oxford University Press, Singapore 1984

Ceylon Tamils' Association Singapore, *Golden Jubilee Souvenir 1909-1959*, Singapore 1959

Choo, Alexandra Avieropolau, *Report on the Excavation at Fort Canning*, Singapore 1986

Churchill, S.Winston, *The Second World War Vol.IV*, Hazell Watson & Viney, London 1953

Comber, Leon, *Chinese Temples in Singapore*, Eastern University Press, Singapore 1958

Convent of the Holy Infant Jesus, *135 Years of Convent of the Holy Infant Jesus 1854 - 1989*, Singapore 1989

Corner, E.J.H., *The Marquis - A Tale of Synon-to*, Heinemann Asia, Singapore 1981

Cuylenburg, John Bertram Van, *Singapore - Through Sunshine and Shadow*, Heinemann Asia, Singapore 1982

Danaraj, T.J., *Japanese Invasion of Malaya and Singapore Memoirs of a Doctor*, Kuala Iumpur 1990

Doggett, Marjorie, *Characters of Light (Early buildings of Singapore)*, Times Books International Singapore

Doraisamy, Rev Fr Aloysius, *The History of the Church of Our lady of Lourdes*, Singapore

Doraisamy, Theodore R, The March of Methodism in Singapore and Malaysia 1885-1980, *Methodist Book Room Publication, Singapore 1982*

Dural Raja Singam, S, *A Hundred Years of Ceylonese in Malaysia and Singapore (1867-1967)*, 1967

Flower, Raymond, *Raffles - The Story of Singapore*, Singapore 1984

Gough, Richard, *The Escape from Singapore* Heinemann Publishers Asian Pte Ltd, Singapore 1988; *Special Operations Singapore 1941 - 42*, Heinemann Asia 1985

Hancock, T.H.H., *Coleman's Singapore,* Monograph No.15, The Malayan Branch of the Royal Asiatic Society in association with Pelanduk Publications, 1986

Handout by the Armenian Church, *The Armenian Church of St Gregory,* Singapore 1835

Handout by the Sri Thandayuthapany Temple, *Sri Thandayuthapany Temple,* Tank Road, Singapore

Harfield, Alan, *Early Cemeteries in Singapore,* London 1988

Harper, R.W.E. and Miller, Harry, *Singapore Mutiny*, Oxford University Press 1981

Holmes, Richard and Kemp, Anthony, *The Bitter End: The Fall of Singapore 1941-42*, Anthony Bird Publications, Chichester 1982

Kennedy, Joseph, *When Singapore Fell Evacuation and Escapes 1941 - 42,* Macmillan, London 1989,

King Edward VII College of Medicine, *The Keviian 1957 - 1987: A tribute and a legacy*, Singapore 1987

Kirby, Woodburn S, Major-General, *Singapore: The Chain of Disaster,* Official History of the War against Japan

Lee, Edwin, *Historic Buildings of Singapore*, Preservation of Monuments Board, SingaporeNational Printers, Singapore 1990

Lodge, A.B., *The Fall of Gordon Bennett*, Allen and Unwin, Sydney 1986

Lim Thean Soo, *The Siege of Singapore*, Educational Publications, Singapore 1971

Lip, Evelyn, *Chinese Temples and Deities*, Times Books International, Singapore 1986

Madrasah Aljunied Al Islamiah, *Mahrajan Kebo 1927-1987*, Singapore 1987

Malayan Branch of the Royal Asiatic Society, *Singapore 150 Years 150th Anniversary of the Founding of Singapore*, Commemorative Reprint, JMBRAS Vol XLII Part 1 1982

McKie, Ronald, *The Heroes*, Angus and Robertson

Media Masters Pte Ltd, *Battlefield Guide: The Japanese Conquest of Malaya and Singapore*, Singapore

Ministry of Culture, Singapore, *Singapore - An Illustrated History 1941 - 1984*, Ministry of Culture, Singapore 1984

Montgomery, Brian, *Shenton of Singapore: Governor and Prisoner of War,* Times Books International Singapore, Singapore 1953

Nathan, Eze, *The History of Jews in Singapore 1830-1945*,Singapore 1986

National Archives, Singapore, *The Japanese Occupation Singapore 1942-1945*, National Archives, Federation Publications (S) Pte Ltd 1985

Nelson, David, *The Story of Changi Singapore*, Changi Publications Company, Australia, Perth 1973

Ong Chit Chung, *The Landward Defence of Singapore (1919-1938)*, Centre for Advanced Studies, Faculty of Arts and Social Sciences, National University of Singapore, Heinemann Asia, Sineapore 1988

Oral History Department, Singapore, Tapes and Transcripts

Palanisamy, K, *A History of Umar Pulavar Tamil School 1946-1982*, B.A.(Hons) Academic Exercise, Singapore 1987

Palit, D.K. Major-General, *The Campaign in Malaya*, India 1971 (revised)

Parliamentary Debates of Republic of Singapore Vol 26, *First Session of First Parliament*, Singapore Government Printers

Pearson, H.F., *Stories of Early Singapore*, University ofLondon Press, Singapore 1955

Percival, A.E.Lieutenant-General, *The War in Malaya*, London, 1949

Probert, H.A. Squadron Ieader (compiler), *History of Changi*, SCORE, Singapore 1955

Ramli, Dol, *History of the Malay Regiment 1933 - 1942*, Singapore 1955

Reith, G.M., *Handbook to Singapore* (revised) Walter Makepeace 1907 and 1985

Saiva Siddhanta Church, Publication, Hawaii, USA, *Benevolent Deity for the Modern Hindu World*

Schweizer-iten, H, *One Hundred Years of the Swiss Club and the Swiss Community of Singapore 1871-1971*, Singapore National Printers (Pte) Ltd

Seet, K.K., *A Place for the People*, Times Books International, Singapore 1953

Sharp, Ilsa, *There is only one Raffles The Story of a Grand Hotel*, London 1981

The Singapore Cricket Club, 1852-1985, The Club, 1985

Sejarah Ringkas, *Masjid Sultan Singapura*

Shorrick, N, *Lion in the Sky*, Federal PublicationsSdn Bhd, Singapore 1968

Siddique, Sharon and Nirmala Puru Shotam, *Singapore's Little India, Past, Present and Future*, Institute of South-east Asian Studies, Singapore 1982

Simson, Ivan, *Singapore: too little, too late (The failure of Malaya's defences 1942)*, Asia Pacific Press, Singapore 1970

Singapore Federation of Chinese Clan Association, National Archives and Oral History Department, *History of the Chinese Clan Association in Singapore*, Singapore News and Publications Ltd, Singapore 1986

Singh, Mehervan, *From Village to City,* Singapore - 1980

Song Ong Siang, *One Hundred Years' History of the Chinese in Singapore*, Oxford University Press, Singapore 1984

Soundara Rajan, N.S.(Editor), *Sri Veeramakaliamman Temple*, Souvenir magazine, Singapore 1987

Sri Krishna Temple, *Consecration Ceremony Souvenir*, Sri Krishna Temple 1989

Stallwood, H.A., *The Old Cemetery on Fort Canning of Singapore*

St Andrew's Cathedral, St Andrew's Cathedral Singapore Pamphlet

St Joseph's Institution, *Memories of St Joseph's Institution*, Singapore 1987

Sunday Times, 14 February 1988

Syonan Times, 11 September 2602

Tanjong Pagar Citizens' Consultative Committee, *Tanjong Pagar: Singapore's Cradle of Development*, Singapore 1989

Tao Nan School, *Tao Nan School Eightieth Anniversary Commemorative Magazine 1906-1986*, Singapore 1986

The Sikh Advisory Board, *Seminar Report on Sikh Youth and Nation Building*, Singapore 19 March 1989

The Straits Times, 31 December 1990

Thomas, T.W.Tan, *Chinese Dialect Groups Traits and Trades*, Opinion Books, Singapore 1990

Times Editions, *Singapore Historical Postcards from the National Archives Collection*

Tinsley, Bonnie, *A History and Guide to the Botanic Gardens*, Times Books International, Singapore 1983

Trenowden, Ian, *Malayan Operations - Most Secret - Force 136,* Heinemann Asia, Singapore 1978

Tsuji, Masanobu, *Singapore 1941-1942 The Japanese Version of the Malayan Campaign of World War Two*, Oxford University Press, New York 1988

Turnbull, C.M., *A History of Singapore 1819-1975,* Oxford University Press, Kuala Lumpur 1977

Tyers, Ray, *Singapore: Then and Now* 2 volumes, University of Education Press, 1986

Warren, James Francis, *Rickshaw Coolie: A People's History of Singapore 1880-1940*, Oxford University Press, 1986

Wijeysingha, E, *History of Raffles Institution (1823-1963)*, University Education Press, Singapore 1963

Winsley, Captain SVC, T.M., *A History of the Singapore Volunteer Corps 1854-1937 being also An Historical Outline of Volunteering in Malaya,* Government Printing Press, Singapore, Straits Settlements 1938

Zoohri Wan Hussin, *The Singapore Malays The Dilemma of Development,* Singapore Malay Teachers' Union, Singapore 1990

Acknowledgments

I am most grateful to Mr Ho Kah Leong, Senior Parliamentary Secretary, Ministry of Information and the Arts, for graciously consenting to write his kind message.

My thanks to my friend, Mr Koh Kong Chia for having read the manuscript and for his valuable suggestions.